Date: 3/10/17

BIO BOZZACCHI
Bozzacchi, Gianni,
My life in focus : a
photographer's journey with

My Life in Focus

My Life in Focus

*A Photographer's Journey
with Elizabeth Taylor and
the Hollywood Jet Set*

GIANNI BOZZACCHI

WITH JOEY TAYLER

UNIVERSITY PRESS OF KENTUCKY

Copyright © 2017 by The University Press of Kentucky

Scholarly publisher for the Commonwealth,
serving Bellarmine University, Berea College, Centre College of Kentucky,
Eastern Kentucky University, The Filson Historical Society, Georgetown College,
Kentucky Historical Society, Kentucky State University, Morehead State
University, Murray State University, Northern Kentucky University, Transylvania
University, University of Kentucky, University of Louisville, and Western
Kentucky University.

Editorial and Sales Offices: The University Press of Kentucky
663 South Limestone Street, Lexington, Kentucky 40508-4008
www.kentuckypress.com

Cataloging-in-Publication data is available from the Library of Congress.

ISBN 978-0-8131-6874-6 (hardcover : alk. paper)
ISBN 978-0-8131-6885-2 (epub)
ISBN 978-0-8131-6886-9 (pdf)

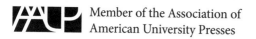

Contents

Elizabeth Taylor on the cover
of my first book, *The Queen and I.*

Foreword

Elizabeth Taylor

In 2001, my dear friend Gianni Bozzacchi asked me to write a blurb for a book he was publishing, *The Queen and I,* a lovely collection of photographs and stories from the twelve years Gianni spent working with me and Richard Burton. Reading the galleys brought back so many wonderful memories of that time, the so-called jet-set era: the glamour, the creativity, the incredible people I spent my life with, people like Gianni. You'd never know it looking at the exquisite pictures he took, but the Gianni I remembered, and the Gianni I was getting reacquainted with through his book, always felt a little like he was outside the party looking in.

Reflecting on that time and those pictures now, I could see that Gianni's insecurities, whether warranted or not, were inseparable from his photographer's eye. By maintaining a certain distance from his own life, and from mine, Gianni found the perspective that made him such an indelible artist. Oh, sure, Gianni enjoyed the glitz, the excitement, the beauty, the allure of that life, but he was never impressed by it, and he never surrendered to it, as so many people did. Gianni, uniquely among his peers, photographed his subjects as people rather than as stars. He had a remarkable gift for seeing past the bright lights, for snapping us when our guard was down, when we were simply and beautifully ourselves.

By the end of *The Queen and I,* I had remembered not just how special Gianni's talent was but how thoroughly annoying it could be, especially to someone whose image was, for better or worse, reproduced and analyzed and debated on every newsstand in the world back then. So I wrote my blurb and sent it to Gianni: "Brilliant, sensitive, Gianni always catches the soul. He is a pain in the ass."

As soon as I'd sent that note I felt bad, and I deleted the last sentence

> *My Darling Gianni,*
> *We did have fun,*
> *didn't we?*
> *Love always,*
> *Elizabeth.*

ELIZABETH TAYLOR

This is the dedication that Elizabeth wrote on the first copy of the book.

before the book went to press. But Gianni was disappointed—he'd loved what I wrote.

Well, now I've read *My Life in Focus*, a book filled with even more stunning pictures, more fascinating, funny stories, more of the man and his work—which, of course, means more of me, too, and the countless celebrities who found themselves in Gianni's sights over the years.

So now I am finally ready to tell the world what Gianni wanted me to say all those years ago: Gianni, you are a pain in the ass. I love you and thank you for it, and I'm sure everyone who reads this wonderful book will too. I love you lots!

Elizabeth Taylor sent me this foreword in January 2011, prior to the publication of the first Italian edition. She passed away on March 23.

Prologue

Rome, June 1976. The hot sun warmed the morning breeze, the Roman *ponentino*. It would not be a morning like any other, although it could have been. I had not been myself for some time.

I left the house, as usual, to go to my studio in Via Margutta, not forgetting my favorite camera, the Leica M2. I took the usual route: Villa Borghese. I had felt annoyed, sad, troubled for a long while. I had to make a decision.

I arrived on the terrace of the Pincio feeling uncertain, kicking stones and leaves. The square was empty except for a young Japanese American couple observing and photographing the panorama of Rome. When the two noticed me, the boy held out their disposable Kodak Instamatic, asking me to photograph them. He gestured very politely, showing me the girl's ring so I would understand that they were on their honeymoon and wanted a picture of themselves with St. Peter's in the frame. I took their strange, fixed-focused camera, looked through the viewfinder, then handed the object back to the boy immediately. They gazed at me, puzzled and sad.

I took out my Leica, posed them, reversing their position so the girl's head rested on his shoulder, stepped back, and began to photograph them. They were amazed. I smiled and handed the boy my Leica, telling him that I would not need it anymore. As I walked away, the boy ran after me and said that he knew who I was.

I told him that was impossible. Even I didn't know.

Introduction

Forty years on, my phone still rings at all hours. Emails clog my inbox. I don't always know the language, but I always understand the questions: "Has Signor Bozzacchi started working again? Can we book him for a photo shoot?"

Photos that I took in the sixties and seventies keep appearing in magazines and newspapers around the world. Even when my name isn't credited, journalists and editors recognize my shots and presume that I've gone back to photography. It is a pleasure to find myself still in demand—but my camera remains hanging nearby on a hook.

When I explain that I'm not back in the business at all, the next question pops out inevitably, a question that has pursued me since 1976: "Why did you leave photography?"

The answer to that question is the story of my life, a story I've chosen to tell through images that have remained imprinted on my memory for so many years. Now, for the first time, the black-and-white life that I led in the sixties and seventies finally appears to me in its full range of color.

The curious thing is that, throughout the fourteen years of my extraordinary career as a photographer, I never truly believed that I had any talent. I was tormented by the thought that my clients might discover where I came from—a very plebeian Roman background—and think of me as a street kid who just got lucky. Which, of course, to some extent, is exactly what happened.

One moment I was retouching positives and negatives and spending my days in a windowless darkroom. The next I was living among the jet set, sailing on Elizabeth Taylor and Richard Burton's yacht, photographing Princess Grace Kelly and Prince Rainier in the royal palace of Monaco, and speeding along French highways in a famous "Bullitt" Mustang, Brigitte Bardot by my side.

One thing's for sure: I was in the right place—Rome—at the right time, when Hollywood fell in love with Italy and our dolce vita. My look—tight jeans, red hair, blue eyes—coupled with a shy and somewhat intro-

3

verted character brought out the best in my subjects, the essence of their sensuality. Remember, it was the sixties. No one wore underpants. They only got in the way.

When I worked, my camera often became an extension of my sexuality . . . or perhaps my sexuality was an extension of my camera? I said very little, instinctively letting my body language do the talking. My personal style became as seductive as it was original, and people would stop me in the street to ask for my autograph. Then they'd read my name and wonder who I was and what I did. Before I even became anybody, I gave the impression of already belonging to a world of famous people. In the end, I really did become part of that world. Deep down, however, I always felt like an outsider.

I should stress that my insecurity didn't stop me from entering the lives of many people who entrusted their image to my care: stars like Elizabeth Taylor and Richard Burton, Grace Kelly, Audrey Hepburn, Steve McQueen, Raquel Welch, Clint Eastwood; artists like Picasso; heads of state like Marshal Tito, the shah and Queen Farah of Iran; and many others in the world of the rich and famous. I'm convinced that all my doubts about my validity as an artist and as a young man in search of an identity were perceived as a demonstration of humility by the people I met. They appreciated that humility. It helped them open up to me and my camera. It got results and, in most cases, the photos were exceptional, even though it sometimes led to psychological consequences that could haunt both photographer and subject for a long time.

It's also true that my humility was born out of fear. I was terrified that the upper class would discover I'd dropped out of school, that I'd never formally studied photography, that I spoke halting English, and that the stunning locations my incredible career took me to were places I was often seeing for the first time. There were so many parties where I kept to myself, hiding behind my camera in order to discourage anyone who might decide to talk to me and thus burn my cover. At the time, all this insecurity left me terribly embarrassed.

However, looking back on those photos, I now realize that my insecurity itself was a key element in my success. The distance I perceived between myself—a street kid—and my extraordinary subjects gave my shots a perspective that made them special. The world was accustomed to seeing movie stars and top models enjoying the jet-set life through the eyes of photographers who enjoyed being part of the same circus. On the other hand, from my vantage point off to one side, at a table for one, all I saw were human beings: men and women, husbands and wives, fathers and mothers, friends and lovers. Those were my subjects: the people behind the legend. My satisfaction as an artist came from capturing with a mechanical eye an image that corresponded to the one seen by my naked eye.

Today it's easier for me to reflect on images imprinted in my memory, now that I have a deeper understanding of life, in and out of the limelight. I've no need to strike a pose, as I did back then. The introvert I was no longer exists.

Clearly I had my reasons for quitting. For one thing, after Elizabeth Taylor and Richard Burton's final divorce, the majority of the prestigious magazines that I'd collaborated with—*Look, Life, Epoca, Stern, Paris Match*—began to vanish. Many others changed their approach to photographs and celebrities. Scandal replaced glamour. Ugly photos were more in demand. Beauty was irrelevant and thus, too, was artistic expression. It all happened because of television, which made printed news old news. Magazines and newspapers needed something new to sell, and that something was photos of stars showing the worst of themselves.

Above all, however, I was tired of living with a triple personality: Gianni Bozzacchi, the photographer who had to have a certain attitude and who'd become introverted in order to hide his ignorance; Gianni, the jet-set photographer, if not playboy, invented by the press; Gianni "Il Roscio," the Redheaded Devil, the street kid who wanted to grow up, learn, and stop pretending to be somebody else.

I'd be lying if I said I didn't enjoy all the attention and privileges that sprang from my success: the headwaiters of luxury restaurants who'd lead me to the best table and later tear up the bill; intimate conversations with fascinating people; the company of a beautiful woman—or two . . . But I was tired of playing the role that I'd carved out for myself, tired of keeping up with its demands.

Nevertheless, forty years later, it's still the role I'm known for. I've since produced, written, and directed movies. I've published books. I've lectured on film and photography at universities all over the world. But even if I got elected president of the United States, I'd still be remembered as the man who was once Elizabeth Taylor's personal photographer.

My wife Kelley and I had been together for four years when, rummaging around in my archives one day, she realized that many of the photos

Gianni Bozzacchi, 1998. (Photo by Kelley Van Der Velden-Bozzacchi.)

she'd admired as an aspiring model and actress had been taken by me, many years before we met. She made me promise that, whatever it cost, I would share the body of my work with the world. She asked me why I'd shut that chapter of my life so abruptly. I tried to make her understand, but she wouldn't have it. "You can't throw away your past," she said. "Maybe you don't realize what you achieved. I'm going to help you!" So she did, and I promised, before her death in 1998, to do everything I could to get this book published.

It was Kelley who provided me with just the right perspective to review my archives and revisit my professional adventures frame by frame, and in so doing, she gave my life back to me.

In dreams one can meet great people. I am honored and awed to think that I not only met them in real life; I immortalized them. I lived with them and, almost always, we became friends.

Chapter 1

War, Hunger, and the Art of Getting By

May 1967. Monte Carlo. I'd met Elizabeth Taylor and Richard Burton in Cotonou, Africa, on the set of *The Comedians* a mere five months earlier. And now here I was, a guest on their yacht.

The moment we docked, I found a public phone, stuffed in a mountain of change, and spoke in the only language I knew, pure Roman dialect: "Hi, Ma. How's it going? I'm on Elizabeth Taylor's yacht with Richard Burton. Grace Kelly and Rainier are coming to visit."

Mamma: "You're okay, aren't you?"

Me: "Sure, Ma, but did you get what I said?"

Mamma: "Don't call me with another string of lies!" *Click.* She hung up.

I can hardly blame my mother for not believing me. She always said I had a vivid imagination . . . from the moment I decided to be born, in the small hours of the night of June 30, 1943, right in the middle of an Allied air raid on Rome.

My father, Bruno, had enlisted in the army and was posted as a photographer with the army entertainment corps, stationed on Monte Mario, Rome's highest hill. The moment he heard that my mother had gone into labor, he stole a bicycle and rode fifteen miles straight, arriving just in time to see me born. You could claim that my father was a fully accredited bicycle thief, given that he served alongside both Vittorio De Sica, the holy father of Italian neorealism, and the actor Amadeo Nazzari.

I'd chosen a bad moment to come into the world. Less than two months later, what Italians know simply as "September 8" happened: Italy severed relations with Germany and the army dissolved, a dramatic moment in our country's history, later immortalized in the classic 1960 Luigi Comencini movie, *Everybody Go Home*.

Taylor and Burton's floating home away from home.

My father was no supporter of the war, nor of the alliance with Germany. But neither was he a guerrilla fighter. He had only two passions: photography and, even more so, his family. He risked a lot for us over the following months, trying desperately to find food in farms while bombs rained on the city like hailstones. With two massive armies—the Germans and the Allies—stalemated in central Italy, Romans remember those days as a time of hunger, even starvation. One day my father managed to purchase a live sheep from a peasant in the countryside and herded it miles home on foot. The poor thing got butchered and cooked on the spot, and our block neighbors descended en masse to share in the feast. Unfortunately, no one had eaten properly in months, and the next day the entire building went down with galloping diarrhea.

Then the war ended, but not the hunger or the suffering. Bombed-out buildings stood as monumental witnesses to the victory of force and stupidity over reason. The air was thick with the acrid odor of victims still buried beneath the ruins, and time beat to the endless buzzing of countless swarms of flies. Curiously, those flies were to prove a resource. I'd sit on the bar of my father's bicycle and watch as the world went by. American army tanks and their crews, now masters of the city, fired my imagination. I watched as smiling, easygoing crewmen, their tank engines running, broke

My family just after the end of World War II. *From left:* my older brother, Giampiero; my mother, Bianca; me; and my sisters, Ofelia and Paola. (Photo by my father, Bruno Bozzacchi.)

eggs on red-hot armor plating and cooked omelets. They were my modern invincible superheroes, though in truth the truly invincible ones were those flies, swarming over the soldiers and their food in a siege that nothing and nobody seemed able to stop. Which is when my father, the veteran of a routed army, had his flash of genius, made a virtue of necessity, and designed and built our family's first-ever flycatcher. Taking a length of stout braided wire, he opened it at one end in the shape of a square-cornered slingshot and then wove a web of netting across it until, voilà, his prototype flycatcher was ready to go. All this, of course, with help from Bianca, his wife and my mother.

At that point I got my first-ever job: as sales assistant, bicycle guard, and flycatcher delivery boy. Every one of the few shops yet open wanted one of my father's contraptions, and in no time our well-to-do apartment block became a factory, where the boss was the pauper in the basement and the workers the wealthy inhabitants upstairs. I remember my father taking them their wages every Saturday and, above all, the table laden with black-market food, until then entirely unavailable to us. Ever since, whenever some fly buzzes around me, I remember all this, smile, and leave it be!

Our house was near the railway line, in the Villa Fiorelli district, which made daily life particularly dangerous. The air raids had finished. But the rail tracks were littered with unexploded bombs, and many people paid dearly for their curiosity or lack of attention, including some of my friends. Others simply disappeared from the district, merely because they were found together with the wrong people in the wrong place or because they said the wrong thing at the wrong time. This was when my antipathy for politics developed. I felt small, alienated from society. I thought more about running away than trying to find a place in the world around me. I didn't want to find another world; I wanted to flee the one I was in.

Many of my contemporaries embraced politics, from left to right, conforming to a system and to dominant myths that, fundamentally, they didn't understand. I could sense the suffering of those difficult and turbulent years, a time when suddenly you could be arrested for simply doing or saying something that only a week earlier had been accepted and even acclaimed.

I remember only one big party in my house, given in honor of the birth of my brother Renato in 1950; I can still see in my mind the gigantic bowl of spaghetti, dripping with butter and parmesan cheese, that my father prepared for the occasion. If I could only reproduce the sounds and

Then we were five: that's me between my sisters, Ofelia and Paola, while my parents proudly present our newborn brother, Renato, all of us posing in the Villa Fiorelli park in 1951. (Photo by my brother Giampiero.)

smells of that day . . . It's now almost impossible to imagine what it felt like to a seven-year-old boy like me. Breakfast for us was rarely more than a crust of yesterday's bread soaked in water and sprinkled with a few grains of sugar, to ward off hunger and "fool the throat," as we say in Italian. It would be years before I got my first taste of a real *amatriciana* pasta. Bacon just wasn't available in those hard times. That mountain of steaming spaghetti looked like Vesuvius to me, the butter a river of golden lava and the handful of parmesan manna from heaven, quenching the steam and giving off a smell of paradise. What a day we had! And when I got the honor of grating on a little more cheese, my father insisted that I whistle the tune to "My World Was My Family." If you whistle—my father would say—then your mouth can't steal the cheese.

To think that my father was of noble birth now brings a contented smile to my face. My paternal grandfather was Angelo Bozzacchi of Cannobio, a title originally from Lake Maggiore in the north of Italy. Angelo worked as a functionary with the State Education Ministry after being sacked from the Bank of Italy for having "ensnared"—as they used to say—my grandmother Liberta. Angelo came from a wealthier family than Liberta, and the wealth difference, together with my grandfather's jealousy, led inevitably to a separation, which he hadn't wanted. It was 1935. You can imagine the scandal! He left Liberta with their apartment and all the furnishings, hoping that she might change her mind. But when this didn't happen, the pain of the separation and the humiliation he felt led Angelo to end his life in a horrible way: he cut his wrists and drank muriatic acid.

In time, though in a less frightful way, my father also had to pay for this class distinction and my grandmother Liberta's wealth. She opposed his decision to marry my mother, Bianca, on the grounds that she came from a family with no title or money. To make her position absolutely clear, she bought a house for my uncle Mario, my father's only brother, simultaneously putting the family inheritance in his name. My father, aged twenty, married my mother anyway and kept working as an army photographer for the National Photographic Collection, which posted him to the Army Film Corps. During the war he was part of a reconnaissance team detailed to photograph target zones before and after bombing, mostly in North Africa, Somalia, Eritrea, and Libya.

My father had to sweat blood to get what he had, but he did it for love of his wife and his work. And he taught us kids that there is nothing more beautiful than doing what you love and living with people you love. Maybe it was thanks to this that we all felt that the little we had was actually a lot. Our apartment was in a basement. Through its windows I could see the street that ran above it, and I felt smaller than a tiny child. Those people outside were walking on my head. Inevitably, I learned to look up at people from the ground up and, as a result, never to lower my gaze.

The apartment consisted of three rooms. Not three bedrooms. Three rooms, total. Plus a corridor, where I slept until I was sixteen. The kitchen had just enough room for a table, a four-ring gas stove, a sink, and a dresser, where we stored our few provisions. The adjoining room, the bathroom, shared the same plumbing: the kitchen sink on one side of the wall and the washbasin on the other. This was a guaranteed source of fun for us kids. Our father would finish dressing and then go into the bathroom to wash his face. We'd race into the kitchen and open the tap. Therefore finding almost no water pressure in the washbasin, he'd open that tap fully. We'd then promptly cut off the one in the kitchen, causing a geyser of water to gush into his washbasin. He'd bellow and storm out of the bathroom like a fury, though in truth he was never really angry. He'd let us have our bit of fun, especially on days when food was short or there was no money, days when we had nothing else to laugh about. And my father always respected our right to be kids.

The third room was the dining room, where there was another table and a fold-up bed where my older brother, Giampiero, slept. He was the only one of us with a lockable bedside cabinet where he kept his things. I would regularly pick the lock and filch any small change. My sisters had their own space in the corridor and slept on a bed that folded out from the wall. My own bed was by the front door, facing the kitchen and bathroom. I remember the cold—we often couldn't afford heating. But that house was everything to me, and it was only at home with my family that I felt that sense of being safe in a nest of union, of belonging. I didn't like the world outside. To me it always seemed an unpleasant and dangerous place.

One day my older sister Ofelia came to get me from kindergarten. We were walking home, hand in hand, when a gypsy woman stopped us. My sister moved to shield me from the woman, but she was actually very kind. She insisted on reading my palm, asking for nothing in exchange. I've never forgotten what she told me: "One day you will have a bad accident, but you've no need to worry, because your lifeline is very long. And your father will have five children."

At the time, my father had only four children. I thought the gypsy woman was making fun of me. But her prediction came true: in 1950 my father had his fifth child, Renato, also known as "butter and cheese spaghetti."

However, it was another thing in that encounter that really struck my young imagination: the gypsy woman wasn't able to find my luck line, which generally runs parallel to your lifeline. Back home, I got a penknife, shut myself in the bathroom, and tried to carve my own luck line across my palm. Hearing me weep with pain, my father rushed into the bathroom, took me in his arms, and said: "Little Gianni, what are you doing?" I replied that I was tracing my luck line. "That's all nonsense," he said. "You are our good luck." He then disinfected my hand and we never mentioned it again. That was my father, too: he respected my decisions, often saying nothing even when he disagreed. I'd love to meet that gypsy woman again one day, just to tell her she got it dead on. Who knows how old she was that day: twenty, thirty, forty? All I know is, more than sixty years have gone by since then . . .

After leaving the army, my father became head of the government

Me, age two and a half, in Villa Fiorelli, the city park outside our home in Rome. (Photo by Bruno Bozzacchi.)

photography department and then went on to work until he retired for the Pathology of the Book Institute, which still has its headquarters in Rome and enjoys worldwide renown. The Pathology of the Book Institute is one of those places that few people have ever heard about, unless you happen to be one of its impressive clients: governments, museums, leading libraries, and top families from across the globe. To them it's world famous, a renowned center of excellence for rescuing, restoring, and preserving priceless books and documents.

These days, the first thing you find on its website are photos: fabulous shots of microscopic fungi that rot books, minuscule insects that eat them, acidic medieval inks that burn them over time. Whatever the problem, the institute has a team of international experts who know what to do about it. Currently, it's involved in restoring a precious copy of Boccaccio's

Decameron, pages of the still-mysterious Dead Sea Scrolls, a key medieval papal decree, and an extremely rare seventh-century copy of the Koran, found recently in the Great Mosque in Sana'a, Yemen.

The institute was founded in 1938, and my father was a central part of its life for decades. Applying a photographic technique using ultraviolet rays, he effectively spent his career bringing back to light images—on paper and parchment—that had faded over time. His work there involved photographing a huge number of valuable documents, with the result that my family came into contact with important people in political and ecclesiastic circles. For instance, I often met Cardinal Stefan Wyszyński, the man who would soon become primate of Poland, and is known by many today as the Primate of the Millennium. My father collaborated with him for many years on restoring the archive of the Polish Catholic Church, making microfilm copies of books destroyed in Poland during the war, using replacements that Polish people from around the world were sending to Rome.

But my favorite priest was Father Karol. I met him on numerous occasions between the end of the 1940s and the early 1950s. He was the goalkeeper for us kids. He'd stand guard between a tree and a fountain, and we would take turns shooting penalties at him. Only later, when the memory matured, did I appreciate the extraordinary metaphor in Father Karol acting as goalkeeper for our best shots.

He was a good-looking man, with penetrating eyes. I'd make fun of him for his Polish accent. One day he got his pronunciation so wrong that I thought he wanted to dance, when all he actually wanted to do was talk. He was always very kind and generous. He always had candy or some little gift for us kids. Intuitive, he had a great sense of humor and a very poetic way of talking about life and God. I didn't understand everything he told me, but I pretended to because I didn't want to appear ignorant.

I saw him as a very spiritual person and, even though I was just a kid, when I heard him talk about God, or politics, or my duties toward my family, I knew that Father Karol was different, that he possessed a special kind of compassion, a greatness and a profound faith in God that would one day be revealed to the world. Indeed, many years later a puff of white smoke emerged from the Vatican's Sistine Chapel chimney announcing that the world had a new pope: our Father Karol Wojtyla had become Pope John Paul II.

Father Karol often questioned me about my faith because he knew my mother attended a different church, the Seventh-day Adventist. But he never made me feel I wasn't a good Christian. One day I told him about a priest who had come to our school because one of my classmates had lost his mother. The priest gave us a long sermon about redemption, telling us that our classmate's mother was in heaven. I raised my hand and asked if the dead were judged immediately. He said they were, so I asked why Catholics believed that Jesus would come to judge both the living and the dead. So it is written in the "Creed," a prayer I'd heard often in church. He didn't reply. But from that day on they wouldn't let me stay in class during the religious education hour. Father Karol was very annoyed about how I had been treated.

Happily, Father Karol's gifts were noticed and appreciated by those above him, with the result that two things happened: he began to scale the ecclesiastical ladder, and—quite understandably—he visited our neighborhood far less often. I remember one or two other teenage soccer matches. But then, in 1963, Pope Paul VI named him archbishop of Cracow, and his visits became increasingly rare. I can imagine what you're wondering. The answer is yes: Pope John Paul II, as well as being an exceptional person, was also an excellent soccer player.

One day in 2005, I met Giuseppe Rusconi, editor of the ecclesiastical magazine *Il Consulente RE,* on a train. He asked if he could interview me about my career, and he published the result in the September issue of that year. It's thanks to him that I began to recall certain dates and details of my relationship with Father Karol. In a life like mine, where you go beyond your dreams, then decide to start again from scratch, certain moments inevitably get filed away in hidden archives, then sit there like bricks, a part of the building, waiting for something to bring them back to light.

I can remember every detail of the day I first started taking photos. I was eight years old. My father had a number of cameras at home, but I wasn't allowed to touch any of them because they were state property. The best was a Rolleicord, just a notch below the queen of cameras, the Rolleiflex. I spent my days looking longingly at the cameras and begging my father to let me use them. He patiently began to explain how to adjust the focus, the differences between the various lenses, and so on. But it was my first shoot outdoors that I remember so vividly. We were sitting outside a bar after my cousin's wedding, and I was on my mother's lap. I asked my father if he would give me his camera. And he did. My first subject was my sister Paola, a beautiful girl with red hair and marvelous brown eyes. This was when it all started.

From then on my father began to take me with him to work. I learned by observing him. And he paid me, teaching me to value time even when you are doing something you love. He wanted me to discover this, and many other things, by myself. There was a changing room outside the darkroom where we'd hang our coats and change into overalls before going inside. He'd leave money in one of his pockets and let me take a little cash after I'd helped out, always checking to see just how much I took and whether it was appropriate to the amount of work I'd done. It was like that rule of giving and receiving, respecting all parties in a deal. He wouldn't let me print my photos on state material. I had to spend the money I'd earned to buy my own paper. But even though I liked learning all that stuff about photography, I didn't want to become a photographer then. I knew my father didn't earn much, and I was convinced there was no future in his profession.

Nevertheless, the more I used a camera, the more it became a passion. I'd watch while my father took endless photos with his enormous wooden-box camera, a huge machine that projected an inverted negative at the back of the box. Since the image reflected on the glass was upside down, and I wanted to see it as I did normally, I'd climb on top of that enormous machine and hang myself upside down, thus making the image look right way up. You could say I learned to take photos upside down.

When I wasn't working with my father, I was out on the streets raising Cain. I was known in my neighborhood as Il Roscio, the Redheaded Devil. My friends and I formed a notorious gang, the Villa Fiorelli Gang, and we were not averse to turning to theft for survival from time to time. We had a system. A lot of families got their groceries home-delivered by young guys on tricycles. We'd hide nearby. When one stopped to make a delivery, we'd run out and steal straight from the basket on his bike: sausages, bread, fruit—whatever we could grab. We had to be careful not to make the theft too obvious by taking too much at one time. So we'd follow the guy to his next delivery, and another bit of his load would vanish. We'd go on like that until we'd assembled a decent meal, and then go off together to eat it.

From ages six to ten, my gang was pretty much my entire life. We'd clash with other gangs in stone-throwing battles, which meant we always made sure to keep our pockets full of good rocks. I lost count of how many times I went home with my head cut by flying stones. Later, when my mother realized that the only thing I used my pockets for was to hold stones, she cut them all out.

My youngest daughter, Astoria, perches on top of my father's old studio camera, just as I used to do as a kid.

Come summer, when our parents would let us go out for a couple of hours after supper, our favorite pastimes were staging battles with water bombs or with paper-cone darts, hand-rolled, licked, and shot through oiled tubes to make the dart fly faster. Often, around dusk, before we'd have to run home, we'd go down to the "arches," the remains of the ancient Roman aqueduct that you can still see alongside Rome's Casilina rail lines. Young couples would use the aqueduct's deep brick alcoves as a lovers' lane. We'd hide, then ambush poor couples, dousing them with a storm of water bombs before racing away. One night I managed to water-bomb my own older brother during a romantic tryst.

Given that our pockets regularly got shredded with all that stone carrying—notwithstanding my mother's sewing efforts—we'd often hide around the fountain and play "touch the bird." This involved waiting for a suitably gullible older girl to come by. One of us would innocently join the girl at the fountain, pretend to wash his hands, and then ask if she could help get his handkerchief out of his pocket. When the trick worked, she got much more than a hanky in her hand.

My best friends were Sergio "the Blondie" and Gaetano, known as Tano. We were inseparable. On more than one occasion we ran away from home together to avoid being punished by our parents. We'd go to the rail depot and sleep in the empty wagons. One night our wagon started moving while we were asleep. We woke in a panic and leapt off before the whole train left.

One day, when I was fourteen or fifteen, Sergio suggested we go up to Via Veneto and take photos of people. I didn't think twice. Without asking permission, I took my father's Rolleicord, leapt onto a Vespa with Sergio, and off we went.

Sergio and I started going regularly to Via Veneto just to look at the people, to be able to say we were there when Kirk Douglas arrived in his Ferrari, or when Sophia Loren passed by. Nothing special ever happened on our own street, an anonymous residential block just like a thousand others in Rome. Via Veneto was another planet, a glittering world of smart cafés, fashion boutiques, and luxury hotels, peopled by those who moved in the most elegant social circles. Before too long, Federico Fellini would immortalize the place and its moment in his classic movie *La Dolce Vita*, and the street now has a square named after the master.

That first day, Sergio and I saw the famous British actor Edmund Purdom coming out of a café with a woman on his arm. As they paused to

My father's prized Rolleicord, the camera I "borrowed" for my first teenage forays along Rome's already famous Via Veneto. (Photo by M&S Materiale fotografico.)

say good-bye he kissed her, and I snapped a photo. The woman told me she wanted a copy of the photo and gave me her name and address. Her name was Anna Magnani. I went home so happy that I told my father the whole story, even knowing that I'd get in trouble for having risked his Rolleicord on a Vespa. He used the camera, he'd explain, but it wasn't his—it belonged to the state. The next day, however, he let me come to his darkroom to develop and print my photo.

I made a contact and was both surprised and disappointed. The image I'd wanted, the one I'd seen with my own eye, just wasn't there. I had no idea what I'd done wrong. The only thing I could do—I thought—was to tell Magnani to her face. I got to her place, rang the bell, and took an elevator to the top floor, sweating all the way. Magnani's son, Luca, a kid my own age who walked on crutches, opened the door. I didn't have time to explain what I was doing there before Magnani herself appeared, wearing little more than a flimsy dressing gown. I'll remember her legs until my dying day. I was a bundle of nerves. I could see her whole body silhouetted against the light. I just handed her my print, mumbling something about being sorry for having ruined the photo.

She didn't seem to care. Instead she asked how old I was. And who had sent me to Via Veneto. Then she gave me a bit of advice: "Remember, every time you do something like that—take a photo of someone—you first have to ask their approval." I didn't reply. I'd no idea what to say. I'd had a chance to see Anna Magnani in a dressing gown—something extremely satisfying for a kid my age—but nothing made up for the humiliation I felt. The first real photo job I'd attempted only reinforced my decision never to become a photographer. I was furious with myself for having failed, for not having captured a marvelous shot.

I've followed the same principle throughout my career, every time I've pushed that button: when you transfer what you see with the naked eye to a mechanical eye, you need to be sure you get the same image you saw first. Click. I knew I had to satisfy not only my subject but also myself. On that occasion, I didn't satisfy anyone. I still didn't know how to follow and use my instincts.

But why did Magnani want that photo in the first place? It was strange that an actress of her standing should have insisted on having a copy delivered. If she'd thought I was merely some kid playing with a camera, or even a real photographer in search of a juicy scoop, she wouldn't have stopped me and she certainly wouldn't have asked to see the photo. Something about my attitude must have struck her.

Via Veneto was always an important crossroads to me, a fundamental place, alive with significant coincidences, like that moment with the gypsy woman. A few years earlier I'd experienced another one of those moments, without realizing it at the time. Back then the guy everyone adored in my neighborhood was an accountant by the name of Marcello Mastroianni. That's right, an accountant. He grew up in Via San Remo, just a few blocks from my house. He, too, was a frequent visitor to Via Veneto's cultural watershed.

In those days, the baker's son—some seven or eight years older—used to take me to our local bar to play pool. According to the rules, I shouldn't have been allowed to play because I was only ten. But every now and then the older guys would let me play anyway. One day Marcello stopped to watch one of our matches. When he got his turn on the table, he asked to play against me and I won. He gave me a 5-lira banknote, worth a loaf of bread or a few pieces of candy back then. That evening I proudly showed the banknote to my father. He promptly scolded me for not getting Marcello to autograph it.

It wasn't until months later that I understood why my father was annoyed. Carlo Lizzani's award-winning 1954 movie, *Chronicle of Poor Lovers*, hit the theaters, and suddenly, up there on the big screen, was our local hero, Marcello Mastroianni. Of course, by then I'd long spent the 5 liras, while Fellini's *La Dolce Vita*—which would make Marcello an international star—was still another ten years off. But my father, along with everyone else, already knew Marcello had something special.

After our pool game, he was always very friendly to me. And over the years I came to know him fairly well. He was a marvelous person, always very elegant, always smiling. Every now and then he'd ask if there was anything he could do for me. He glittered like a rising star, a vision, someone destined for fame. On one occasion he took me for a drive in his Jaguar convertible. People stopped just to watch us go by. In truth, all we did was take a turn around Piazza Ragusa, hardly Rome's most famous square. But I felt like I'd flown around the world.

The more that cinema came looking for me, the more I went looking for it. I'd skip school and hang out in cinemas, catching any movie I could. I don't recall ever going with my mother or father, and I never went to any theater drama productions. I was fascinated by American movies, so different from Italian neorealism. The people, whether beautiful or ugly, driving luxury cars or beaten-up old wrecks, always looked happy. And the movie that struck me more than any other wasn't Italian. It was the 1956 Robert Wise movie, *Somebody Up There Likes Me*, starring a young Paul Newman as boxing champ Rocky Graziano. What got me was the story, a boy struggling to find his way up in the world. I could identify with the same sense of exclusion, with the many trials Newman had to suffer to find his way in life, to find an identity. The character Newman played doubted that he shared his father's vocation to be a boxer just as I questioned the idea of following in my own father's footsteps as a photographer.

Meanwhile, between skipping school and spending afternoons out stealing with my gang, I watched American cinema evolve from the westerns I'd loved as a kid to different kinds of films starring my favorite actor, James Dean: *East of Eden* and *Rebel without a Cause*. Years later, Elizabeth Taylor told me that one of Dean's favorite sayings had always been: "Dream as if you'll live forever, live as if you'll die today." It's been a favorite of mine ever since.

I started toying with the idea that maybe I could become an actor myself. For me and other kids my age, cinema was a way out, especially

American cinema, with its luxury and its immortal heroes. I didn't like my world, and school was part of that world. I thought cinema might provide an alternative. Back then, however, the only place you could study acting in Rome was at the famous Cinecittà Studios. And the price was exorbitant. The students were all rich kids, people like Prince Orsini. I lost all hope. I didn't think I had a chance.

I felt like a prisoner of war plotting my escape, trying to find some gap that I could squeeze through, never losing the feeling that I could fly, the feeling Mastroianni had given me with that spin in his car. I racked my brain, imagining and dreaming of ways to flee the real world. Meanwhile, I was stuck with the one I had.

That summer vacation, aged thirteen, I went to work with my father in his darkroom and began to get a taste for real money—or what seemed like real money to a teenager. Come autumn, I couldn't figure out why I should sit still in class all day instead of going out to work. I liked the hands-on learning I got from my father and thought school was just a waste of time. Mine was more of a technical college than a high school, designed to introduce youngsters to a work environment. I signed up for the photography course. But I was more capable than my teachers. And they knew it. So they wouldn't include me on fun day trips away from school. They wouldn't give me the interesting homework that they gave the rest of the class. They knew I was better than they were and they resented it. The lack of humility typical of a teenager got the better of me, and I quit attending class.

I'd leave home in the morning, go to school and then, when the bell rang, slip out of a side door in the gymnasium and spend my day hanging out in the park with the other kids who'd skipped school. Or I'd slip into a cinema through the service door and watch one movie after another until some attendant nabbed me.

From time to time I'd work for Beautiful Babies of Italy. This involved me knocking on doors and taking free photos of people's babies. The organization paid me by the roll. They'd make prints of the little guys, and then send sales staff to flog contact prints of my shots to the parents. It was kind of a scam, really. I'd manage to do the work before school ended and get back in time for the bell, when I'd slip in through the gymnasium and leave through the front door.

This couldn't last, of course. Eventually the school wrote to my parents asking where I'd been. The next day my father went to school before classes ended and confirmed my absence for himself. When I reappeared later that afternoon, he exploded. He wanted me to follow in his footsteps at the Pathology of the Book Institute, and I couldn't do that without a high school diploma.

I knew only one sure thing about my future: I wasn't going to end up like my father, leaving home early in the morning, spending his days in a blacked-out darkroom, and getting home late at night, all for a pittance of a salary. That's what a photographer's life looked like to me. I didn't realize there was a difference between artistic work and technical work, and that you need to master both. Everything I knew about photography I'd learned from my father, and I couldn't imagine how a camera would lead me into any other life than one like his. I told him to his face that he didn't earn enough, that he was letting himself be exploited by the government, and that I didn't want to end up like him. He slapped my head so hard that he fractured his wrist and little finger.

Shortly before I turned fourteen, my father and I sat down to talk and he asked me straight: "What do you want to do? Do you want to leave school? I won't let you do that until you graduate."

I replied, "Okay, let's cut a deal. If I get top marks this year will you let me leave?"

My father laughed. "I accept the bet. You'll never, ever finish the year with top grades."

That autumn I threw myself into my books, and my grades began to improve. I had a lot of trouble with the woman who taught math and chemistry. She was convinced I was cheating, and the other teachers were highly suspicious too. They kept making me change my desk. They made me sit right up in the front row so they could find out what my trick was. But there was no trick. I'd simply never studied before. Now I was determined to show my father he was wrong.

When he saw my grades, he didn't believe me either. "How have you done this? You must have cheated."

He kept saying the same thing every time I brought him my latest school report. In the end, though, I finished the year with top grades and my father, to his regret, had to let me leave school and go to work. We'd made a bet and he kept his word. But did I really win? I still ask myself that question. I came to regret leaving school, because dropping out meant I missed out on a lot of learning and culture.

My father could claim a smaller victory. I was as determined as ever never to work in his darkroom, but I did want to earn money. And the only thing I knew how to do was develop photographs. In one sense, my dilemma was the same as ever: either go to school or go to a darkroom.

But now it was my decision, and that was enough for me. My dreams were the same as any other fifteen-year-old's: get rich, leave a mark, be the best in something. Right then, however, I didn't have the slightest clue what that "something" might be.

Chapter 2

A Roman Rebel without a Cause

One week after my final grades were posted, I found work in the Magicolor photo shop. The moment I arrived on my first day they gave me a mop and I spent the entire day cleaning the floor. The next day they made me wash the whole place: the equipment, the workbenches, the windows, everything. The third day they told me I was going to have to mop the floor again. I dunked a sponge in my bucket of water and threw it in the owner's face. "Clean it yourself," I said. "I quit."

If I absolutely had to work in a photo shop, at least I wanted a proper job, not work as a cleaning boy. So I found a job at a different photo shop near the Trevi Fountain. It mostly handled amateur photos. I developed and printed one hundred rolls a day. It felt like a jail sentence. I was basically doing exactly what my father did, spending my whole day in a darkroom. I clocked in early in the morning, when it was still dark, and left in the evening. I didn't see the sun for months and months. But I was happy to be making a bit of cash. Then summer came to an end, and work began to tail off. People had quit taking vacation photos for the year.

Then I heard about a job with Telephoto, a photo shop near Trinità dei Monti and the Spanish Steps. It specialized in cinema film. The pay was good and the work constant throughout the year. What's more, I'd be developing professional film set photos, which I considered much more interesting and demanding. Telephoto was on an entirely different level. Instead of turning out hundreds of amateur 10 × 15s, it handled images of extremely high quality, enlargements of all sizes, different lenses, different formats, glossy, matte, posters, everything. The company developed and printed a lot of Italian movies. I remember two by Pietro Germi: his 1958 movie *A Man of Straw* and the 1959 *The Facts of Murder*, starring Germi himself along with a young Claudia Cardinale. We also handled a lot of famous foreign movies, like *Ben Hur* and *Spartacus,* and everyone was on pins and needles when the negatives of *Cleopatra* arrived from England. In our own small way, we worked with the biggest movie ever made as well as with the world's biggest movie star, Elizabeth Taylor.

Unfortunately, the work at Telephoto proved harmful to my health. I did a lot of retouching of positives and negatives using solutions and gels that gave me bags under my eyes and wrinkles like the ones I was magically removing from prints with scalpel, brush, and Indian ink. I didn't realize that Telephoto was using those substances at concentrations of 100 percent in order to speed up the developing process. In the end, what with me developing all that film by hand, I got seriously ill. My bosses begged me to come back when I got better. But my father, outraged at the risks they'd exposed me to, insisted I find another job. So I was obliged to quit and get by on whatever odd jobs I could pick up around town: a retouch here, a photo there. I collaborated with the Luxardo and Cantera studios and, for a while, got steady work with the famous Canadian archaeologist-photographer Roloff Beny. He toured the world photographing ruins in places like Tuscany, India, Mongolia, Iran. It gave me a chance to handle fascinating, exotic images. Beny used very large negatives and closed the stop right down in order to capture as much detail as possible. My job was to hide the errors, correct the imperfections, sharpen the focus, and produce absolutely perfect prints. Beny adored my work. And he adored me too . . . rather too much. I was seventeen. In Europe at that time you still didn't see many people in tight jeans and running shoes. My red hair and American style gave me a very special look, especially on the streets of Rome. And— to guys like Beny—that look clearly conveyed the wrong impression. Eventually he became a tad too friendly. Once again, I was obliged to quit.

I kept learning whatever I could from famous photographers I'd meet, such as Ivan Tchicanovich. It was he who taught me how to exploit light, which became one of my most valuable techniques. The word *photography* comes from the Greek *phōtos* and *graphé,* which together mean "drawing with light." If you use light in the right way, you don't need to retouch the image with chemicals or ink—nor with a computer, as they do today. Adjusting the light to smooth out imperfections confers a truth and purity to images that is lost if you rely on retouching later in the darkroom. I learned that lesson so well that, throughout my career, I rarely had to retouch my own photos.

Tchicanovich was very demanding and meticulous. He wanted everything to be very fluid, bathed in light tones of gray. He'd underexpose and overexpose his film in order to give the photos very little contrast. It was a style suited to the glossy tourism and nature magazines that published his photos. To my mind, however, the lack of contrast produced prints that were flat and dull. There was less of the realism and clarity that I was accustomed to seeing in my own photos, in those of my father, in neorealist cinema, and out on the street. Tchicanovich said I was young and presumptuous. It took me years to realize that, in reality, the object of our argument was his style compared with what would become mine: the glossy fashion magazines against the naked eye, which goes beyond artifice and celebrity, penetrating the intimacy of its subject. At the time I knew I was right because my father shared my opinion about Tchicanovich's technique. So, I was putting in eight, nine hours a day in a darkroom, with no artistic satisfaction, printing photos I didn't like. What did I do a few weeks later? Sure, I quit.

It goes without saying that I felt frustrated. My first experience with professional photography only seemed to reinforce my conviction that this wasn't the career for me. But what else could I do?

One day a friend convinced me to go to a casting call in a Via Margutta studio, the one that featured Gregory Peck in *Roman Holiday,* near Piazza di Spagna. A new director was preparing his first movie, and they were doing open casting. I had nothing else to do, so I figured, why not?

After pre-casting, they sent me to the Arco Film offices, where I met the producer, Alfredo Bini, and the director, Pier Paolo Pasolini, in a room full of mirrors. Pasolini was wearing a weird painter's jacket, dark pants, and zipped boots. I was wearing a custom-tailored outfit: beige pants and a bolero-style jacket. I didn't look Roman. I didn't even look Italian. Pasolini studied my red hair, cupid face, and wide blue eyes and said, "So who painted you?" Then, turning to the actress Laura Bettie: "What do you think? He's unusual, almost American. Looks like he came straight out of *Rebel without a Cause.*" He took my hand and added, "Let's give him a screen test."

While Laura was shooting the test, Pasolini kept moving around me, caressing me every time he came close. The moment the test was over I ran out of there. I'd no idea what he was doing. But whatever it was, I definitely knew I didn't want it.

Pasolini was already a leading figure in the emerging Roman cinema.

Me, age seventeen, screen-testing for Pier Paolo Pasolini's *Accattone*. Unfortunately, the great director found me far too attractive for comfort, and I fled. Ten years later I managed to get this copy from photographer Alfredo Bini.

He's remembered today as one of the major intellectuals of the entire twentieth century, not to mention celebrated as a gay icon. Back then, however, I'm afraid he had to do his groundbreaking movie—*Accattone*—without me.

A few days later, ever fascinated with cinema, a friend and I rode our bicycles to Via Veneto to watch Federico Fellini shooting *La Dolce Vita*. And who should I see in front of the camera but the accountant I used to shoot pool with, Marcello Mastroianni? That was the first time I fully realized he really was a famous actor. More, in fact—he was a star. At one point Fellini and Mastroianni moved away from the set to discuss something in private and passed close by. Marcello saw me, gave me a hug, and introduced me to Fellini. The only clear memory I have of that moment is that I blushed.

I went to see the movie when it came out and didn't understand a thing. Which is rather ironic given that, like Marcello's character in the film, I didn't have any clear objectives myself either. I was dreaming of money and beautiful girls, and trying to make some sense of my life.

Meanwhile, Cinecittà was enjoying a wave of glory. Besides Italian movies, the Roman studios were welcoming a growing number of international productions, attracted by low costs and the expertise of artisans who were building the best sets and creating the best costumes in the world. Scores of producers, directors, and actors, eager to enjoy a slice of our "dolce vita," were shifting their shooting schedules to Rome, the most fashionable place to be at the time. And, since stars never travel alone, a swarm of friends and relatives trailed in their wake. Suddenly the world's top stars were adopting Rome as their second home.

Then word spread that production of *Cleopatra* would be completed at Cinecittà. Shooting in England had been suspended. Elizabeth Taylor had fallen ill and undergone an emergency tracheotomy. Her doctors said she would recover quicker in a warm climate, so the entire production moved to Rome. While Elizabeth was convalescing, they rebuilt all the sets and shot new scenes with minor actors. If something similar were to happen today, Hollywood wouldn't think twice about replacing the star, no matter how famous. Which gives you some idea of Elizabeth's greatness, of just how important it was to have her name on the poster of such a colossal production. Throughout the shooting of *Cleopatra*, the movie dominated conversation in Rome. Elizabeth was on the front cover of every magazine and pretty soon another face joined hers: Richard Burton's.

History's legendary love story between Cleopatra and Mark Antony stepped right out of the big screen into real life. Both Elizabeth and Richard were married to others at the time, and people of the older generation were scandalized at the mere hint of adultery. Those of the younger generation, on the other hand, were glued to the unfolding soap opera. In no time, the tale of the glittering Hollywood superstar who fell in love with the brooding Welsh actor became even bigger than the biggest movie ever made. Print editors eagerly rode the explosion of interest in celebrities and gossip and, before you knew it, scandal sheets were outnumbering every other publication for sale.

Television lost no time in following their example. Photos of Elizabeth and Richard, whether alone or together, sold for rafts of money. For the first time, you could really make a living as a photographer. All it took were a few spicy photos. Federico Fellini created the word *paparazzo* and made it famous in *La Dolce Vita*. But it was the feeding frenzy around Elizabeth and Richard that really gave birth to this new business, and to this new breed of photographer.

Everyone in Rome wanted to be involved in the shooting of *Cleopatra* firsthand and to come into contact with Elizabeth and Richard. It was a gigantic production, and lots of Romans found work on the set. There was a constant demand for extras to fill the enormous crowd scenes. I was still looking for work and went to the set to try out for the role of an archer. I knew I was too thin, so I'd submitted doctored photos, with my head stuck onto the much stockier body of my friend Massimo. It must have been the one time I botched a touch-up job, because I didn't get the part.

An enormous open space behind the Cinecittà Studios was packed with thousands of extras, all in costume. I spotted Elizabeth in the distance. A golf cart was taking her from her dressing room to the set. Only people who were actually part of the movie and authorized to be near the star could go any closer. Everything was organized in an almost maniacal fashion.

Years later I became friends with Alberto De Rossi, the makeup artist on *Cleopatra*. We talked about the movie on a couple of occasions. He told me how one day the director, Joseph Mankiewicz, pointed at a crowd of thousands of Italian and English extras, their faces all darkened to look Egyptian, and shouted, "Alberto! What's wrong with you? The third man from the left is not made up!"

To which Alberto replied: "Go fuck yourself."

Alberto would get up at 2 in the morning to do all the makeup. Elizabeth was accustomed to having hers redone during the shooting. But Alberto was a perfectionist: he'd dedicate an hour and a half to her face and ten minutes to the rest of her body, and having to redo a perfect job made

My friend Massimo (*left*) and me, age sixteen, holding aloft my great friend Tano. I took this shot on auto-remote with my very first camera, a Bakelite-encased Agfa Pioneer.

The camera that started it all. (Photo by Kristy Tayler.)

him angry. "My makeup has no need of retouching!" he'd shout. However, since he didn't speak any English, he had a hard time speaking directly to Elizabeth. In the end he got so fed up he threw a wet sponge in her face and left.

I kept having one disappointment after another. My career as an actor was over before it began. Nevertheless, since I didn't consider myself a real photographer, I never even dreamed of looking for work with my camera. But I didn't want to go back to developing. I was terrified of ending up like my father, grinding his life away in a darkroom.

The only way of avoiding that fate was money. But I didn't have any. Then I became friends with Giacomo, the son of a newspaper distributor. He was only one year older than me, but he already drove a convertible and happily squandered money left and right. I decided to join him and his job, delivering newspapers—which didn't mean just going round the neighborhood on a bicycle. It was quite another operation altogether. We handled a lot of leading publications: *Tuttosport, La Gazzetta Dello Sport, Il Resto del Carlino, Lo Stadio, La Nazione.* But they were all printed in the north of Italy. Getting copies to Rome's 530 newsstands on time was a problem. In those days planes weren't allowed to take off or land after midnight in coastal cities, which ruled out airfreight. Yet trains were unreliable and too often arrived late. And when that happened, sales plunged below the threshold of costs covered by advertising. There was only one solution: deliver by car. So, to guarantee a dawn delivery, we began driving back and forth between Milan and Rome, well over six hundred miles a night.

The papers would come off the presses around 1:15 a.m. By 5:00 we had to be in Rome. We went fast, dangerously fast, especially given our poor brakes and heavy loads. But the risk to our lives was worth it—the plan worked. We'd make 15,000 liras a night (around $300 today), and at some point people began talking about the crazy newspaper deliverers and their mad dash from Milan to Rome. We became famous on the semiprofessional racing circuits, in part thanks to a few exaggerated anecdotes. We were lucky, it's true. But we were also very good.

Nevertheless, none of us involved seemed to realize the dangers involved in racing six hundred miles by night at full speed through snow, rain, fog . . . and all just to stay in business. This new passion became a kind of vocation in itself. Without trying, we set a new speed record for the drive between Milan and Rome. And when money began coming in, we acquired faster cars with appropriately modified engines that could race to

125 miles per hour, an exhilarating speed at a time when even the latest Ferraris were topping out at 140 mph. Whenever anyone asked me what line of work I was in, I'd say, "Journalism."

One night, in bad weather, I was driving the two-lane Autostrada del Sole highway across the Apennine Mountains. Right after the Bologna viaduct there was a long downhill stretch. I hadn't anticipated how the newspaper load that had previously slowed my car would now act as an accelerator on the downhill run. I hit a bend at top speed and found myself slap in front of two trucks coming the other way, one in the process of passing the other. Braking would have been pointless, so I swerved into the emergency lane, only to find that blocked by a parked car. As if someone had put it there on purpose. My last hope was to rack the handbrake and slam the steering wheel, which sent me into a spin. The front wheels skidded and the back of my car smacked into the rear of the outside truck. My Opel Kapitan split in two. When what remained of the wreck came to a halt, I crawled out on all fours, sure I'd broken every bone in my body. But I didn't feel any pain. Newspapers filled the air, fluttering down like ghosts in the headlights of other oncoming cars, which luckily all managed to stop in time. Someone asked me if I was still alive. I said, "Yes," and then fainted.

I had other, even more dangerous accidents, but driving gave me my first taste of fame. Minor fame, for sure, but fame all the same. I soon became a regular visitor to the semiprofessional racecourses. Fans noticed me, and the Fiat Giannini team offered me a tryout. People bet on me across Italy—illegally making far more money than I ever earned winning the races.

My father wasn't at all happy about my new career. He thought I was wasting my time and talent, and kept asking me, "Don't you know you've got a gift?" which only made me angry. "What gift?" I'd reply every time. "I'm a failure! I've got nothing and know nothing!"

My photography was instinctive. It came easy to me. I didn't realize this could constitute a gift, a talent. My father had shown me all the essential technical aspects: how to use a stop, a shutter, calculate ASA grades, frame a subject properly in order to get a printable result. But photographing documents for restoration purposes is not the same as photographing a person. No one had ever taught me how to position a face so as to have the light strike it in the right way and then reflect into the camera, creating a beautiful image. There are a lot of rules about how to obtain a good photo. One simple example: if someone is short, they should be shot from below, so as not to emphasize their lack of height. And you don't use the same lens to photograph someone with a long face as opposed to a round one.

However, since I'd never formally studied photography, I didn't know all this stuff. All I knew was how to obtain the image I wanted. My father, on the other hand, knew all the rules and saw in me the same special something that Anna Magnani had noticed. He recognized the artistic quality in my photos and knew that professionals and critics would react in a way that I wasn't able to understand at that point in my life. Only years later, well after I'd retired from the profession, was I able to look back at my work with a critical eye and see what he had seen. And only now do I fully appreciate the technical decisions I made. Because, back then, and throughout the first part of my career, I didn't even realize I was making them.

My sports car racing widened the gap between my father and me. We argued a lot. Once he even slapped me. I felt so humiliated I didn't go home for two days. On another occasion, I heard my parents arguing about a book my brother needed for school. My father said he didn't have the money and my brother was crying. So I just dumped a fistful of crumpled banknotes onto the table, far more than the sum required. The gesture offended my father. He threw my "dirty money" onto the floor and began pulling 1,000-lira banknotes out of his wallet, each one looking as if it had just been starched and ironed. I left my cash where it lay and stormed out of the house. My mother cleared it up and used it later. But I didn't care what my father thought about my money, nor how I'd earned it. The gift he saw in my photography, I saw in my skill at the wheel. And even if part of it was sheer luck—more than I realized—I was earning enough to aspire to a life beyond our basement, maybe somewhere along the brightly lit streets around Via Veneto.

Then, on September 20, 1962, my luck ran out. Doing well over 140 mph in an Alfa Romeo GTA, I hit a wet patch on the road. The car flipped into the air, slammed back onto the asphalt like a rock, and began spinning out of control. A moment later my life stopped. I heard a doctor say there was little they could do. I fought in silence, sensing the presence of someone watching over my involuntary sleep. After weeks of slipping in and out of a coma, I came back to the light. The first thing I saw was the figure I'd sensed beside my bed all that time. My father, so emotional that he had tears in his eyes as he caressed my face, was sitting in the light that I'd been following all those weeks, the light that was now leading me back to life. All my brothers and sisters came to visit me, though I don't remember it. I was still in another world. One day my girlfriend Patrizia came too. I remember her, but not my sister Paola, who'd accompanied her to the hospital.

A nun, Sister Elena, looked after me. Dressed all in white, she looked radiantly beautiful to me, like an angel, and I was so shy. I said she looked like Simonetta Vespucci, Botticelli's famous model, and that she was sexy. She blushed easily. I'd make fun of her, teasing her with sexy pranks, like sticking my fingers up beneath the sheets, at which she'd flee the room.

When I finally returned home I had no strength. A friend suggested exercises I could do to re-form my muscles and resynchronize my reflexes. I spent hours lying flat on my back moving my legs and arms in various ways, struggling to restore communication between my brain and my limbs. As soon as I was well enough to drive I went back to visit Sister Elena, to thank her with a little gift but also to see her again. At first I didn't even recognize her. Not only was she not the beauty I'd printed in my mind, she was actually rather ugly. Saying good-bye, I instinctively tried to give her a hug. That was the last time I saw her flee a room.

I knew my racing career was over—assuming it had ever actually begun. My injuries would eventually heal completely, and there'd be no physical obstacle to me going back to racing with the Giannini team, nor to resuming the Milan-Rome newspaper delivery business. But I would never recapture the mental attitude—courage combined with lightheartedness. The moment you start asking yourself if you can take a bend at a certain speed, instead of just doing it, the race is over. Worse still, you become dangerous to yourself and to others. Even if I did try to return to racing, I knew I'd never again feel that inner rush, my mind one with the roar of the engine. What I'd hear instead would be the voice of that young man in a coma, confined to a hospital bed, begging me to brake when I needed to accelerate, hesitating at every bend and every straight. I'd feel fear. So I quit racing.

There would be other moments: gunning a "Bullitt" Mustang through the streets of southern France, or the time I took a Ferrari from Milwaukee to Chicago in forty-five minutes, no kids or wife on board to worry about. But even back then, at just nineteen years old, my body and mind still recovering, I realized that I'd always felt fear, that fear had been what attracted me to racing in the first place. But now that same fear would become a demon rather than a lure.

Nevertheless, photography to me was still that terrible government

My beloved Pentax Asahi, with its 28 mm lens. (Photo by M&S Materiale fotografico.)

job my father did in a darkroom. Even when I was convalescing at home, I rarely saw him. He'd leave at 7 in the morning, come home for a quick lunch, and then go back to work until 8 at night. That was his life. And if that was my "gift," I didn't want it. I'd tried to convince myself and others that I was a race car driver in order to flee that prison, that miserable salary, and those long hours.

Back in our basement apartment there was a little alcove at the end of the corridor covered with a curtain. We all used it as a kind of closet. Before the accident, I'd bought a brand-new Pentax with two lenses and had hidden it back in there, where my father wouldn't see it. One morning, convalescing at home, my mother at the market and my father at work, I got it out, still in its original packaging, took it into the bathroom, and opened it up.

I began a dialogue with that camera, weighing it in my hands, studying the aperture, the two lenses, the exposure meter. I felt confused, but I knew that camera and I had to get along, had to go somewhere together, although the road we took was going to be radically different from my father's.

To be absolutely honest, I have to confess that I feared photography for another reason. Despite the natural talent with a camera that everyone recognized in me, I had never done any formal study. I'd observed and imitated my father. The rest was instinct. What I didn't know at the time was that a path was actually already opening above my head, right outside, in the streets of Rome.

Chapter 3

After the Neorealism

It's not easy trying to describe major cultural change. At school they taught us that a series of small events eventually gives rise to something new. In movies, there's a major event, then a fade to black, and everything's different in the next scene. I've always felt more at ease in a cinema than a classroom. What's more, I'd just faded to black myself, almost literally. Which is why, for me, it felt like the sixties began overnight. I went to sleep beneath the clouds of De Sica and Rossellini and woke in the sunshine of Pietro Germi and Federico Fellini.

Returning to the streets of Rome after my accident, I discovered that *La Dolce Vita* was the movie of the moment. So I went to see it again, and this time I understood it a bit better. On the one hand, it exalted the widespread sense of excitement and liberation that was in the air at the time. Simultaneously, it put us on guard against the decadence that could follow. What had captured the imagination of the world was not just the beautiful people, the clothes, the restaurants, the wild parties and carefree sex, but also the ease of "the sweet life" that Fellini had brought to the screen. After a decade spent rebuilding cities, brick by brick, Italians had had enough. We didn't want to scrimp and save just to buy bread anymore. We wanted to buy restyled French or American jeans and designer shirts. We didn't want to be slaves to a corrupt government anymore. We wanted to party in the best restaurants. And then, of course, "the pill" arrived, and suddenly everyone was talking openly about sex, without feeling afraid or guilty. It was as if everyone took one deep breath, then let everything out at once. And all this despite the fact that the Vatican dome still loomed over not just Rome but over much of Europe too.

Fellini went straight to the heart of this new feeling in the famous opening scene of *La Dolce Vita*, in which a statue of Jesus, suspended from a helicopter, soars over a snarled-up traffic jam. In a city so dominated by the Vatican and religion, we all grew up with the constant refrain that God was looking down on us from on high, and would judge us for everything we did. Fellini broke with all that, making use of that sense of irony that we Romans are masters of, dangling Christ on a rope above our heads. It goes without saying that the Vatican didn't appreciate his sense of humor and soundly condemned the movie. But that only served to reinforce the split between the old Rome and the new, a fissure that the Catholic Church would start trying to heal a few years later with Vatican Council II. Fellini's Christ became a symbol of an irreverent search for pleasure and of the flowering of a new culture that would characterize postwar Rome.

I'd watched Fellini shoot his masterpiece in 1959. Now, in 1963, it felt as if I'd punched a hole in the big screen and stepped right into the movie itself, wandering through the streets of the same glorious Rome anticipated by *La Dolce Vita*.

The epicenter of this renaissance was Via Margutta, a street of artists just around the corner from Piazza di Spagna. Imagine the potent concentration of Hollywood glamour offered by Sunset Boulevard all compressed into just a few short blocks, and you'll get an idea of what Via Margutta felt like in those days. It was the place to go to see Rome's beautiful people, the place to be seen if you were one of them. Or—as in my case—if you were trying to be.

One of the leading figures in the Via Margutta scene was Johnny Moncada, the famous fashion photographer and business entrepreneur. His family owned a lot of buildings in that unique, extravagant, exceptional street. Moncada looked like Jack Lemmon dressed as a European aristocrat. The Moncada family belonged to Italian nobility and Johnny was actually a titled count. At some point he'd decided to become a photographer, bought everything he needed, and opened a studio in Via Margutta.

You could see Johnny was rich. More important, however, he had class. Almost anyone can make money, but not many people know how to do it with Johnny's style. Always impeccably dressed, with beautiful cars and an American former model as a wife, it was he who launched Ali McGraw and Veruschka. Nicola Pietrangeli, the leading tennis player of the time, was one of his best friends and a frequent customer in the same bars and restaurants.

I recognized people with class easily and was convinced that my family's humble background, along with my lack of schooling, separated me much more from Moncada's world than money. I was acutely aware of the difference between the Via Margutta community and my own.

Word went around that Moncada was looking for an apprentice, someone good not only at retouching but also in other areas of photography. "Okay. Go for it," I said to myself, spurred on by youthful arrogance as much as the hard life I was having to deal with. I went to his studio and told him straight: I was the guy he was looking for. He thought I was too young but gave me a photo to retouch. I did an excellent job. A few days later he rang, and I began work the next morning.

Moncada had a lot of important customers and a lot of beautiful models. Definitely one of the perks of my job was watching all those stupendous women wander naked around the studio. Moncada had an original style that distinguished him from other fashion photographers of the time. He used a lot of contrast, giving mobility to the immobility typical of standard fashion shots. On one occasion, for example, he shot a collection with a sports car race in the background. He was the first to use 35 mm film for fashion, instead of TMX 120 film or other large formats. And he never used a tripod. He worked hard on 400 ASA film, pushing it up to 1600, creating a heavily grained effect, very unusual for a fashion shoot in those days. He was also very creative with light. With the help of an umbrella flash, he'd project light first off the ceiling and then onto the models, rendering it much softer and suffused but with the same high contrast. Moncada effectively found a way to illuminate shadow. His photos winked at critics and the public, but also turned off a lot of people. At all costs, he wanted to be considered an artist, not merely an aristocrat in search of recognition. Consequently, he did everything he could to produce unusual and provocative photos with great artistic flair. The result was a very innovative style, very different from that of other photographers, and the fashion industry respected this.

Working with Moncada, I saw the how and why of his flirting with models. The aim was to make them more attractive and sensual, from the inside out. In those days, models were almost mannequins. It was up to the photographer to tell them what expression to assume, how they should pose, everything. The girls were all incredibly thin. They didn't eat, they didn't drink, they all looked sad. Moncada was the first to penetrate their veneer, stimulate their intimacy, and make them feel like real women. I watched him do a shoot for a Permaflex mattress commercial that became famous. He got the model Pupa Baldieri to stretch out on a bed and then addressed her in an almost obscene fashion, or at least that's how it sounded to a young guy like me. But the result was so successful that Baldieri became known forever as "the Permaflex girl." These days you can regularly see more explicit scenes on prime-time TV. But at the time, I felt scandalized. Moncada wanted Pupa to look like she felt she was in heaven on that bed, a symbol of relaxation—but also a nod in the direction of sex. His veiled sexual innuendos brought out Pupa's sensuality, rendering the photos provocative but at the same time classy.

In the same period, I made friends with the character actor Mario Brega, a huge, kindhearted, rough diamond of a guy, almost famous. He got me a bit part in a B movie he was in, *Buffalo Bill: Hero of the Far West*. He was forty, six foot four, and almost three hundred pounds, a crazy monster. We once fought because he couldn't bear wearing socks that didn't match. I dared suggest that it didn't matter and he flew into a rage.

One day Mario took me to the Café de Paris, where he had to meet a director about a part in a western. The director was Sergio Leone. And he was in a foul mood because the actor they'd given him for the lead role seemed too young and inexperienced. He'd wanted Eric Fleming, the star of the highly successful American TV series *Rawhide*. Instead he'd got Fleming's supporting actor, a barely known American by the name of Clint Eastwood. We met them sitting at the bar with cameraman Massimo Dallamano. Clint looked out of place, irritated because nobody spoke English. A full-on American, he was wearing a short-sleeved shirt, tie, and tennis shoes, which looked very funny to us Italians. Sergio just sat there looking black as thunder, chomping on a Toscano cigar. At one point, he offered one to Clint. The scowl of disgust with which Clint brushed it aside caught Sergio's attention. Gesturing to make himself understood, framing a camera angle with his fingers, Sergio made it clear that he wanted Clint to repeat the scowl. Which he did. We'd be seeing that look on screen for years to come, marking an era and a personality.

Clint was so shy that it took me a while to realize just how smart and ambitious he was. He knew exactly what he wanted. "One day I'll win an Oscar," he told me, and I had no trouble believing him. Nevertheless, nobody took him seriously at the time, either as an actor or as a person, mostly because he worked in spaghetti westerns—but from these he would proceed to build a majestic, lasting career crowned with success.

He was the first American I'd met: calm, relaxed, simple, precise, completely himself, all the qualities we associate today with Clint's best roles and with the movies he's directed. He was a natural-born star; the rest of the world just didn't know it yet. And there I was, without a camera. It's a good memory and a bad one. If I'd had a camera, maybe then I'd have taken my first step toward that fabulous life I felt excluded from. But I was just a kid without a story, still struggling to create one.

Mario later invited me onto the set of *A Fistful of Dollars*, which had been built at Cinecittà after shooting ended in Spain. I hoped to get work as an extra in the movie, but I was too young. Instead, I got two days' work serving drinks.

I adored westerns, but it was weird watching all those Italians, who didn't speak a word of English between them, playing cowboys. Not to mention how odd Sergio seemed to be. No one understood why he shot the way he did; no one could fathom what he wanted. I was sure the movie would turn out ridiculous. Then I saw it: all those incredible angles, the Ennio Morricone soundtrack, Sergio's mastery in handling tension. Sergio had the entire movie in his head before he even began shooting. He couldn't care less whether anybody else understood a particular frame. He already knew how it would fit into the whole picture, and he was right.

When I turned twenty, the army interrupted my work with Moncada. Everyone had to do an obligatory fourteen months' military service. I figured my family already did enough for the government, considering the long hours my father spent at the Pathology of the Book Institute. But I had no choice. At the medical exam, I tried to get myself rejected, faking convulsive breathing. But the draft card came all the same, destination Bari, an Adriatic port city some three hundred miles south of Rome. Anywhere was pretty much the same to me.

What upset me most was the thought of wasting all that time. I turned up for duty slouching and depressed. I had eight to ten weeks' basic training to do before the army decided where to relocate me. But even there, something I knew how to do was waiting for me. Three days in, one of the officers asked if any of the recruits was a photographer. I raised my hand, and that was the end of my training. I was transferred immediately to Rome. My father couldn't believe his eyes when I turned up back at home. Nobody did military service in his own hometown. But I did. I was sent to the army school of photography, run by a field marshal who knew absolutely nothing about the subject. He asked if anyone knew how to do retouching. Again I raised my hand. They made me do a test. "You're not

Before and after my military service, age twenty and twenty-one.

going anywhere, son," said the testing officer. "You're too good. Stay here with us." Every time I raised my hand, the army promoted me.

My first job in my new post was to photograph one of Italy's top generals. I used everything about light that I'd learned from my father to smooth his face. When I'd finished retouching the photo, he had the skin of a newborn baby. The general was so impressed by my talent and my photo that, from then on, when I wasn't in service I was free to do whatever I wanted. I went home, visited my friends, even kept in touch with Moncada, hoping to go back to work for him after my military service.

What I didn't realize was that one of my "promotions" had landed me in an espionage department. Had I raised my hand once too often? One month before my discharge, someone noticed that I hadn't done any military training. That wasn't allowed, so they sent me to complete my training in Bologna with the elite Arditi assault corps. The very word *Arditi*— "audacious"—got on my nerves.

The day I arrived at the base, the place was swarming with scary-looking guys leaping from helicopters on ropes, shooting machine guns, and chucking hand grenades. But when I registered at the office, I realized it was they who were scared of me, including the general. Nobody believed I was just some kid close to discharge. They couldn't understand how I'd come so far in such a short time, why I'd been allowed to serve in my hometown, and why I'd been sent for basic training after working in an espionage department directly under a top-ranking general. I tried to explain that I was just a photographer and the army had merely wanted to exploit my skills. But to no avail. They were all convinced that I'd been planted there as a spy and were determined to make me do my basic training, so that I'd submit a favorable report to the people I really worked for.

On my first afternoon off duty in Bologna, I drank ten strong coffees, plastered my uniform in mud, and, doubling up in simulated pain, presented myself at the military hospital, telling doctors that I'd fainted. They put me in a bed and subjected me to every analysis in the book. Naturally, they found nothing. Someone thought maybe they should remove my appendix—a strange diagnosis, given that my appendix had been taken out when I was five. While they kept me under observation, I discovered that the nurse needed someone to develop their X-rays, a process still done manually in those days. I raised my hand, which by now was a key part of my military training. As a result, I spent my last four weeks with the army working in yet another darkroom. I can even claim to have worked as a radiologist, since one night I developed X-rays that I took of myself. I wanted to check the injuries I'd suffered in my accident. I couldn't figure out a thing.

By the time I was ready to go back to work with Johnny Moncada, he'd transformed his photography studio into an advertising agency. There was a lot of money in that business, and Moncada could boast prestigious clients like Alitalia airline, which could guarantee regular, long-term work. I knew that if I stayed with Moncada, I'd be condemned to do what I was trying to avoid: retouching, lighting, occasional developing, and a few prints. But the idea of becoming an independent professional like Moncada felt like an unachievable dream. Financially, he could do whatever he wanted. He bought cameras like I bought cigarettes. What's more, although I'd accumulated a lot of experience collaborating with top photographers, I still hadn't made a name for myself, so I couldn't just set up shop on my own. Which wasn't necessarily a good idea anyway. When Moncada went into advertising, his longtime assistant had left to set up his own shop as a photographer and had ended up doing provincial weddings. I sure didn't want that. I wasn't even sure if I wanted to be a photographer at all. But I definitely needed a job.

My friendship with Mario Brega and time spent on Sergio Leone's set had reignited my interest in cinema. One day I read an article about the photographer Pierluigi Praturlon, who had a private studio in Rome and an international advertising agency. He'd been the guy responsible for taking the set photos of *La Dolce Vita,* photos that had proved fundamental in promoting the wonders of Rome, Fellini, and the movie itself in America and abroad. In fact, the famous scene of Anita Ekberg in the Trevi Fountain was based on a photo that Pierluigi had taken himself some years before the movie. That story goes that he and Ekberg had been walking back from a restaurant to Ekberg's home when she stopped to bathe her aching feet in the fountain. Pierluigi quickly got a car owner to shine his headlights on the scene and, with that as lighting, took a series of photos. Fellini saw them in a magazine and used the idea in his movie.

I called Pierluigi's office to ask if they needed anyone. They said they already had a lot of photographers but needed someone who knew how to do retouching. Not again, I thought, but I put a brave face on it, shrugged my shoulders, and told them I was the best in the business. They asked me in for a test. At the time, Pierluigi was in Spain working on *Tony Rome,* a Gordon Douglas movie starring Frank Sinatra, so I was interviewed by his brother. He gave me a photo of Elizabeth Taylor to retouch. I did what needed doing and gave it back to him. He began looking at it from various angles. He got another copy printed and compared it with the retouched one. I knew I'd done an excellent job. Nobody could tell where I'd intervened. When Pierluigi got back from Spain, he called, asked me to come in to see him, and gave me the same photo of Elizabeth to retouch. He wanted to see if I was capable of doing it again. When I'd finished, he examined both retouched photos and couldn't find any difference between them. "You're hot shit," he said, unable to believe I was so good so young. I got the job.

Pierluigi showed me around his studio, and I watched while he photographed a number of actresses. He had the most astonishingly sophisticated equipment: the very best cameras, lights on electrically operated mountings. But in my opinion, despite the surroundings, Pierluigi was a mediocre photographer. Even with my limited professional experience, I already knew how to recognize the technical superiority of a Beny and the innovation and creativity of a Moncada, all of which Pierluigi clearly lacked.

Some truly exceptional 35 mm cameras were coming out in those days. But the majority of photographers weren't able to use them to their full potential. And Pierluigi was one of them. He'd always been more of a paparazzo than a professional studio photographer. His photos never had that touch of quality that you could see in work by better photographers. The latest cameras made it easier and cheaper to produce modern, sophisticated, artistic photos. But Pierluigi didn't care. He didn't know where to begin with the new technology. He told all his photographers: "Shoot, shoot, shoot. Don't worry, we'll fix everything in the darkroom." But when you looked at the negatives, only one or two were any good. Those were the ones he printed, retouched, and then signed himself. He wasn't precise. He didn't design any sets or dream up creative photos. All that mattered to him was doing, doing, doing. Quantity, not quality.

Yet Pierluigi had built his studio from scratch. He'd begun as a paparazzo, and when he acquired enough money, he'd opened a studio, then a darkroom, then an international agency. Thanks to this, along with famous photographs he had taken on all the most important Italian movie sets, he enjoyed a lot of respect in town. Neither handsome nor fascinating, he was always surrounded by beautiful women. One evening I stayed behind to talk. I wanted to sketch out a theory I had, a way of avoiding retouching by making certain adjustments to the lighting during shoots. He was irritable; we talked about it but only tested it when everyone else at the agency had gone home.

I'd begun as a retoucher, but slowly I began taking photos. Pierluigi worked for a lot of production companies: MGM, Paramount, Warner Bros. He handled photo shoots and layouts for big stars. He wasn't managing a mere photography studio but a major enterprise with as many as ten apprentice photographers working under him, plus correspondents in major cities throughout the world, just like a newspaper. But the buyers of celebrity magazines or 18 × 24 photos of stars never heard anyone talk about other photographers—guys like me—because the only name to appear on photos coming out of Pierluigi's studio was Pierluigi's. He took all the credit and the copyrights, regardless of who'd taken the photo. Years later I discovered that a number of photos I'd taken for Pierluigi had appeared in important publications like *Look*. At the time I didn't know where the photos ended up. Pierluigi was the one who signed, sold, and archived every photo produced in his studio. Our job was to do what he told us to do. What happened to the work later was not our business.

At some point the *Tony Rome* job in Spain began turning into a nightmare for Pierluigi. Sinatra kept getting sick on account of the wild life he was leading in Madrid, forcing frequent production delays. The on-set photo service started taking much longer than planned and began to overlap with another job Pierluigi had taken on. So he returned to Rome and sent me to Madrid, though word went around that those delays weren't the only reason why Pierluigi had left Madrid. It seems he'd argued with Sinatra, who'd told him to get out and not come back.

It was only the second time I'd been out of Italy and only the second time I'd flown in a plane. I'd never been to Spain, and like the rest of the world, I adored Sinatra. What a job! But when I got to Madrid, no one was waiting for me at the airport, and I had no idea where I was or where I was supposed to go. Plus, my Spanish was worse than my English. I changed enough money to phone Pierluigi, who told me to wait where I was. Four or five hours went by before a car finally showed up. Pierluigi had told no one I was coming, even though I had all the cameras they needed in my luggage. The car took me to a hotel, and that was pretty much all I saw of Spain. Sinatra still didn't feel well, so shooting had been interrupted again. They told me they hoped to restart in a couple of days. But two weeks passed, during which time I didn't take a single photo. No one knew who

I was or what I was doing in Madrid. I had no one to talk to, and my hotel room didn't even have a television. A couple of times I found the courage to leave the hotel to buy something to eat. But I got lost. And with production in such chaos, I didn't dare go far in case they needed me suddenly.

Whatever the true story was about Sinatra's health, it seems he also got arrested. He was out drunk one night in a bar and started hurling insults at the Franco regime. "Fuck off, Franco! Franco's a piece of shit! Look what he's doing to his people!" and stuff like that. I never heard for sure whether Sinatra got sick or whether he really did cause a minor diplomatic incident and irritate the government. Or if there were other problems I knew nothing about. In any case, the production was a disaster. I went home without taking a single photo.

A few months later, Audrey Hepburn came into the studio for a shoot. She was a little early, and Pierluigi was busy on the phone. I set up the lights while she went to the dressing room with makeup artist Alberto De Rossi. When she finally got on set, Pierluigi was still on the phone. She was dazzlingly beautiful and elegant. Given my sketchy English, I was too intimidated to strike up a conversation. So, instead of standing there like a mute, I started photographing her. I must have given the impression of being a professional photographer because when I stopped, she hugged me good-bye and left, just as Pierluigi came into the room. He was furious. Until he saw the prints.

One of the photos I took of Audrey that day became so famous it was printed and sold as a poster. Pierluigi signed it, just like all the others. He never told us who commissioned a service, maybe to avoid giving us some way of claiming authorship. In fact, he was so good at taking all the credit that, just a couple of years ago, in a cinema souvenir shop in New York, I spotted a poster of that very same photo of Audrey that I'd taken forty years earlier—and it still carried Pierluigi's signature. I bought the poster, cut Pierluigi's name out, framed it, and hung it in my studio.

The incident with Audrey made me realize just how jealous Pierluigi was, and how distrustful he was of his collaborators. I got the impression that he kept an even closer eye on me after that, like he was trying to catch me stealing something.

One day I was busy photographing one of the many models and actresses who constantly hung around the studio, each hoping to get into a shot that might result in getting a commercial or even movie work. For this particular shoot, I had the girl stretch out on the floor while I stood

I nearly got fired for taking this shot of Audrey Hepburn on my own initiative. But then my boss, Pierluigi Praturlon, signed it as his own and took all the credit.

The camera I used to capture Hepburn was this Hasselblad. (Photo by M&S Materiale fotografico.)

taking photos of her from above. I then got down on my knees, straddling her, while I kept shooting. I liked the sexual tension that developed between a subject and myself. It was a technique I used often throughout my career, sometimes clothed, sometimes not. Pierluigi was standing off to one side with a man I didn't know who was watching me closely. From the way Pierluigi was talking to the guy, I could tell he was someone important. But I'd no idea who he was, or why he seemed so interested in me. When I was through with the shoot, Pierluigi called me over and introduced me. It was Michelangelo Antonioni, the great director, in the studio reviewing some work that the agency had done on his movie *The Three Faces*, featuring Princess Soraya of Iran. We'd also handled a number of photos of his girl-friend, Monica Vitti, which Pierluigi had shot, we'd printed, and I'd retouched. From the expression on Pierluigi's face, it seemed I'd done something wrong. I figured I was in trouble. When Antonioni asked if I'd like to go to London to work on his next movie, *Blow-Up*, I realized why Pierluigi was so put out. It was possibly the first time someone had come to his studio and asked for one of his employees. It wouldn't be the last.

Michelangelo didn't want me to take photos but to work with the star of the movie, David Hemmings, who had replaced Terence Stamp at the last minute. My job, in secret, was to help the actor play a photographer in the movie as authentically as possible. What I really had to do was teach him how to move, teach him my "body language." So that's what I did. I showed David how to hold a camera, how I'd move in order to get the right angle, how and why I made models lie on the floor. Michelangelo liked the angle so much he got Hemmings to repeat it with the model Veruschka in what became a famous scene, later called "the most sensual cinemato-graphic moment in history" by *Premiere*. In the scene, while Hemmings is photographing Veruschka, his shutter starts opening faster and faster, in time with her growing excitement, until in the end she almost seems to have an orgasm. The scene, however, is as emotionally empty as it's sexu-ally charged. Hemmings and Veruschka are physically very close, but they couldn't be farther apart, which was Michelangelo's genius: his portrayal of the sad poetry that he sensed within our inability to relate to others.

Michelangelo portrayed this void best in the famous last scene of *Blow-Up*, something that would never have occurred if he'd been as pre-sumptuous and self-indulgent a director as many accused him of being. In reality, producers found working with Michelangelo far easier than you could ever imagine. He never complained about feeling held back and never attempted to squeeze extra money out of anyone. For example, his 1960 movie, *L'avventura,* which made Monica Vitti an international star, was a true miracle. It ended the way it did simply because Michelangelo had run out of money and just edited what he had. One of the greatest movies ever, winner of the 1960 Cannes Jury Prize, has no real "ending" because Michelangelo couldn't afford to shoot one.

I witnessed something of his genius in London. The last scene in *Blow-Up* involves a game of tennis. We went to shoot it in a park one Sunday, which turned out to be the only day in London that I didn't spend shut away in some hotel showing David how to hold a camera. When we got out of the car, Michelangelo didn't look at all happy. The weather wasn't good for shooting exteriors. But that was nothing compared to what came later: the prop master had forgotten the tennis balls. We scoured the park, hoping someone had left some behind. Nothing. And this was 1960s London on a Sunday. You couldn't just pop into a Walmart and buy a few tennis balls. And Michelangelo had permission to shoot the scene only on that one Sunday. What's more, the English production people were decidedly unhelpful, possibly on purpose. The impression was that someone in the government or the British cinema department was worried about how Michelangelo intended to portray the nightlife and drug culture of "swinging London," and word had gone out that the Italian wasn't to be trusted.

When Michelangelo finally calmed down, he decided the actors should simply mime the tennis game, hitting an imaginary ball. It sounded crazy, but the cast and technicians listened to the master. Michelangelo's improvisation turned out to be even better than the scene he'd planned. Mimed, the match became amusing and surreal, a snapshot of the playful madness of the last years of the 1960s. And it portrayed perfectly David Hemmings's existential problems in the movie, the nothingness of his existence, the way the more he looked at life, the less he saw. Had the props guy done his job, the end result would have been just a long shot of a man walking past people playing tennis.

On my return from London, Pierluigi figured he'd concocted the perfect punishment for me. I was to be sent to Dahomey (now Benin), where Elizabeth Taylor and Richard Burton were filming *The Comedians,* a Peter Glenville movie based on the novel by Graham Greene, who also wrote the screenplay. Nobody in the studio wanted to go to Africa, me included. But Pierluigi persuaded me that it would be good experience. He said I'd handle every aspect of the job: I'd photograph Elizabeth and Richard, costars

Alec Guinness, Peter Ustinov, and James Earl Jones, and retouch and print all the photos on location. All this sounded good, so I accepted. When I said good-bye to my girlfriend, Patrizia, she cried, as if she'd had a premonition. And possibly she really had.

So, at the end of November 1966, I packed all my stuff, including a full darkroom kit, and flew to Paris, along with one of Pierluigi's printers, Franco. Once we picked up our visas from the Dahomey embassy and suffered a string of vaccinations, we set off on the long flight to Africa. I knew Pierluigi had no interest in giving me any extra experience. My trip to Africa was merely punishment for stealing Antonioni's attention. But what I didn't know was how, when I eventually returned to Rome, Pierluigi would have even more reason for annoyance. And I didn't know I was about to soar clear out of my basement life forever.

Chapter 4

Jet-Set Jungle

The plane landed in the middle of nowhere. Cotonou airport consisted of a single landing strip surrounded by jungle. Being so fully immersed in nature was beautiful, exciting, and terrifying all at the same time. The entire town boasted precisely two hotels: La Croix du Sud, a five-star place carved out of a half-star hotel, where most of the production lived, and the Hotel de la Plage, a smaller establishment run by French staff.

Franco and I stayed in the latter, though we also had a house rented by the production where, a couple of days later when all the equipment arrived, we set up a darkroom. We shot and developed a few trial photos to make sure everything worked properly. But the climate was so humid that the pictures took forever to dry, which meant we weren't able to retouch them. So we decided to work at night, when it was a little cooler and the humidity less oppressive.

The intense heat obliged me to sleep naked. One morning I woke to find two large eyes staring at me. They belonged to a young African woman who worked in the hotel. She addressed me in French, asking if I had any laundry that needed washing. A couple of days later, the same thing happened, only this time she asked if I needed washing. Not sure if I'd understood correctly, I managed a strangled "Oui" and let myself be led under the shower. She didn't waste a second shedding the multicolored sheet she wore for a dress, revealing a stupendous body, which made mine look even more pasty and pallid. I wondered if this kind of thing also happened to the classy people in other rooms, whether they got the same "room service." But I wasn't complaining, and she said that they didn't. She was just infatuated with me.

Wandering around Dahomey left me feeling very ill at ease. Everywhere I went, people would stop me and touch my hair. I don't believe they'd ever seen anyone with bright-red hair like mine. A few days after we arrived, we

Pierluigi wanted me dead for taking unauthorized photos like this of Elizabeth Taylor and Richard Burton on the set of *The Comedians*. However, when Elizabeth saw them, she hired me herself. Richard signed this print for me.

heard the sound of explosions coming from outside the city. A new president had just come to power. After that, all of us who'd served in the military or knew how to handle weapons were authorized to go around armed. In fact, the movie's production company, MGM, quietly distributed guns to any employee who wanted one. I called Pierluigi to tell him what was happening and he replied, "Don't be stupid, don't take unnecessary risks." So I got a pistol. I must say it felt strange the way a sense of vulnerability could turn so easily into potential aggression.

In reality, the "revolution" wasn't such a big deal. The Italian ambassador to Ghana, the Ivory Coast, and Dahomey came to my hotel and asked me to accompany him to meet the new president, mostly because I was one of only a few Italians in the country and he wanted to turn up with an entourage. So I went although, to tell the truth, I didn't have a clue what was going on. At the time, being in such an unstable country was a little scary. I acquired the unusual habit of never going out without my pistol.

During those days I got to know Umberto Betti, an engineer from Genoa, a well-known figure in town. He'd worked in a lot of African countries and had set up a plantation in Dahomey, along with a processing plant that produced a textile obtained by crossbreeding two species of plant fiber. It was called K-NAP, a commercial material similar to jute. He invited me to visit the plantation and I accepted. The moment we left Cotonou, we plunged straight into deepest Africa, the one you usually see only in nature magazines. We drove hundreds of miles through countryside alive with giraffes, lions, zebras, elephants, and—every now and then—a village or two. Finding myself in the middle of untamed nature stirred strong emotions in me, the same mixture of awe and fear that I'd felt the first time I got off the plane, though now far more heightened. The plantation was run by four Italians, with ten thousand Africans working the fields, for God knows what pay. But the Italians were much loved by the Africans, thanks to engineer Betti and other entrepreneurs who'd invested in local infrastructure, launching construction projects and creating industries. The Africans who worked on the plantation knew how to say only two things in Italian: "Fuck off" and "I swear to God." Every time I passed one of them, they'd give me a huge smile and say one phrase or the other, convinced they were saying something more like, "Good day, how's it going?"

On my first day at work I met Bob Penn, the movie's set photographer, and realized that Pierluigi had been lying to me from the start. Elizabeth Taylor's press agent, Jean Osbourne, told me what I'd actually already guessed: under no circumstances could I photograph Elizabeth. It seems she'd liked a number of photos that Pierluigi's agency had printed and retouched and had asked them to send the person who'd done the retouching. Me. I later learned, in fact, that the only reason the production had hired Pierluigi's agency at all was because Elizabeth had wanted the retoucher. Me.

I could take whatever photos I wanted of anyone else, but not of Elizabeth who, at that stage in her career, had total control over who could and could not photograph her on set. I was to retouch Penn's photos—nothing else. It was like taking a kid into a candy store, putting a dollar in his hand, and then telling him he couldn't buy any candy. Endless hours of travel, vaccinations against everything from malaria to yellow fever, and I couldn't take a single photo of the most famous woman in the world. And even if, by chance, I happened to produce a beautiful image of Richard Burton, Peter Ustinov, or Alec Guinness, no one would give a damn. Penn's official set photos would be the only ones published.

I would never have agreed to go to Africa just to touch up someone else's photos, and Pierluigi had known that. Every last doubt as to why he'd sent me to the set of *The Comedians*, every glimmer of hope that maybe he really had wanted to give me experience on a true Hollywood set, evaporated on the spot. That was Pierluigi's way of putting me in my place, reminding me who was boss.

I was furious. But Franco and I had no choice, doomed to hang around on set, twiddling our thumbs, waiting until Penn handed us a roll to develop, print, and retouch. So I buckled down, set to work as one of Pierluigi's employees, and started taking a few photos of my own—of Richard, Alec, Peter and, yes, Elizabeth. With or without permission, I'd acquire the experience Pierluigi had promised me. Besides, I got the impression that Jean wasn't all that worried about what some twenty-two-year-old kid was up to, whatever his qualifications. My presence was so irrelevant that no one bothered to complain about my shooting to Pierluigi either. Elizabeth had the last word on every single photo, and it was clear that no photos other than Penn's would ever see the light of day. However, since I wasn't there to work as a photographer, I wasn't obligated to shoot pictures that corresponded to the framing that the director and camera-man set up for every scene. In one sense, by lying to me, Pierluigi had given me the freedom to photograph the way I wanted to: spontaneously, without my subjects knowing they were being shot, in natural situations, from whatever angle I preferred.

Whenever I wasn't wandering around snapping photos, I spent my time with the rest of the crew. On set everyone spoke two languages, English with the cast and French with the crew. I couldn't speak either. The most I could do was flirt with the girls on set, retreating behind my camera whenever the language barrier became insurmountable. The only person I was able to communicate with reasonably was a splendid Corsican girl named Claudye, Elizabeth's hairdresser. She'd trained under Alexandre de Paris, possibly the most famous hairdresser in history, the man who'd been there when Elizabeth got sick during the filming of *Cleopatra* and is said to have flown to her bedside, creating her famous "artichoke cut" while three nurses held her steady. The first time I met Claudye I was trying to start a Solex, a French electric bicycle with an engine mounted on the rear wheel. I'd never seen one before, and Claudye offered to show me how to use it. She was blonde, with big, very sexy chestnut eyes. Claudye thought she spoke Italian, but actually she spoke a Corsican dialect, and I knew no more than a dozen words of French. We made all kinds of mistakes but eventually understood each other. Pretty soon, whenever Claudye wasn't busy with Elizabeth, she'd take me for a spin on her Solex. This flirtation with Elizabeth's hairdresser made my presence even more irritating to the cast and crew.

A family atmosphere develops on every movie set, especially among the people behind the scenes, the people who do the heavy work and make life easy for the stars. When work for the day ended, everyone usually went to some club or bar. One evening, Richard Burton sat down beside me and ordered a drink. He introduced himself and asked me who I was and what I was doing in Dahomey. He'd never noticed me on set. I tried to reply with my nonexistent English, but all he understood was "MGM." He excused himself politely and left. That was my first conversation with Richard.

On those nights in Cotonou clubs I heard African music for the first time. I loved it, as did a number of others on the crew. For me it was a new rhythm that got right under my skin. However, going back to the hotel after leaving those clubs could get scary. It was usually very late at night. The town was so dark you felt you were in deep jungle. I'll never forget the avenue that led from the street to our hotel entrance, walled in with thick ferns and other exotic plants. You felt as if you were forging through virgin jungle toward the distant light of civilization. The sensation turned dramatically acute one time around 3 a.m. when I had just started up the avenue. I suddenly heard rustling in the bushes. "Who's there?" I demanded in Italian. No reply. "Hello?" Still no reply. But I knew for sure someone was lurking back there, so I grabbed my gun and cocked it loudly, determined to make sure that whoever was in those bushes heard it too. Pointing the pistol straight ahead of me, I began moving backward. "I'm armed," I stuttered. "Come out slowly or I'll start shooting!" In truth, I was terrified. Marlon Brando came stumbling out of the bushes, followed by Christian Marquand. Both were drunk. They'd wandered off together into the shadows. Everyone in cinema already knew that Brando and Marquand were lovers—except me. It was stunning news to me. I felt like I'd done something wrong just by being there and seeing what I'd seen. I thrust my pistol back into its holster and hurried toward the hotel entrance. Just think about it. If I'd been a tad jumpier that night, or if my finger had slipped . . . No *Godfather*, no *Last Tango in Paris*, no *Apocalypse Now*.

Brando's unexpected arrival in Dahomey was classic jet-set behavior. It seems he'd been staying in Elizabeth and Richard's house in Switzerland when news came that Elizabeth had won the New York Film Critics award for her role in *Who's Afraid of Virginia Woolf?* Elizabeth had called asking him if he could collect it for her, which he did, and then Brando just popped down to Africa to deliver it in person. "If you please," as Richard would comment in his diary.

A couple of days later Brando appeared on set, snuck up behind her, brushed Elizabeth's shoulder while she was getting made up, and grabbed her ass with both hands. Elizabeth turned, smiled, and exclaimed, "Marlon!" Richard wasn't nearly so amused. He ran over and pulled Marlon away. They argued and started punching each other. I immediately started snapping photos, imagining them published in some top magazine. I barely got a glimpse of my fantasy before Jean Osbourne grabbed my camera and tore out the roll.

The only other occasion when anyone paid attention to me was during a difficult exterior road scene. Alec Guinness was dressed as a woman in the role of an ambassador trying to flee, and Richard Burton was chasing him. The car was supposed to skid around a bend and go into a spin. But the stunt men couldn't make the car perform the way the director wanted. Shot after shot, the car wouldn't spin. Frustration mounted. At a certain point I went over to them, introduced myself, and said, "I know how to do it." The director and stunt coordinators ignored me. But Richard, tired of repeating the scene, told them to let me try. I crawled under the car and unhooked the rear brake, then took my place in the driver's seat. At my first attempt, I skidded so violently the car spun twice. Too much. At the second attempt, I took the bend exactly how they wanted. Marvelous, but that was it. As so often happens, the scene was later excluded from the final cut, and my moment of glory expired in the jungle.

I never spoke with either Elizabeth or Alec Guinness while in Africa. But Peter Ustinov was very friendly. The first time I saw him on set I'd no idea who he was. All I thought was, there's Nero (from the movie *Quo Vadis*). But one evening we were talking—as far as that was possible with me—and the conversation turned to cars. Peter immediately launched into a wild imitation of a Formula One race, complete with roaring engines and commentators shouting in every language under the sun. Everyone watching just collapsed laughing.

When shooting ended in Africa, I returned to Rome, where I developed and printed my photos, made a few small touch-ups, and handed them over to Pierluigi. Without telling me—and maybe by mistake—he had all of them sent on to the production company along with Bob Penn's official photos. Elizabeth immediately noticed that a number of unfamiliar shots had been taken and wanted to know who'd done them. When she found out, she asked the producers to have me sent up to Nice, in southern France, where new sets had been built at the Victorine Studios to continue interior shooting on *The Comedians*. Pierluigi tried to send another photographer in my place, but Elizabeth vetoed the idea. She wanted me and all my equipment in Nice immediately, just like in Cotonou.

I was delighted but kept asking myself, "Why me?" Was it because she liked the photos I'd taken without permission? Or because my images were better than those of the set photographer? Why me? It was a question I would ask myself often throughout my career. It's a question rooted in insecurity, my lack of a proper education, and what I used to feel was my lack of class. It was the question at the heart of my long argument with my father.

I'd enjoyed freedoms that a twenty-two-year-old rarely has on the set of a movie featuring two of the biggest stars in the world. Not being the official photographer was a blessing. He or she is obliged to stay close to the camera and take photos that correspond to individual scenes, with no freedom to choose any other angle than whatever the director wants. Actors know they are being photographed while they work and inevitably pose, even if unconsciously. Which is why any "spontaneous" photo of a star at work isn't spontaneous at all. Those were the kinds of photos that Elizabeth had expected to see.

When I was on set, my technique had been to not be seen. If you don't see me, you don't think that someone is photographing you. You feel freer, more relaxed. A lot of people are intimidated by a camera. They block, consciously or unconsciously, concerned about how they look. But in my case, since no one cared what I did and didn't realize that I was taking professional photos, I didn't have that problem. I was able to photograph Elizabeth and Richard being natural without worrying about their poses.

My long experience with printing had taught me the best system for photographing a woman. I learned from observing how light bounces off a subject through the lens and is then imprinted on film. The negative. The aperture of the stop is inversely proportionate to the contrast obtained in the final photo. Thus, at the retouching stage, you realize that some of the defects could have been avoided with a different stop aperture. Skin and color tonality are merely a question of light, and thus of contrast. In Africa, the light was very strong, so I knew I had to close down the stop and use film with a low ASA. To get better photos, I exposed a small quantity of light (stop closed) over a longer time lapse (shutter).

All these considerations contributed to me getting unique photos. But I don't believe that that was what made them special, nor why Elizabeth appreciated them so much. Stops and exposure times mean nothing when you're dealing with a woman as beautiful as that. If you took a Polaroid shot of her neck she'd still have looked like a star. She was the most famous and photographed woman in the world. The world had literally watched her grow up through movies and photographs. Ever since she shot to stardom in Clarence Brown's 1944 classic *National Velvet* at just eleven, Elizabeth had been shot from every conceivable angle and in every imaginable circumstances, often alongside crowned heads and superstars. How can you take an interesting photo of a woman like her? What more can a photographer come up with?

In the end, while shooting dozens of photos of her in Africa, I realized where the real challenge lay in photographing Elizabeth: how to make people looking at my photos feel as I'd felt, as if they were seeing Elizabeth—the world's most photographed and famous woman—for the very first time. I'd spend the next twelve years trying to solve that problem. My photos were not of a movie star but of a woman and her husband behaving normally, unaware of my lens. And those were the kind of photos I'd keep trying to take throughout my career.

But back then, on my way to Nice, my career was the last thing on my mind. What career? I still didn't have one. All I kept thinking was, "Why me? Is she bringing me all the way to France just to chew me out for taking unauthorized photos? Does she really like my work? Is my father right, even though I still can't see what he sees? Does Elizabeth see it? And why is Pierluigi always so angry with me?"

Franco and I got to Nice and went straight to our hotel. But before we even had time to unpack, Elizabeth's people came to get us and set us up in an apartment behind the famous Hotel Negresco. Elizabeth's driver then picked me up and took me to her yacht, where she was waiting for me. The second I stepped onto the yacht I could tell she was annoyed with me.

"You're good," she said. "But you're an asshole for taking these without my consent."

Despite this opening, she offered me a drink. Then, with Claudye helping translate, I explained the false promises that Pierluigi had used to persuade me to go to Africa, adding that I'd merely done the job I'd been sent to do. Elizabeth already knew about Pierluigi's methods, and this helped ease the tension between us. Richard, on the other hand, was not very friendly. When I saw him, I stuttered, "Hi, Mr. *Bar*ton," and he immediately corrected my mispronunciation. I felt so embarrassed that I didn't dare try to say his name again—and spent the rest of my time in Nice practicing my English vowels.

When we weren't developing and retouching the set photos, Franco and I lived like kings in that apartment. In addition to *The Comedians*, the same studios were shooting an Italian movie, *Arriva Dorellik*, with Johnny Dorelli in his first lead role. And Nice had a lot of women's colleges, where the nascent feminist movement was making itself heard, which inevitably led to a constant flow of girls through our apartment. We even had our own darkroom, which of course we didn't use only for developing film. We were having the time of our lives while Pierluigi, back in Rome, was struggling to work out what the heck we were doing and where we were living. When he eventually learned from Franco that Elizabeth had moved us into a luxury apartment and that I spent most of my time with her and Richard, he sent another of his photographers, Roberto Biciocchi, to spy on us. But Roberto promptly moved into our apartment and joined in the good life. Pierluigi went nuts, consumed with jealousy.

There was a lot of competition between the French and Italians working on the two movies, especially when it came to women. The most sought-after girl was Elizabeth's stand-in, a beautiful girl whose job was to take Elizabeth's position on set so that technicians could adjust the lighting while Elizabeth was dressing. Every single man on both sets, French and Italian, tried to go out with her. But she turned down every invitation. One of the assistants was the super-rich heir to a cosmetics empire, the son of Madame Rochas. He'd cruise around in a Mustang convertible. She turned him down too. The Italians insisted I give her a try. And the truth is, I didn't even like her that much. From time to time I'd joke with her on set, but that was it. In the end I gave in and invited her out. And she accepted.

It turned into an embarrassing night. She was in a bad mood, didn't want to do this, didn't want to do that. In the end I said, "Let's drop all this and go to my place." She agreed. I found a phone and rang the apartment, asking Franco and Roberto if they could clear out for a bit. They congratulated me and made themselves scarce. Back in the apartment, we stretched out on my bed half dressed and started making out. But then she stopped me, saying she didn't want to. Did that "no" mean "yes," or was it a real "no"? I didn't bother to find out; I just took her word for it and fell asleep. When Franco and Roberto got back they found me asleep and the girl fully dressed, offended and angry. She asked them to take her home immediately, which they did. When they came back they let me have it: "You'll ruin our reputation!" they shouted, and even rang Pierluigi to tell him I'd bombed with the girl. They went on and on about it, insisting I repair the "damage." So, even though I still didn't like the girl, we went out again. This time, the "no" of that first night turned out to mean "yes." I don't intend to boast about being some kind of playboy. I was just a kid, and it was the sixties. This is the way it was.

After a while I began spending time at Claudye's apartment, picking up the thread of what we'd started in Africa. We spent a weekend in Saint-Tropez with other members of the crew, and when we got back I taught her to drive my Fiat Giannini. I knew she liked me and the attraction was mutual. We went out together on numerous occasions and I'd spend the night. But commitment took time. I still wasn't ready for a serious relationship, and there were a lot of nights when I told Claudye I was too busy, when actually I was out with other girls. But all I thought about was her, and Claudye was very patient with me as well as persistent. She'd always come to find me on set.

One night I was in a bar with two girls. A woman came over, said she liked my eyes, that I had a beautiful profile, and that she wanted to kiss me. I didn't stop her. Then suddenly this guy appeared, shoved her off her stool, and pulled out a knife. I tried to dodge it, but he cut me. Out on the street, I ran into Claudye. I was still bleeding. She took me to her apartment and bandaged my wound. In that moment I realized that Claudye truly cared for me, and I cared for her. We got a lot closer after that night.

When shooting ended on *The Comedians,* Elizabeth invited me to spend a weekend with her and Richard on their yacht, which was actually rented at the time. They wanted to get to know me better. She also liked the idea of me and Claudye together and wanted to give our romance a little nudge.

Our first stop was San Remo. Elizabeth, Richard, Claudye, and I got off the boat to go to a restaurant. We'd barely set foot on shore when we were assaulted by paparazzi flashbulbs. Richard was walking behind Elizabeth and me, alongside Claudye, and for who knows what reason, Elizabeth grabbed my arm. Paparazzi followed us all the way to the restaurant. The next day, photos of Elizabeth on my arm were all over the place. Overnight I'd become Elizabeth's new personal photographer. Seeing my face in newspapers and magazines made a big impression on me.

I was still news when we got to Monte Carlo for the Monaco Grand Prix. But the real story turned out to be the tragic death of top Italian driver Lorenzo Bandini. He lost control of his Ferrari when his left rear wheel hit a guardrail. The car went into a wild skid, hit a straw-bale barrier, and burst into flames, rolling over with Bandini trapped beneath it. He died of his injuries three days later. Richard and Elizabeth's yacht was moored only yards from where the crash took place. We were so close we could hear Bandini's screams as he desperately tried to escape the wreck. To witness such a tragedy firsthand was a revelatory experience. The universe seemed to be showing me how my own life could have ended . . . in the precise moment that a new life was opening up.

My face was in all the papers alongside Elizabeth's and Richard's. Photos that I'd taken on a Hollywood set appeared with my name. I had a beautiful new girlfriend. My head was spinning. Instead of going back to work after the weekend, I called in sick. I went straight to my parents' house, where my father said Pierluigi had been phoning at all hours. He wanted to make sure I knew that I'd been fired.

Fired? Why? According to Pierluigi, I'd cut a deal with those paparazzi to make newspapers talk about a new photographer in the Taylor-Burton entourage. He refused to believe that I'd merely accepted an invitation to dinner and taken a stroll with my future wife and another couple. The truth is, Pierluigi was crazy with jealousy. For the first time ever, one of his photographers had done something extraordinary, something over which he had no control and for which he could claim no credit. From the moment that photos of Elizabeth and me, arm in arm, had appeared on the front page of every newspaper and magazine, Pierluigi's phone hadn't stopped ringing. But no one was calling to book Mr. Praturlon. The man everyone wanted to talk to was Elizabeth Taylor's new photographer. Me.

I called the office, and a friend told me that Pierluigi wanted to fire everyone. He was going nuts because he'd seen my photo on the cover of *Eva Express*. I didn't even know the magazine he was talking about. Outclassing Pierluigi was the last thing on my mind. I was still his employee and I thought I owed him something. Without him I would never have gone to Africa. I wanted to talk to him in person, tell him it was all a misunderstanding. I didn't want to be fired, especially because I knew I hadn't done anything wrong. When we finally met, Pierluigi didn't even give me time to open my mouth.

"You're fired. I created you and I can destroy you. Get out of here."

At the time, I felt as if Pierluigi really had destroyed me. I wasn't Elizabeth Taylor's personal photographer. I was just a kid caught in paparazzi crossfire at the wrong moment. And now I was just another unemployed photographer. I didn't even tell Claudye that I'd been fired, let alone Elizabeth or Richard. I feared that if I lost my association with an established professional photographer, they wouldn't want anything more to do with me.

Claudye came to find me in Rome. We spent a couple of weeks by the sea before she went back to Elizabeth and Richard's home in Switzerland to talk about their next movie. When Elizabeth and Richard left for Sardinia, Claudye phoned to tell me she'd just had a wonderful *scopata*—which in Italian means "fuck." Hurt, I asked her with who. She said she'd done it on her own. I insisted. Had she started a relationship with someone new? But she just went on about some famous chef, Henri Belin Close-Jouve. Turned out she actually meant *scoperta*, a discovery. She'd found these amazing recipes and wanted to know if I'd like to come up and stay for a few days—if I had nothing else to do, that is. Something else to do? I'd just been fired. So I said yes, of course, and jotted down the name of the town she was in the way I heard her say it: Stet. I asked her how long it would take to drive there, and she said I'd arrive in time for dinner.

Once I crossed into Switzerland, I studied the map, found this place called Stetten, and set out across country, arriving around 10 p.m., when I stopped a man in the street and asked him where I might find Elizabeth Taylor's chalet. The guy burst into laughter. "That's not Stetten," he said, "it's Gstaad," and proceeded to give me directions, way over on the other side of the country. When I finally arrived at Elizabeth's place it was 3:30 in the morning.

The thousand-mile trip had melted my car's muffler. Unable to find a replacement, Claudye rang Elizabeth and asked if we could use one of their cars. Richard told her to give me their Mini Cooper S and bring it to them in Sardinia. It was a perfect plan, since he and Elizabeth wanted me on the set of the movie they were preparing in Capocaccia, Joseph Losey's *Boom!* They wanted me not as Pierluigi's employee nor even as a photographer—they wanted just me for who I was. The one drawback was that this time I couldn't take any photos, not one. Bob Penn's contract with

Elizabeth was still in force, and he'd been very embarrassed by all the attention Elizabeth had given me on account of my photos from the set of *The Comedians*. All I'd do was retouch Penn's images. It wasn't exactly the job I wanted, but it was a job, and I needed one. It was also a chance to spend more time with Claudye. We loaded the Mini Cooper and set out from Stet . . . I mean, Gstaad.

The production company in Sardinia had built an exotic house on rocks jutting out from a beach, where Elizabeth's character was supposed to live with a whole menagerie of animals: cats, dogs, parakeets, monkeys. They hadn't even started shooting yet when one morning we got to the set and the house was gone. It had fallen clean off the rocks and simply vanished into the sea. All that was left were a bunch of African monkeys and parrots.

Ten years later, researchers would flock to Sardinia to study the strange phenomenon of monkeys all over the island. But because the movie took place in an imaginary world—not Sardinia—no one connected the monkeys to that accident on set. Had they asked me, I could have saved them time and trouble. But I wasn't in the movie's credits, so no one would have believed me anyway. Those original house-wreck survivors had spread out over the island and multiplied.

The set had to be entirely rebuilt, which left us with a lot of free time on our hands: Elizabeth and Richard on their yacht, Claudye and I in our hotel. One day the man insuring the movie, Prince Spada, brought his niece to look at the new house they were building by the sea. As she wandered around the rocks, she suddenly slipped, banged her head, and fell into the sea. Everyone stood frozen in shock. I'm a useless swimmer, but for some reason I impulsively dived in and pulled her to shore. After that I was like a god around the set.

Then one day I went to Alghero, and while I was strolling around town a local jeweler stopped me. He worked with coral, gold, and diamonds to produce objects of great beauty. When I told Elizabeth about his work, she said she wanted to see it and asked me to drive her to Alghero myself. I asked whether we should take her bodyguard. There'd been a rash of kidnappings in Sardinia and even though nothing sinister had happened on set, security was tighter than usual.

"No," she said. "Let's go on our own."

So off we went. Suddenly, rounding a sharp bend, I found both lanes up ahead blocked by a car parked in the middle of the road and flanked by

Elizabeth shopping during a break in shooting Joseph Losey's *Boom!* (1968).

two men armed with hunting rifles. I yanked the handbrake. The car spun around. Men with machine guns appeared out of nowhere, and I sped back the way we'd come as fast as possible. All that newspaper delivery work hadn't gone entirely to waste.

After this episode, Elizabeth was surrounded by security guards for the rest of the shoot—Italian police, FBI, Scotland Yard. We never did discover what those guys were up to, whether it really had been an attempted kidnapping, a robbery, or even worse. Either way, I was now a hero twice over. Or I was at least as far as the Italian police were concerned, who treated me wonderfully. But the FBI, Scotland Yard, and the production were all mad at me for taking Elizabeth from the set without informing anyone. I even got the impression I was under suspicion myself. However, from that day on something changed in my relationship with Elizabeth.

Boom! is a cult movie today, both for the outlandish tone of every aspect of the movie and especially for Elizabeth's performance. Watching the shooting, I realized it would be a strange movie, which was appropriate because the director, Joseph Losey, was a strange guy. His mother was a Native American from the Winnebago tribe, and he'd spent most of his childhood in Wisconsin. He was one of those American directors considered a communist, one of the undesirables, registered on the blacklist. No one managed to communicate with him much, on or off the set. He wasn't friendly and was very focused on himself. Elizabeth respected him and did what he said, but I don't think she appreciated his directing much. More than once, at the end of a scene, I heard Losey call, "Cut! Good." But Elizabeth would then say that she could have done better, and an argument would follow. Richard never intervened. But Elizabeth always won anyway. Mostly because it was thanks to her that the production had the funding it needed in the first place.

Strange things kept happening, almost as if the production was taking its cues from Losey's odd personality. First the house collapsed. Then there was the presumed kidnapping attempt. Then Michael Dunn's wife, Joan Talbot, a fabulous dancer from Las Vegas, dumped him out of the blue. She simply vanished. No one knew where she'd gone, and a few months later they divorced. One night, drunk out of his mind in a bar, Dunn clambered onto the counter and shouted, "Do you want to know why my wife stayed with me?" Then he pulled out his willy. Dunn may have been a dwarf, but naked it looked like he had three legs.

As if all this wasn't enough, Richard discovered that the captain of their yacht had been stealing and fired him. By way of revenge, the man stole Elizabeth's dog, Georgia. Elizabeth was devastated, so I offered to get her back. I'd made friends with the captain before he got fired, so I told Elizabeth I'd handle it. I flew to Nice in her private plane; then a limousine took me to the captain's house in Beau Soleil, a village just outside Monte Carlo. When I knocked, no one answered. I started calling his name, and

My future wife Claudye (*top right*) fixes Elizabeth's dress while director Joseph Losey cheers and Richard glares into the sun (or maybe at me—I still wasn't sure).

a voice yelled back, "Fuck off!" So I kicked the door down and burst in. The captain grabbed a knife, held it to the dog's throat, and yelled: "One more step and I'll cut him to bits." I lunged forward, fists clenched, ready to flatten the guy. At which point he simply dropped the knife and handed me the dog. What a coward.

I took the poor thing straight back to Sardinia. Elizabeth was delighted. When I told her the whole story, she laughed and said, "Gianni, you're a real gangster!" As an Italian I felt offended and shot back, "I'm just a kid who grew up on the streets. Maybe you don't know what that means." I don't think Elizabeth understood just how sensitive Italians can be to Mafia stereotypes, and I still didn't know her sense of humor very well. But when she kept calling me "gangster," I eventually tried to fight back by quipping, "Okay, have it your way, Baby Boobs." It was a common gangster expression at the time referring to buxom women like Elizabeth. From then on we always used those nicknames with each other. As for Georgia, eventually she got handed off to me because she didn't get along with Elizabeth's other Pekingese, O'fie (Shakespearean English for "get away").

Elizabeth adored dogs. They'd respond to her calls and commands, yet seemed to ignore Richard's. This bugged him, since he liked dogs too. Then one day he showed up with a Pekingese named E'en So (Shakespearean English for "even so"). The dog was blind in one eye, and Richard claimed he'd rescued it. Strangely, Elizabeth had trouble communicating with the dog, although it seemed to pay rapt attention to Richard, leaving Elizabeth wondering what she was doing wrong. Only much later did Richard confess that he'd bought the dog already trained—but only to commands spoken in Welsh, which he spoke fluently.

Claudye and I were together all the time. We visited nearby Corsica, where I met her family. Corsicans can be very rough and ready, just like Romans, so we got along wonderfully. Elizabeth was thrilled. A true romantic at heart, she found the love story between her retoucher and her hairdresser just perfect.

Work on *Boom!* was going to finish in the Dino De Laurentis Studios just outside Rome. So we all flew out of Sardinia on Elizabeth and Richard's private plane. During the flight I asked if I could take a photo of the three of us together. When they agreed, I set my camera on automatic and plonked myself down beside them, wearing the biggest smile I could possibly manage. Journalists swarmed all over us when we landed, everyone asking who I was and what I was doing in Elizabeth and Richard's entourage. Elizabeth introduced me as her private photographer, which wasn't true. But what else could she say? That I was the guy who retouched her photos to make her look more beautiful? No way. The journalists took their photos, asked more questions, and off we went. In a flash, word spread around Rome that Elizabeth Taylor had taken some Italian guy into her entourage.

One day, during a break in shooting, I stepped outside the studio for a cigarette and bumped into a beautiful American girl also smoking. She was dressed in this weird, space-age bikini, so I took her for an extra and told her—in Italian—that she was *bella*, beautiful. She quipped right back, with a foreign accent, "You're not so bad yourself." Then a man came up and asked her, in French, if I was bothering her. No, she replied, and they left. Later I figured out the guy was director Roger Vadim and the girl his wife, Jane Fonda. They were shooting *Barbarella*—a movie later renowned for its opening scene featuring Fonda undressing in zero gravity. Sadly, since I didn't know who they were at the time, I don't have any photos.

By the time shooting on *Boom!* came to an end, I'd become an official member of the Taylor-Burton entourage. Elizabeth liked having me around, partly for my talent and partly because I was with Claudye. But if Claudye had earned her full-time job and standing, I was still just an unemployed photographer with little idea what to do about it. Nevertheless, off set and far from Bob Penn's ill will, I snapped a bunch of spontaneous photos of Elizabeth, Richard, and their kids. I showed Elizabeth every shot I developed, and she allowed me to sell some of them. She'd never had a personal photographer who'd take those kinds of shots of her and her family. But she responded immediately to mine and trusted me. She appreciated my eye.

At this point, Elizabeth and Richard had a few weeks' break before beginning their next movie, and Richard was due to give an important speech at his alma mater, Oxford. Elizabeth wanted to take her hairdresser friend with her, so I was invited along too, but forbidden to take any photos of the event. The university had granted exclusive rights to some English newspaper in exchange for it covering all the costs. We arrived at the outdoor site where the university had organized the event. A couple of thousand students were already there waiting—strangely, in dead silence. The rector introduced Richard with a brief biography, whereupon Richard sprang to his feet, stepped up to the dais, took the microphone and said: "My name is Richard Walter Jenkins . . ." There was a long pause, which was greeted in silence, before he continued, ". . . in art, Richard Burton."

Thunderous applause followed, lasting some minutes. I didn't have a clue what was going on. It was only later that night that someone explained to me how Richard, a miner's son from south Wales, had been unofficially adopted by his schoolmaster, Philip Burton, a well-known BBC personality and famous as the man who had tutored Richard all the way through Oxford.

That evening, after his speech, Richard told Elizabeth to go home with Claudye and the others. He and I were going on a pub crawl. Elizabeth agreed and they left. Richard put his arm around my shoulders, and off we went. I think we went into every pub in Oxford, with Richard putting one beer after another in front of me. I had never drunk beer before. I was stunned by how much we had to go pee! At one of countless urinals, Richard told me that I wouldn't have the same problem in America. "The beer there is all water. You'll see," he said, though the comment didn't really mean anything to me at the time. I was too busy peeing.

After a couple of hours knocking back endless beers, me struggling just to keep up, Richard moved on to vodka. I don't mean a vodka cocktail or a martini. Just vodka, straight, with a cube of ice. He ordered one for me too. When he turned away for a moment, I managed to tell the barman to slip me water in an identical glass. Richard swigged his shot down straight before I had time to take more than a sip of mine. He scolded me for being slow, grabbed my glass, and took a slug from it. Then he studied it pensively for a moment and said, "I must be drunk. This vodka tastes like water."

Being drunk didn't stop Richard from continuing to drink, not even when his hands shook so much he couldn't hold his glass steady anymore. Since this was a recurring problem, he'd even developed a system for dealing with it. He'd take his belt off and tie it to his wrist. Then he'd pass the belt around his neck, grasp his glass with the hand tied to the belt, and pull the other end of the belt with his free hand, creating a pulley that raised the glass to his lips. He'd happily do this sitting in front of everyone in a packed pub, without giving a damn what it looked like. If anyone commented, he'd just sway back and forth by way of answer. I knew very little about Richard's past in those days. I had no idea that his natural father had been a heavy drinker himself, a "twelve-pints man" as they say, and that Richard had started drinking at age twelve. All that kind of stuff was new to a Roman street kid like myself.

Pretty soon I found myself begging to go home, but no sooner did I drag him out of one pub than he'd suggest "just one more pub"—and then just one more. The next day, shortly after dawn—I have no idea how or why we were up so early—I met Richard in the kitchen and he invited me to share breakfast with him: a fat sandwich of white supermarket bread spread thickly with hot mustard and filled with a generous helping of French fries. "Eat," he said, "it'll make you feel young."

Richard was what you'd call a sad drunk. Sad about what? Well, think for a moment about who and what Richard was before he met Elizabeth. He was a classically trained theater actor, well known and in demand—though not much so outside of England—married, with two children. *Cleopatra*—or, more precisely, the actress who played the legendary queen—transformed Richard's life overnight, much as my trip to Africa changed mine. He and Elizabeth were truly in love. But the press didn't give him a moment's peace from the very start. Once he'd divorced his wife, the actress Sybil Williams, and married Elizabeth, Richard led a very different life. In his heart, he never quite felt he earned the private jets, five-star hotels, and million-dollar checks all by himself. He was never sure if what had made him a major movie star was his own talent or his wife.

As time passed, I felt increasingly comfortable with the world that now surrounded me. Oddly enough, the person who should have made me feel most uneasy, Elizabeth, the most famous star in the world, was actually the one who made me feel most at home. She had a great sense of humor, was very affectionate, and loved having fun. She never set herself above the people in her entourage. She never harbored the reservations that I did about my class, or lack of it. She liked my style, the way I moved in her prestigious circle without airs. I never felt sexually attracted to Elizabeth. I can't tell you how many times I've been asked, "Did you sleep with her?" But the honest truth really is—for whatever reason—that the thought simply never crossed my mind. We became friends so quickly, so easily, that for me she was—and always remained—just a friend.

Richard was imposing. His voice inspired silence. I didn't understand what he spoke about in his speech at Oxford. It was Oxford English and I didn't even understand the English on television. But I was impressed by the way his voice was able to impress itself on that huge audience. Whether you'd known him for a minute or a year, his presence always inspired a cer-

Richard and Elizabeth pose in front of an entrance to the coal mine where Richard's father had worked in Pontrhydyfen, his hometown in Wales.

We were on holiday, and all I had for a camera was a Kodak Instamatic. (Photo by Kristy Tayler.)

tain awe. To me, he was everything I wasn't: he had class and an excellent education, even though I knew he was the son of a miner. He was a successful and seemingly confident artist, a man who inspired respect even when he said nothing, a man who had no need to impress anyone. I, on the other hand, could barely manage to pronounce his last name.

Chapter 5

Introverted
in America

Wait . . . What was it that Richard had said about America? Was it just drunken rambling?

No, that conversation in the restroom about America's watered-down beer was actually a formal invitation. The Burtons still had some time to kill before their next movie, and Elizabeth hadn't seen her parents in a while. So they were going to go to the States and wanted Claudye and me to go with them.

Preparing for my first trip to the United States, my biggest concern was what to wear. I was convinced I had nothing suitable for traveling with Elizabeth and Richard. "You're going to America," I kept telling myself, rejecting one item of clothing after another. I wanted to look right, appear like one of them. I knew how much Elizabeth cared about appearances. She was even taking her personal hairdresser with her across the Atlantic. Richard, on the other hand, couldn't care less.

The world acquired an entirely different dimension when traveling with Elizabeth and Richard. It was like stepping inside an enormous Technicolor cinema screen. Life suddenly became extremely easy. No waiting in line, no lost luggage, no delays—unless, of course, the delays were Elizabeth and Richard calling the airport to make a plane wait. No one was impolite. If you had a problem, someone solved it. If you forgot something, someone went and got you another. If you saw something you liked, it was immediately given to you as a gift. When Elizabeth and Richard traveled on commercial flights, they bought out the entire first class section which, in the case of our family trip to the States, left four people with a third of the plane at our disposal.

Generally, of course, the entourage was considerably bigger, as many as forty people on some occasions. And invariably almost everyone in it was gay. Elizabeth and Richard were surrounded by gays. Richard's personal secretary was gay. So was Elizabeth's. The man who looked after their yacht was gay. Alexandre, the hairdresser, was also gay. This may have been the sixties, with us heterosexuals liberating like wildfire, but remember— back then, the very word *gay*, in the sexual sense we now use it, barely existed. Homosexuality in Britain, for example, was a criminal offense until 1967. One day I finally asked Richard why he and Elizabeth had this preference for gays. I wasn't prejudiced, just curious.

"Gianni," he replied, "they don't have any family following them around. If our staff had spouses and children, we'd have to maintain even more people than we do already."

It was that simple.

When we landed in New York, the cabin crew let us leave the plane before everyone else. The moment we stepped into sight, we found ourselves facing a sea of journalists, photographers, and police. Security guards escorted us to a car that took us to the Regency Hotel on Park Avenue. I was dumbfounded by the extreme kindness shown me by the drivers, the hotel staff, everyone. Their care and attention was as overwhelming as the contrast between my simple street culture and the five-star service that I now received wherever I went. When I woke on our first morning in the hotel, I started to make the bed. Claudye had to tell me to stop. When I got out of the shower, I hung my towel on a hook. Claudye told me I was supposed to drop it on the floor.

The night before, after we'd checked in and unpacked our bags, we'd gone for dinner with Aaron Frosch, Elizabeth and Richard's lawyer. He had a penthouse apartment. I'd never been so high up in my entire life. I was used to the view from our Roman basement. Now there I was on top of the world, almost literally. I kept looking right and left, fascinated by everything. After all, I was just a tourist trying to absorb as much as possible, to remember every tiny detail. Being up in those buildings, I felt like I was suspended in air. Everything looked exaggerated and big, yet easily accessible.

On another night, I was in our room in the Regency when Claudye phoned me from Elizabeth and Richard's suite, telling me to put on a jacket and tie and join them. Robert Kennedy was coming to visit. The approach to their suite was, of course, swarming with bodyguards. It took more than a moment to convince them that I really was with the Burtons and to let me through. Once inside, I shook Bobby's hand. But what could I say? I could barely manage to say anything in English to anyone, let alone a Kennedy! I believe he was there that night hunting for Elizabeth and Richard's endorsement in the upcoming elections. I kept looking at him and thinking, "Wow! This is the brother of the president, who was assassinated in Dallas." Though, to me, he looked more like a young boy than a political candidate. I was fascinated and, strangely enough, didn't even think to go get my camera. Elizabeth invited him to stay for lunch. But Kennedy said he didn't have time, so she called room service and ordered a dozen club sandwiches. When they arrived I wasn't hungry, which is when I finally realized what a tremendous opportunity I was missing and raced downstairs to get my camera. It took me forever to get down and back. Only one elevator was working, and secret service agents insisted on frisking me and checking my camera on my way back. By the time I reached the suite, Kennedy was already in the hallway on his way out. So I didn't get a single shot. But at least I got to shake his hand.

Before leaving New York, the agent Jack Painter contacted me, asking me if I was interested in photographing a young actor everyone was talking about. It seemed like a good opportunity, so I went to the address he gave me, a commercial office building on Fifth Avenue, and got into the elevator with this strange, short guy wearing a long, black coat complete with hood. When we got off at the same floor, he went one way and I went another, but it turned out there were two separate entrances to the same set of offices. So when a secretary showed me into a room, the guy from the elevator was already there, sitting by a window waiting for me. His name was Al Pacino. Faced with my camera, he was very shy, almost embarrassed. It was raining, and I'd have preferred to photograph him outside. But he refused to move. So, without insisting, I photographed him as he was, with all his shyness.

Over the years, I've met Al on a number of occasions, and he's always thanked me for being kind to him when he was a young emerging actor. Once, during the eighties, I went to his home with Michelangelo Antonioni, and Al received us wearing nothing but his underpants. Michelangelo was very embarrassed. But I remembered that day in New York and realized that this was the same shy guy from twenty years earlier, despite all his stunning success. Being in underpants was actually part of that same shyness, his way of showing—without being aggressive—that he wasn't in the least bit intimidated by such an important director.

A young Al Pacino in New York (December 1968), showing his timid side.

After our stop in New York, we flew on to Los Angeles. During the flight, I kept thinking, "This could be the trip of my life." I still had no idea where my work would take me. I was a well-known retoucher, and a major star had appreciated some of my photos. But that was it. I didn't know if this was the beginning of something extraordinary, or just nothing. In any case, I decided to enjoy the moment.

When we landed in Los Angeles, the plane stopped a long way from the arrivals gate. I got worried. Had something happened? Then I saw a limousine drive onto the landing strip, followed by a mob of reporters and photographers. Elizabeth and Richard posed for a number of photos and answered all their questions. I was in a daze as we climbed into the limo. I'd never been in anything like it. It felt more like a cruise ship than a car. Valerie Douglas, Richard's secretary, who'd told me she'd be my "American mom," pulled out a bottle of Dom Pérignon to toast my first trip to the States. Richard tried to open it, but he couldn't. The bottle passed from hand to hand, but that stubborn cork defeated everyone's best efforts. Then someone spotted a bar on the other side of the street, and the limo did a sharp U-turn, stopping right outside.

Elizabeth and Richard asked me to go see if it was open. I'd barely stepped inside the place when the owner yelled, "We're closed!" To which I replied, "Are you closed for Elizabeth Taylor and Richard Burton?" So we stepped outside. Richard was standing by the limo, smoking. The bar owner saw him and promptly went out of his mind. "We're open!" he screamed. "We're open! We're open! Please, come inside!" We all sat down. Claudye and I admired a lamp on our table. The owner gave it to us as a gift. Then an ashtray. The drinks were all on the house. Richard tried to give him $50 for the lamp. He refused, so Richard left the waiter a $100 tip. On our way out, we saw the guy tell two assistants to put aside the chairs that Elizabeth and Richard had sat on. One hour earlier they'd just been two chairs. Now they were holy relics. The whole thing felt like a sketch from a TV comedy show.

We moved into a bungalow at the Beverly Hills Hotel. Richard asked me if I wanted a car to get around in. I told him I'd love to drive the new Mustang that had just come out in the States. So he got me a Mustang, and off I went on a high-speed spin around town. I promptly got stopped by the police and—as you do in Europe—I got out of the car. Two policemen sprinted forward, their guns aimed right at me, and slammed me against the car. "Beverly Hills Hotel!" I cried, trying to explain. "Elizabeth Taylor!

Richard Burton!" They cuffed me in a flash. Things got better once we were in the police car. I managed to explain who I was and why I was in Los Angeles, so they took me to the hotel. When one of the officers asked Richard if he knew me, he looked at me and answered, "No," which wasn't a funny joke. Then Elizabeth appeared. "Gianni, what have you done!" That was my welcome to California.

I never understood the American frenzy over Elizabeth and Richard. Maybe I'd lived in Rome too long. Romans aren't impressed by anything, or at least they don't show it by racing after celebrities, screaming and crying hysterically. Marcello Mastroianni or Anna Magnani could stroll down

Whenever Elizabeth made this face, Richard would be butter in her hands and concede anything.

Elizabeth with the black cat that adopted her (and she it) when she found it abandoned on the terrace of the Dorchester Hotel in London.

Via Veneto without ever getting mobbed the way Elizabeth and Richard were in Los Angeles. When the Burtons moved, everyone moved with them, from police and journalists to fans and private detectives. Yes, even detectives. One night I decided to get a breath of air in the hotel garden. To my surprise I saw a large tropical plant move, then stop. A man poked his head out from behind it and smiled at me. He was a detective up to who knows what. But I realized he was interested in Elizabeth and Richard because, before running away, he said, "Bye, Mr. Bozzacchi. Have a good day." He must have really studied up on everyone to know who the heck I was.

I met an even more absurd individual at a Beverly Hills party thrown in Elizabeth and Richard's honor. We were in an enormous house owned by one of their friends when I found myself sitting opposite a fat, taciturn stranger with shifty eyes. I couldn't work out whether he was a producer, a journalist, or what. Finally, at the end of the evening, I introduced myself and he did the same. I apologized for my English and asked if he was an actor. His reply was ice cold, which was pretty much how he came over in general. "I'm an arms dealer," he said. When I stared back in silence, he added calmly, "Oh, nothing illegal, you understand. I just buy arms from one country and sell them to another." By way of conversation, I asked if there was much competition in the business, to which he answered dryly, "My biggest competitors are epidemics." I had no idea what else to say. He chilled me. I looked him in the eye, and his icy gaze made my flesh crawl. I still wonder what that squalid individual was doing in such a firmament of stars.

We went for dinner with Elizabeth's parents, Francis and Sarah, at their hillside home in Bel Air. Francis had recently had a stroke and they'd moved from England to Southern California on account of the climate. He'd lost a lot of weight. Elizabeth was very close to her parents, and her British accent blossomed when they spoke together. On our way back, Elizabeth wept almost all the way. You don't often meet a man as distinguished as Francis. He was one of the world's leading art dealers. And now he could barely speak. Elizabeth was left emotionally drained.

During dinner I took photos in the dim light. I realized how important the photos were when I developed them. No one had photographed Elizabeth with her mother and father since she was a child. And, given that no one had said anything to me while I was taking them, I imagined I was authorized to sell them, as I'd already done with other photos of Elizabeth and her family. But when they were published, Elizabeth got angry. I thought she'd appreciate them, that she'd be happy to show that side of herself to the world. But she was furious that I hadn't been more considerate of her father's condition. I've never again published or shown those photos to anyone, and even now I wouldn't violate Elizabeth's wishes again.

Then there was the day they took me to Frank Sinatra's place. I'd barely stepped out of the car with my camera when Frank looked at me and said, "He stays in the car." I was crestfallen. Mia Farrow was there. And Peter

Lawford. A photo of Frank, Elizabeth, Richard, Mia, and Peter all together . . . It would have been crazy. Anyway, the Burtons explained who I was and Frank, addressing me in Italian, asked, "You Italian?" "Yes, Italian." "Sicilian?" "No, Roman." "Boot boy?" "No! Photographer." I showed him my bag. "I'm a photographer. That's why I've brought my cameras." He gestured imperceptibly to a waiter—who looked more like a bouncer—and he took my bag. End of conversation. Then they all began drinking and laughing about stuff I didn't understand.

Late that night we went on to eat at one of Sinatra's favorite restaurants, up on Little Santa Monica Boulevard, called, strangely enough, La Dolce Vita. The place was very dark. They seated us at a table, leaving all the other tables around us empty. It was the first time I'd tasted Italian American cuisine. The portions were enormous. Quantity over quality.

I wasn't able to follow the conversation there either, and over the years I've come to the conclusion that the fault was definitely more mine than Elizabeth and Richard's. I'd "won" that bet with my father all those years ago. So now I just had to grin and bear it, and laugh whenever they laughed, whether I understood what they were laughing about or not. Every now and then I'd catch a name, but mostly I had no idea who they were talking about. Sometimes Claudye would try to translate for me. But you need to bear in mind that she was born in Corsica and grew up in Paris; she translated in Corsican dialect, which is basically a mix of Paduan, Genoese, Sardinian, and a dash of French. I'd have been better off pretending to be deaf and dumb. I was confused and embarrassed. I was a street kid in a foreign country, light years from my own world in terms of class and culture. I believe Elizabeth and Richard—Claudye too—were convinced they were giving me a gift, offering me an extraordinary opportunity to spend time with all those fabulous people. Which is true, of course. They were. But it was a gift I wasn't able to enjoy. All I was able to do was smile, nod, and sit there feeling I didn't deserve this, feeling like a total idiot.

Toward the end of the trip, we went to see a screening of Mike Nichols's *The Graduate*. Even though I didn't understand everything, I liked it a lot—the images, the sense of confusion, the abuse of power. And I loved the Simon & Garfunkel soundtrack. I'd never heard pop music used that way in a movie, and no one else had either. It was actually a rare and bold move at the time, and clearly it worked. Other moviemakers quickly recognized the legacy of *The Graduate*, and pop music soon started appearing frequently in soundtracks, contributing to the success of classics such as *Butch Cassidy* and *Midnight Cowboy.* I watched *The Graduate* again, often—always in English—until I understood everything. It became one of my favorite movies.

When the lights came up at the end of that first screening, I saw Dustin Hoffman sitting silently at the back of the theater. He was incredibly shy and kept to himself. Mike had first noticed Dustin when he was playing Hamlet in an off-Broadway production. During post-production of his 1966 movie, *Who's Afraid of Virginia Woolf?* Mike asked Richard to go with him to watch a performance, and Richard had been very struck by this little guy who put so much depth and drama into the role.

I wondered why Elizabeth, Richard, and Mike hadn't worked together again after the huge success of *Who's Afraid of Virginia Woolf?* an important triumph for all of them, winning Elizabeth and Mike Oscars and going into Academy Awards history as one of only two movies ever nominated in every eligible category. Elizabeth and Richard had, in fact, asked Mike to handle the direction of a movie about the famous Welsh poet Dylan Thomas, a project proposed to them by his widow, Caitlin Thomas. Richard was a huge admirer of Thomas and had known him personally. But with dozens of people claiming rights to his estate, the movie never took off. That project aside, the three of them could definitely have done something together. Mike was one of the world's leading directors, and Elizabeth and Richard were among his closest friends. So why didn't they develop a major Hollywood production instead of returning to Europe? Why did they live and work at such a frantic pace?

Slowly I began to realize that Elizabeth and Richard didn't have much choice. They were trapped inside their own fame. A helicopter, a plane, a luxury car, an entourage, a yacht, homes in various countries, lawyers all over the place, not to mention children . . . All this had to be paid for, which meant work. Lots of it. Richard was already getting ready for his next movie, *Where Eagles Dare,* and confessed to me that he was only doing it for the money. Plus, they had endless tax problems. Neither of them could reside in England or Los Angeles for more than ninety consecutive days, otherwise they'd have to pay taxes on their movie revenues. Which is why they stayed in hotels in London and LA. On the other hand, in order to maintain their homes in Mexico and Switzerland as well as enjoy tax benefits, they were obliged to spend a certain number of days every year in both of those countries. Elizabeth and Richard enjoyed being citizens of the world, but what looked like carefree wandering actually followed a precise plan.

All this came to me slowly over time. Meanwhile, I struggled to work out how I could find a place for myself inside Elizabeth and Richard's world, should the opportunity ever arise. When I'd worked for Pierluigi or Johnny Moncada, I'd been loquacious, extroverted, and sure of myself, even with famous people. But it was one thing being myself when celebrities came to a studio—inside my own territory—for a couple of hours of professional work. It was quite another thing being part of Elizabeth and Richard's entourage, where the relationship was personal as well as professional. On that trip to America I discovered that going out at night was far from the lighthearted affair I'd known in my own life. You had to take care of appearances, behave in the right way with the right people, live up to expectations that the world had for people who were part of Elizabeth and Richard's entourage. A certain level of class and sophistication was expected, and I knew I didn't have either.

I began to think back to my old battles with my father, the clashes between his advice and my ego. I became increasingly conscious of the fact that I'd left school at thirteen, that my English was poor, and that the world was a lot bigger than my ability to understand it. I'd grown up in an unpretentious way, in an honest and solid family. Now I'd been hurled into the jet set.

I wasn't even comforted by my own work. I was too young and inexperienced to be able to appreciate my abilities. The compliments I received sounded too exaggerated. When you spend a lot of time with celebrities, you get tired of hearing that everything is "amazing" and "brilliant." That new book was "brilliant," even if the reviews had been terrible and you hadn't read it. That new movie was "amazing," even if Hollywood had condemned it as a flop. I was always fearfully anxious that all the compliments I received were dictated by the mere fact that I was close to Elizabeth and Richard, who were "amazing" and "brilliant" in everything they did. That said—and maybe I didn't yet understand the industry very well—it seemed to me they hadn't done an important movie since *Who's Afraid of Virginia Woolf?*

In any case, Elizabeth and Richard were now counting on enjoying a brief rest in Gstaad before Richard began work on *Where Eagles Dare.* So I returned to Rome. I barely had time to unpack before I was contacted by DEAR Movies, the production company set up by the influential Rome-based producer Robert Haggiag. They wanted me to work as special photographer on their next project, a sex farce entitled *Candy,* directed by Christian Marquand. I remembered Marquand as the man I'd met in Africa hiding in the bushes with Brando. I accepted, even though I knew nothing about the movie except that the actors would include Orson Welles. However, shortly after DEAR hired me, Welles left the movie and Haggiag offered the part to Richard.

So before *Where Eagles Dare,* Richard came down to Rome with Elizabeth to fit in ten days' shooting on *Candy.* Haggiag had nursed the project for some time; it was an adaptation of a Terry Southern novel written by Buck Henry and, in part, by Anthony Burgess. Haggiag was a very shrewd producer. To get the funding he needed, he put together an exceptional cast—Richard, Marlon Brando, Ringo Starr (in his solo movie-acting debut), Walter Matthau, James Coburn, John Astin, and Sugar Ray Robinson—and then shot everything in his own studios to cut costs.

As special photographer, my job was to take photos for advertising layouts, both on set and backstage—with actors getting ready or fooling around, little episodes that happen on every set but that people rarely see. If a producer uses his special photographer well, he can save a lot on advertising because the public will see his photos in advance and know all about the movie before it comes out. It's a bit like doing a photojournalist report on a movie under production without being chained to the director of photography and the cameraman, the way an official photographer always is.

Brando was the hardest person to photograph on that set. He was always very aware of the camera's presence. The young idol of *On the Waterfront* and *A Streetcar Named Desire* had already begun to show signs of considerable eccentricity. No one knew this better than Brando himself. He'd been such an Adonis in his youth that he now hated to see himself looking ugly in movies and photographs. He kept a close eye on me—controlling where I stood, what angle I was shooting him from—and that made it very difficult for me to get the natural photos I wanted. I never chatted with him, so I don't know whether he remembered seeing me in those bushes in Africa, and whether that had anything to do with his awkwardness in front of my camera.

One day Elliott Kastner, the producer of *Where Eagles Dare,* visited the set to tell Richard that Paul Newman wouldn't be taking part in the movie. His place as Richard's costar would be taken by Clint Eastwood. Richard shook his head and said, "No, I don't want an Italian actor . . . he has to be American."

Ringo Starr ready for his role in the 1968 Christian Marquand erotic comedy, *Candy*, in which he starred with Burton, Brando, and a string of other top names.

Richard still hadn't seen any of Sergio Leone's westerns—*A Fistful of Dollars, For a Few Dollars More, The Good, the Bad and the Ugly*—and, from what he'd heard, the star rarely spoke, which made him think that Clint was some Italian who spoke no English. I told Richard that I knew

Swedish actress Ewa Aulin, the title character in *Candy*, clearly has no trouble keeping Richard's eye on the prize.

Clint and offered to call Sergio and organize a screening while we were still in Rome. Richard said he'd view no more than ten minutes of film. But when Sergio brought a reel to DEAR, he laughed like crazy throughout the opening scene, even though *A Fistful of Dollars* still hadn't been dubbed into English. When the ten minutes were up, Richard complimented Sergio on his work, adding that he would have liked to have had time to see the rest. However, he'd seen enough to convince him that Clint was good. Before leaving, Sergio told Richard that he'd got the idea for the movie from Akira Kurosawa's *Yojimbo*, a claim he would later categori-

Marlon Brando (here on the *Candy* set with Ewa Aulin) was probably the most difficult-to-shoot star of my career. He could never stop thinking about himself (and maybe how to shoot me).

cally deny when Kurosawa and his producers sued—and won—over the issue.

One day I went to Haggiag's studio to show him some of my photos. I followed him to an editing station where Orson Welles was sitting at a console watching a reel of Haggiag's movie *Don Juan in Sicily*, directed by Alberto Lattuada. Robert asked him, "What do you think? Do you have any idea how I should recut it?" Welles replied with a gesture: "Like this," he said, imitating a pair of scissors cutting the film lengthwise down the middle. Robert just burst out laughing.

Candy seemed destined to end the same way. No one understood the movie, not the director, not the actors, not the genial director of photography, Giuseppe Rotunno, and probably not even Haggiag. Throughout the movie, the protagonist, played by Swedish actress Ewa Aulin (known principally for having won Miss Teen Sweden) basically goes to bed with every man she meets. Brando plays a mystical Indian. Richard is an eccentric

Me communicating with my trademark body language. I'm using my Leica M2, a camera that Elizabeth gave me and that seemed to bring both of us good luck.

poet called MacPhisto. Ringo is a gardener. The shooting was in such chaos that when Richard completed his ten days, he asked Elliott Kastner to hire me on *Where Eagles Dare,* just so that I could get off the set.

Elizabeth and Richard invited Claudye and me to spend Christmas and New Year with them in Gstaad. At this point I began to wonder if I'd ever go home. But I had no intention of refusing the invitation. It turned out that the cook at Chalet Ariel was on holiday during the festivities, and Elizabeth, without really asking, told me to make pasta for everyone. I had no idea where to start. I'd always lived at home with my parents and had never cooked for myself or anyone else in my life. Of course, I didn't have the courage to tell Elizabeth this. I already felt out of place with those people. I could hardly reveal that I didn't even know how to be an Italian. "No problema," I said, adding that I wanted the whole kitchen to myself, no assistance, just space and time. The moment everyone was out of the room, I grabbed the phone and called my mother. She proceeded to give me step-by-step instructions for two simple dishes, which everyone later said were exquisite. Of course they were. My mother had cooked them by phone.

One thing Elizabeth really seemed to like doing at Christmas was making pancakes. She adored making pancakes. She got me to fry bacon, which had to be American bacon. That was the only kind she'd eat. She had it personally delivered from the States. For the rest of the time, she made sure we bought food as locally as possible. I remember we ate a lot of Swiss *viande des grisons*—a kind of Italian bresaola—and fondue bourguignonne, usually with beef and, of course, lots of melted cheese. She adored cheese too. Her kitchen always smelled of fresh Gruyère.

One evening, after a brief quarrel with Richard, Elizabeth went to bed. And so did Claudye, leaving me alone with Richard, who proceeded to get even drunker than usual. I tried more than once to follow the women's example and excuse myself, but Richard kept stopping me. Suddenly, he hurled his empty glass to the floor, looked me straight in the eye, and said, "I'm a millionaire. Me. I'm a millionaire."

I quipped back that I, too, was a millionaire. Which I was—in old Italian lira terms. "It depends on your point of view, no?"

But he didn't like the joke and got enraged. "No you're not, you damn liar! I am. Me, Richard Burton. I'm a millionaire."

I understood exactly what he meant, that he was a millionaire in his own right, not just as the husband of Elizabeth Taylor. I'd just been joking, in an ironic, Roman way: I really did have a couple of million lira, more or

Self-portrait (1968), taken with a Nikon F.

The Nikon F.
(Photo by M&S
Materiale
fotografico.)

less. But they, of course, were multimillionaires in US dollars, which is quite another matter. But Richard just got angrier. He staggered toward me in a fury and tried to grab me. I ducked away. Then he tried to throw a punch. I ducked again, and as bad luck would have it, he hit the mantelpiece instead. I realized immediately that he'd injured himself. Laughing, he mumbled something that I didn't understand, but he let me tend to his hand. I could see he'd possibly dislocated or broken his wrist, so we headed for the hospital. Outside it was snowing a blizzard, and getting Richard's Mini Cooper S through the streets was an adventure in itself. The next morning, he came to wake me and asked what had gone on the night before. He didn't remember any of it. I never told him that he'd tried to knock me out.

Later that day Richard gave me a speech that I wasn't expecting. He asked me what my intentions were regarding Claudye. He said she was family, as far as he and Elizabeth were concerned. Elizabeth called her "little sister," and Richard treated her like a daughter. I tried to reply with self-assurance: "Intentions will come later. For the time being, we love each other and are happy that way."

Richard nodded. Then he said something that would change my life forever: "Would you like to work for us?"

I couldn't even manage a reply. I couldn't find the words in English. I tried to explain myself with gestures, shaking my head. Richard helped me out with a few words in Italian, and then understood that, yes, I would love to work with the greatest stars in the world. I just needed to find the cour-

The children and grandchildren at Chalet Ariel, the Taylor-Burton home in Gstaad, 1972. *From left:* Maria Burton, Michael Wilding, Beth Wilding (holding Laela, Michael's daughter), Liza Todd, and Christopher Wilding.

age. I was racked with uncertainty. Then Richard said, "Elizabeth needs you. Why don't you join our family?"

I felt like leaping out of my chair. Instead I tried to keep calm and composed. Richard took my timidity and my difficulty in finding the right words as a sign of coldness. He asked another couple of times: "Do you want to work with us or not? Yes? Can you leave your job with Pierluigi?"

There was no way I could talk in English with Richard about this, or anything else. I was too ashamed to even try. I was embarrassed to have such a special relationship with the famous Richard Burton and not even be able to communicate with him. We were sitting right next to each other.

But the distance between his life and mine was so huge we might just as easily have been at opposite ends of the earth. I could have said something in Italian, just so I expressed what I was thinking, feeling, even if Richard couldn't understand it all. Instead, I quit trying to speak altogether, which today I regret. I shook my head and managed a strangled "Yes." He gave me a strange look. Surely he didn't think I thought I was doing him a favor! Then he gave me a clap on the shoulder and, in perfect Italian, said, "Bene. Non dimenticare che io sono il figlio di un minatore" (Good. Don't forget, I'm the son of a miner).

Richard had understood my dilemma perfectly. He stood up and left me to join Elizabeth in their bedroom. They could have worked with dozens of photographers more experienced than me, photographers who hadn't just been fired from one of Italy's biggest and most prestigious journalism agencies. At some point, surely this ride would come to an abrupt halt. I'd be thrown from the saddle and they'd gallop on without me, as if we'd never met. I was overwhelmed by a sense of insecurity. I couldn't understand. I was being offered the chance of a lifetime and I felt so awful? My thoughts went back to my childhood, me skinny with rags on my butt. Then I caught sight of my reflection in the large living room windows of the home I was in, that of Elizabeth Taylor Burton (as she liked to be known in those days), and sat there admiring the extraordinary view offered by my new world. "But I'm a photographer," I kept saying, and maybe I even managed to convince myself.

Chapter 6

"The New King of the Camera"

Where Eagles Dare was filmed in Wolfern, northern Austria. Every morning, for a month and a half, we toiled up a steep mountain road to the set, located in a castle an hour by car from Salzburg. It was so cold that my cameras froze and my lenses fogged over. I wore two overcoats and tried to protect my cameras by slipping them between the layers. But it didn't help much. Licking the lenses was the only way to effectively defrost them. And wearing gloves made correcting the focus a clumsy operation. There were no automatic functions in those days. You had to constantly fuss with all the various mechanisms to adjust the levels.

The members of the cast and crew were almost all English. To keep warm, they drank—cognac in their coffee, gin, whatever. But I didn't drink. So I froze. One morning I woke in my hotel room, put one foot out of bed, and fell to the floor. I was stunned. When I took my temperature the thermometer almost exploded. I withdrew from the battlefront for a couple of days before returning to that icy mountain.

The director, Brian Hutton, looked familiar, but I couldn't remember where I'd seen him before. Then someone told me he used to be an actor and I remembered: he'd been in all those westerns that I'd gone to see when I skipped school in the afternoons. At the time, few actors had ventured into directing, and it was interesting to watch Hutton at work. The more I frequented movie sets, the more I became passionate about the whole dynamic of realizing a movie, how the various phases converge, the entire mechanism of production. I realized there were basically two directing techniques: either the actor followed the camera, or the camera followed the actor. The majority of the directors I'd seen at work made the camera follow the actor. Hutton worked the old-fashioned way—the actor following the camera—but the many small roles he'd played had given him a chance to study in depth the behavior of other directors and actors, with the result that he displayed a high degree of skill.

I heard a story about how Hutton, as a young, penniless actor in New York, had decided to open a restaurant with his friend Al Lettieri (who later played Sollozzo in *The Godfather*). It was an international restaurant, offering all kinds of food: Chinese, German, Italian, French, Japanese. But no food was prepared on the premises. Hutton and Lettieri paid guys to go by bicycle to various nearby restaurants and buy takeaway dishes, delivering them to the door labeled "Kitchen" in an alleyway behind the restaurant. The meals were then served to patrons at a higher price. For a while they were very successful. But then restaurants caught on to the scam and started refusing to sell to the bicycle boys. Soon enough, the enterprise folded.

The weather in Austria was very unstable. One day we were forced to evacuate the set when it was swept by a blizzard. Half of us were taken out by helicopter. The others drove down to the valley by jeep. So much snow fell that the following day our location was unrecognizable.

There was one scene where two actors came down by parachute, and the one with the radio had to fall and die. Hutton then wanted Richard to walk out over the virgin snow and retrieve the radio. Richard took two steps and vanished. No one had realized that there was a huge ditch in his path because Hutton had forbidden anyone to disturb that snow by walking over it. Everyone rushed to pull him out. It was a very funny moment. But Richard flew into a rage with both the director and cameraman, who were both doubled up laughing.

For some reason unknown to me, the same cameraman took great pleasure in making my life difficult. He was a huge guy, and he loved to come up behind me and give me a hearty slap on the shoulder—bang! "Gianni! How's it going?" It hurt like hell. He kept this up for weeks, seeming to think it was funny. Then one day I was taking some photos when he shouted, "Shadow in the shot!" and pointed at me, gesturing for me to shift because my shadow was in the camera's field of vision. But what I caught was "Shut up!" and besides, I was already annoyed with him. So I went straight over and punched him in the head. He collapsed and almost vanished in the snow. Richard smiled, winked at me, and gave me a thumbs-up. Surely he didn't think I'd hit the guy on his behalf?

During a break in production, I went with Richard to Salzburg to meet Rock Hudson, who was there shooting a movie with Claudia Cardinale.

Claudye and I had met Claudia and her husband, the producer Franco Cristaldi, in Paris. I went to greet her, and she introduced me to Rock, who replied with a curt "Hi," as if he were far from pleased by our visit. We stayed no more than half an hour, during which time I got the distinct impression he was flirting with Claudia in an exaggerated fashion. That bothered me a lot. I considered Franco a friend and admired him. Back on set, I mentioned this to Clint, who calmly told me not to worry: Rock was homosexual. "But he's been married!" I said, flabbergasted. As if that had anything to do with it. Remember, we were still light years from the mid-1980s, when Rock would become the first major celebrity to die from AIDS, a tragedy that would help transform public awareness of a still highly stigmatized disease and push his good friend Elizabeth to the forefront of AIDS activism.

From Austria, the production of *Where Eagles Dare* moved to England, where filming was completed at the MGM Studios in Elstree. Elizabeth had already signed to act in another Joseph Losey movie, *Secret Ceremony*, which was being shot across the street in another part of the studio. As a result, I found myself photographing the sets of both movies. This was Elizabeth and Richard, remember. You've got to work. And now I had to work as well! I ended up being so busy doing *Secret Ceremony* and *Where Eagles Dare* that I barely got a moment to enjoy London. A car would take us to the studios in the morning before it was even light. And by the time we finished it was already dark. On a few occasions we went out for a nightcap. But mostly we went straight to bed, hoping to grab as much sleep as possible before that car came to get us again in the morning.

In Elizabeth and Richard's case "bed" was on a rented yacht moored in the Thames. Elizabeth had insisted—as she usually did—on bringing her dogs along. But this was England, which had a six-month quarantine period for any dog brought into the country. So Elizabeth's typically extravagant solution had been to get the yacht and keep her dogs on board. Thus they never had to go through quarantine. One day, flipping a finger at the British government, she had me take a picture of them propped up on the yacht's railings, with London Bridge clearly visible in the background. Then, rather than sign it myself, she had me send it out to the press as if some paparazzi had snapped it.

I didn't like Joseph Losey any better the second time around. *Boom!* hadn't been much of a success, but Elizabeth still admired him for his earlier work and because he'd been blacklisted. I knew nothing about all that.

All I knew was that Losey was still weird and grumpy. "I liked some of the photos you took on the set of *Boom!*" he said, emphasizing the word "some." Then he started calling me "Guillotine" because of the noise the motor on my new Hasselblad made. That was about as friendly as Losey got.

Years later, I had a chance to see just how unfriendly Losey could be. It was 1982, and Michelangelo Antonioni and I were going to a preview of his latest movie, *Identification of a Woman,* which I'd already seen and didn't think worthy of Antonioni. Regardless, I'd persuaded Michelangelo to give a speech, which we'd written together, before the screening. My girlfriend at the time, Tahnee Welch, read it through with him beforehand to help him memorize it. We got to Lincoln Center in a limousine and climbed into an extremely slow elevator from the garage. When it stopped on the first floor, Losey stepped in. And before the elevator could crawl to our floor, he made one of his comments I'd come to know so well: "Michelangelo, this elevator reminds me of one of your movies."

It took all my self-control to keep from laughing. I was amazed Losey could be so spiteful. Michelangelo was furious. I could see his facial tic accelerate. He refused to give the speech we'd planned, and the screening was a disaster. Having worked with Losey on two movies, I knew exactly how Michelangelo felt.

On the first day of shooting *Secret Ceremony,* I arrived at the set around 7:30 in the morning and was walking down a corridor when Mia Farrow stepped from her dressing room. She had a bottle of Italian wine in her hand, a Verdicchio. "Can you open this for me?" she asked, waving the bottle in the air. Her marriage to Frank Sinatra had just ended. It was

Mia Farrow had just left Frank Sinatra when she invited me for an impromptu 7:30 a.m. drink in her dressing room on the London set of *Secret Ceremony.*

"Why didn't it work out with Sinatra?" I asked. "Because I like the Beatles," she explained, bopping to *Sgt. Pepper's*.

Mia Farrow (1968) and her mother, Maureen O'Sullivan, otherwise famous—especially to me—as Tarzan's companion Jane.

strange to think of this actress and Sinatra ever being a couple, although I'd actually seen them together in Los Angeles. We'd all heard the story of how he'd served her divorce papers right while she was in the middle of shooting *Rosemary's Baby,* apparently furious that, as his wife, she'd dared to go back to work. So while I opened the Verdicchio, I couldn't help asking her why they'd separated. "Because I like the Beatles," she replied. I took a photo of her posing with the album *Sgt. Pepper's Lonely Hearts Club Band,* which she then put on a turntable and began dancing to, right there in the dressing room.

One Saturday Mia called asking if I could take a photo of her with her mother, Maureen O'Sullivan. We met in the street, and as they were coming toward me, I thought, "But that's Jane!" Which indeed Maureen was: Jane of *Tarzan* fame. I'd seen her so often as a kid, up there on the silver screen alongside the legendary Johnny Weissmuller, that I couldn't help calling her "Jane" all day. We took a stroll and I snapped a number of shots of the two of them together. In some photos I took of Mia she looked very sad. I don't know if her sorrow was connected to her breakup with Sinatra or not.

I enjoyed a good rapport with Mia. She was like a child, sweet, kind, and innocent. I never felt out of place with her. She never criticized others and never made a big thing about her celebrity. At the same time, although I liked her, she was strange, enigmatic. You couldn't have a real conversation with her. She'd keep jumping from one thing to another. I never really understood her personality. Maybe it was because she was so young. Or because I was so young. Or maybe I just couldn't separate her from *Rosemary's Baby*. I hated that movie, its darkness, its abstract quality. I'd come to cinema through neorealism and American epics.

Another star of *Secret Ceremony* was Robert Mitchum. He seemed to behave a bit like Losey. He came and went as he pleased, without getting close to anyone. The attitude fitted with the image he wanted to give of himself—tough, distant, cynical, like a lot of his characters. But after I'd spent some time with him, I actually found him very friendly. I'd chat with him in my stumbling English, and he'd tell me dirty jokes in his equally stumbling Italian.

He asked me a lot of questions about Italian women. He'd been out with a few and found them confusing. He'd say, "I can't work out how they think. It's impossible to understand them. They're sexy. They're beautiful.

Secret Ceremony star Robert Mitchum, one of cinema's leading men, who liked to project a tough-guy image, but we became friendly anyway. He asked me a lot of questions about Italian women.

But I've never understood their way of thinking. They say 'no' when they mean 'yes.' They desire you. But when they've had you, they pretend they don't care anymore. Why do they do that?" Of course, Mitchum was a man from the previous generation, one who still found the free love of the sixties unpalatable. I thought he was very funny. There was absolutely no point trying to explain the women's liberation movement to him.

Mitchum never liked to pose, which was just perfect for me. He had a very interesting face. Light sculpted it. He didn't have conventional good looks—like Richard. His features were more consumed than defined, and he had a shrewd air, which didn't inspire trust. Photographing him made me understand more clearly the difference between having a woman as a subject and a man. The exposure can be the same, but the stop has to be different. With the right light, you can smooth a woman's face without having to resort to artificial retouching (or a computer, as they do today). With a man, on the other hand, you have to close down the stop in order to highlight the features of his face.

In Mitchum's case, that meant highlighting all the marvelous crevices in his face, the furrows of a survivor, his gangster's grimace. Mitchum appreciated my photos. He said he was never conscious of my presence, never noticed when I was on set, and he liked that. A lot of photographers only worry about pleasing their subjects. I concentrated on the overall context of a photo, on its artistic quality.

I surprised everyone with my work on *Secret Ceremony*, including myself. For the first time, I got huge compliments from the producer, the actors, and even Losey, who never seemed to like anything I did. It was the movie that made me feel I'd grown as a photographer. And the fact that so many important people had appreciated my work instilled a great sense of confidence in me. Around then, an interview with me appeared in the *London Daily Mirror* under the headline "The New King of the Camera." The newspaper asked me to provide a self-portrait, which I did with a sense of irony, using a double exposure.

The world seemed to be trying to convince me that I'd succeeded, that I'd reached the peak of a photographer's skill. But the only opinion I really trusted was that of the best photographer I knew, my father, who simply said, "You're getting better, but you're still not there . . ."

Naturally, he was right. And I needed his honesty to avoid losing my bearings. Immortalizing the life of the jet set, being in daily touch with all those extraordinary people, was already hard enough. Sharing that kind of

The self-portrait I took for the *London Daily Mirror* when that newspaper dubbed me "the new king of the camera" (1968).

life felt like an impossible task for a street kid like me. I'd only ever felt at ease behind a camera, and it was there that I hid. I became a full-on introvert, a guy sitting in a corner observing the most famous people in the world enjoy life, snapping photos when my instinct told me to.

During the shooting of *Where Eagles Dare* and *Secret Ceremony,* Claudye and I decided to get married. I completed the layout of the two movies before shooting ended, and Elizabeth and Richard gave me time off to plan my wedding. It is Italian tradition that the breadwinner, the father, should help with the wedding arrangements, so I rang my father to give him the news. "Hi, Dad, I'm calling to tell you that I'm going to get married."

"Why?"

"What do you mean, why? We've been together for a year and . . ."

"If it's fine by you . . ."

"Of course it is. We've got to organize everything, so you've got to come to London."

"What?! Have you gone crazy?"

My father didn't sleep a wink for a week before the trip. He and my sister Paola used to take the same bus to work, and according to her he told everyone he met on the bus that he was going to London because his son was getting married. He was very excited, and very nervous. I had to call friends in Rome to help him prepare for the trip and apply for a passport. Then I had to call him just two days before he was due to leave to tell him there'd been a change in plans. He had to stop off first in Paris because Claudye's family wanted to meet him. He went off his head: "You can't do that to me. I'm only ready to go to London."

I went to meet him at the Paris Orly airport in my future father-in-law's little Deux Chevaux Citroën. He was as white as a sheet. He'd never been on a plane before. I tried to find out what had happened, but he just kept saying: "It's all *fine,* just *fine.*" Whatever problem he might have had, he had no intention of telling me about it. When we got to passport control, my father refused to give his passport to the agent. Someone in Rome had told him to be very careful about his passport and not to let anyone touch it. I had my work cut out convincing him that he absolutely had to give it to the agent. Finally, my father presented his passport, shouting, "Hey! Hey!" and pointing his finger until the guy stamped it.

Shortly after we left the airport my father asked if we couldn't maybe get a taxi. "Why?" I asked. "Because I feel like I'm still on the plane," he said, referring to the Citroën's bouncy suspension. After a while he calmed down and then proceeded to ask me to take him to the Louvre. I told him that Claudye's family was waiting for us.

"No!" he replied. "When Bruno Bozzacchi gets to Paris, he goes immediately to pay homage to art! Take me to the Louvre."

"All right!" I cried, and took him to the Louvre. He wanted to go in on his own. I said I'd come by and get him later, but he insisted on having the address of the restaurant where we were to meet Claudye's family, saying he'd get there by taxi. When he finally got to the restaurant, he was again as white as a sheet and gasping. I ran over to him and asked what had happened.

"Sortie, sortie, sortie!" he said. "There's no way of getting out of that place!"

Sortie means "exit" in French, and in Roman dialect we say *sortire*. But in the Louvre, those signs only mean that you're leaving one gallery and going into the next. The museum is organized as a one-way route. When my father realized it was getting late, he began running toward those signs hoping to find a way out. He lost count of the number of galleries he raced through in his desperate dash. All the same, we spent a lovely evening with Claudye's family. Then we left for London.

Elliott Kastner knew I was arriving with my father and put a Rolls Royce at our disposal. The driver was waiting for us outside the airport— bald, with a black overcoat, black boots, and an icy stare, an authentic English character from the sixties. My father took one look and said, "Is that our driver? He looks more like a Nazi. I'm not getting into a car with a Nazi. Look at his face. He's not English, he's German." He was determined not to get into that car. I had to go to the driver and ask him what his nationality was. English, he replied, in a strong Cockney accent. I told my father. He remained suspicious, but he got into the car all the same.

On the way, I said, "Dad, we're going to the studios to meet Elizabeth and Richard. They asked me to bring you. Is that okay?" He got agitated: "Do I really have to?" I said we couldn't avoid it; they were going to be best man and matron of honor at my wedding. He hesitated. He was worried that he didn't know any English. "Dad," I said, "we have to go. Just shake their hands and say, 'Nice to meet you.'" Throughout the rest of the drive he kept practicing: "Nice to meet you."

We got to the MGM Studios, where Richard met us. He hugged my father, apologizing that he had to run back to the set to finish shooting a scene. So we crossed the road to the Elstree studios and got to Elizabeth's dressing room, where I told my father to wait by her secretary's desk while I went to get Elizabeth. He just stood there tugging nervously on his thin moustache until Elizabeth arrived wearing nothing but a negligee. "Hi, Bruno!" she cried, rushing forward to hug him and kiss him full on the mouth. My father broke into a stutter, "Nnnnice . . . to . . . mmmeet you . . ." I could see he was embarrassed and stepped next to him. His knees were literally buckling, as if he was slowly turning to water. I grabbed one of his arms. His eyes were glazing over. He was in ecstasy. "You are coming to dinner with us tonight, aren't you?" said Elizabeth, whereupon she hugged him again, and once more kissed him full on the mouth. If I hadn't held him up, he'd have fallen to the floor. We left the studios with my father moving like a zombie, in shock, bewitched by Elizabeth's charms. In the car, all he could manage was: "Damn, she's so beautiful! Oh! And don't say a word to your mother that she kissed me on the mouth!"

That night we went to dinner with Richard and Elizabeth at a beautiful restaurant in Hampstead. Away from the set and far from their fans, they were very affectionate, friendly, and simple people. So they got along well with my father. But before long he vanished. After a search, I found him in the kitchen helping the cooks. My father didn't easily adapt to this world either, so "revered and spoiled," so different from our own in Rome.

The following evening, we all went out together with Marilù Tolo, a friend who was in London studying English. She was a well-known actress in Italy at the time, and my father's reaction was very similar to the one he'd had meeting Elizabeth. He was so proud to be out in public with her like that. And infuriated that he couldn't make the most of it. "Christ, I'm out walking with Marilù Tolo and won't meet anyone I know!"

We went to a very popular Polynesian restaurant. My father studied the menu, but didn't have a clue what to choose. There was no pasta and no other food that he knew. I ordered him a scorpion, a cocktail with three types of rum mixed with fruit juice. He took one sip and said, "This is crazy, you've ordered me fruit juice." He wanted wine, but they didn't have any, so he slugged the scorpion and ordered another. I warned him to go slow. But by the end of the evening, when we got up from the table, he exclaimed, "Mamma mia, I've lost my legs!" He was drunk from the belt down, and I had to physically carry him to the car. He wasn't raving; he simply couldn't walk.

When my father returned to Rome, I finished developing my negatives from *Where Eagles Dare* and *Secret Ceremony* and began getting ready to go to Paris to organize our wedding. Before leaving, however, I was contacted about doing an album cover for the Rolling Stones. I believe they were interested in me because I wasn't English. In those days, Paris was the world's fashion capital. They'd read the *Daily Mirror* article about

Elizabeth Taylor's personal photographer, an Italian who lived in Paris, and they thought it was cool. So I met Mick Jagger and Bill Wyman, along with some of their managers. They were two young, arrogant kids, a bit like I was. But they didn't make a good impression on me. Their version of celebrity was very different from the style I'd become accustomed to with Elizabeth and Richard. They were rock stars, not members of the Hollywood nobility. We didn't understand each other. They offered me the job, but I was so busy with preparations for our wedding that in the end nothing came of it.

The Beatles also wanted to hire me to do the cover of what would become their last album together, *Abbey Road*. I had what I thought was a good idea: the four of them walking in single file across the street. I talked about it with their agent and took a few Polaroid shots. But then they said they wanted to do something else, when in fact they hired another photographer and stole my idea. I complained to the Beatles PR man, Jerry Pam, who later became one of my good friends, and I even thought about suing. But it would have been so difficult to prove the whole thing, so eventually I gave it up. There's so much copying in photography that it becomes impossible to resolve situations like that. Maybe someone else really had had the same idea. And when the Beatles heard it for the second time, they liked it better. In the end, the credit goes to who took the photo. Maybe the end result was better than what I would have done anyway. Or maybe I really would have done a better job. Who knows?

Claudye and I married on June 22, 1968. The wedding was supposed to take place in Paris, but when the famous May Revolution broke out, we decided to move to a countryside location in Lower Normandy, Claudye's close friend Alexandre's country house in the village of Saint-Lo. Elizabeth and Richard, as our matron of honor and best man, came and went the same day by helicopter. As their wedding gifts to us, Claudye got a Dior dress and I got a Mini Cooper S! Our bridesmaids were Liza Todd and Maria Burton. Our page was John Heyman's son, David.

The ceremony was held in a Catholic church. The priest didn't want to marry us because I wasn't baptized. Then Elizabeth gave a "donation" of $10,000 to his church, and suddenly he no longer seemed worried about my faith. Nor his own, it would seem, given that soon afterward the good father disappeared, along with Elizabeth's donation. Who knows what happened to the man, into what world he vanished? I often used to ask Alexandre, because he lived in the parish and knew everyone. But all he

Claudye and I married in France, June 22, 1968, flanked by our honor guard, Elizabeth and Richard. My former boss Pierluigi took the (exclusive) pictures.

could say was that the priest never returned and no one had since heard a word about him. I believe he felt rather embarrassed about the whole affair.

We wanted a small, private wedding. But of course that was totally impossible, given the presence of Elizabeth and Richard. The entire village turned out to watch the bridal procession in front of the church. The reception was held in Alexandre's house and fabulous garden, an old restructured mill on an island in the Vire River. I'd never seen so many photographers all in one place. They'd come from all over Europe and, in order to steal their shots, had donned fisherman's waders and were standing half submerged in the river. That way, by staying in the water, they weren't trespassing on private property. The only photographer I authorized to come inside was Pierluigi. Marie Elaine de Rothschild invited herself. Top fashion executives, artists, total strangers, people I'd never met, all turned up to swell the crowd.

The only guests I really cared about were my own close friends and family: my father, my mother, my sister Paola, my brothers-in-laws Robert and Tonio, and my brother Renato. And, of course, Richard and Elizabeth,

Pierluigi took this shot of us newlyweds. I'd love to have a copy of the photo you see Elizabeth taking, but oddly I never got one.

who were very affectionate with all of them. At one point, Richard invited my father to sit next to him while he continued to drink and chat with everyone around him. Then he noticed something strange about my father's socks. The elastic had snapped and they'd slid onto his shoes, so my father had rolled and tucked them back up around his calves. Richard burst out laughing. "Bruno, you're fantastic," he said, and hugged him. My father was a simple man, just like the son of a Welsh miner. Then I saw my mother go over to Elizabeth and give her a pinch on the cheek. "You're a right sweetie, you are," she said, at which Elizabeth laughed and hugged her back.

Every time I'd approach my mother she'd ask, "Who are all these people?" I don't know if I was more delighted that day, or confused. My wedding was everything a wedding should be, full of joy, dancing, good food, and lots to drink. But Elizabeth and Richard's presence, even though it was extremely appreciated, made it seem to me like the event had spiraled beyond Claudye and me, had become something that wasn't entirely ours.

The following day, newspapers around the world—with photos supplied by Pierluigi—publicized the love story that had blossomed inside the world of Elizabeth and Richard, a love story inside the biggest love story on the planet.

Claudye was much more at ease in this vortex than I ever was. We were in her close friend Alexandre's house. Elizabeth and Richard had been her employers and friends for ages. Claudye knew all these important people whom I'd never met. She was used to a lifestyle that was still so new to me. What was I doing there? Did I belong to this group of people simply because I'd taken a few beautiful photos? And were my photos really so extraordinary that they deserved all that prime space in top magazines? Or were they only "good" because they were exclusive, or because I was part of Elizabeth and Richard's entourage? I was happy and excited about beginning a new life with Claudye. But it still didn't feel like my life—not yet, at least.

Chapter 7

Black and White in Color

Claudye and I spent the better part of 1968 on our honeymoon. From Paris, we went to relax for a few days on the Côte d'Azur in southern France. Then we went to Corsica, where locals came to serenade us under our hotel window. Then we went to Rome, where we hired a car and drove to Naples, crossing over to Capri. Our next stop was Saint-Tropez, where we stayed in another of Alexandre's homes. Then we met up with Elizabeth and Richard in Villefranche-sur-Mer, a little town between Nice and Monte Carlo. Their yacht was moored just off the port, and as we approached it by sea, I noticed that they'd changed the name. They'd bought it and rebaptized it *Kalizma*, an acronym of the names of their three daughters: Kate, Liza, and Maria. We proceeded to enjoy a long cruise on that beautiful yacht.

When Richard originally rented the boat in London it was already old. First launched in 1912, it had done service for the British navy throughout both world wars. When it was associated with the magic couple Taylor-Burton, however, the press dubbed it the "Love Boat," and it became one of the world's most exclusive aquatic residences. It had seven bedrooms and could sleep fourteen passengers plus accommodate a crew of eight, which included a cook, a maid, and a waiter. We had a lot of fun over the years on that yacht: Richard, Elizabeth, their children, and everyone's friends. It's since been bought again and fully restored by a wealthy Indian industrialist. He spent good money revamping the yacht from stern to prow but took care to maintain the name *Kalizma*. After all, the name was what made it famous in the first place, and its association with Elizabeth and Richard remains a significant reason why it's still worth a lot of money.

Life quickly became more surreal. Total strangers stopped me in the street, called me by name, asked for my autograph. Paparazzi followed us everywhere. Yet all I could do was keep wondering, "Why me?" I didn't

Elizabeth takes a dip from the *Kalizma,* suggesting one reason why paparazzi dubbed it the "Love Boat" . . . because they were in love with its leading lady.

think I deserved so much attention. Worse still, I wasn't at all sure it would last. I was convinced Elizabeth and Richard would eventually figure out I was a fraud. And if they didn't, Claudye would. I'd spent half my life trying to avoid photography. Now, without even trying to, I'd become the most in-vogue photographer on the planet.

During that trip, I tried to picture my future life as a married man. I was used to the freedom that came with my work and the climate of those times. Well before our marriage, we knew that our lives were different, that our world of work was different, that I was different. Certain things were part and parcel of my job. "It was the sixties!" people my age still say, especially if they worked in the entertainment industry. It has become a short-hand way of summing up the situation, an excuse for being young and free to do whatever we wanted, whenever we wanted. If you never personally experienced the repressive forties and fifties, you'll never truly understand the cultural shock of the sexual revolution that followed. Especially how it felt to a young twenty-four-year-old guy who suddenly found himself front-page news around the world. And, of course, it wasn't just us guys. The pill had given women a way to control their sex life. And they were using it, aggressively.

At first I thought women were just reacting to my camera. I knew how to recognize someone's beauty when I saw it through the lens of a camera. It took me some time to realize that, without me knowing it, I was sexually provoking women. I acted on instinct. It came naturally to me to behave like that in order to get the image I wanted. I had no precise intention of taking them to bed. I just wanted to stimulate them in order to get a beautiful photo. Eventually I realized that while I was photographing women, I was manipulating their inner sensuality. It's something you have to experience in order to understand it properly. For example, if you know how to touch a woman, you can stir certain feelings in her. If you don't, she can end up turning you down. Exactly the same thing happens with a photo. A good photographer has to bring the best out in his or her subject, make the person feel good in order to create the best possible image. I was a young Italian guy photographing beautiful women. During photo shoots in a studio, I couldn't hide in the background like I did on sets or at parties. Inevitably the exchange became personal. If I'd ignored my subjects or tried to hide behind my lens, I'd have made them feel intimidated, insecure. I had to interact, chat, encourage, compliment. I flirted with women in my studio, trying to get inside their minds with feelings, expressions, body language. My cameras became an extension of my sensuality, and this created a certain intimacy between me—the artist—and my subjects.

I have to confess that my system worked so well that it transformed me into a sex symbol. Women stopped waiting for the end of a photo shoot to proposition me. They'd stroll straight into my studio and strip naked before I could even say, "Hi." Turning them down only seemed to make them more aggressive. Some got offended and left. In the end I quit trying to stop them. After all, we're talking about a procession of amazing models and fabulous actresses. Like I said, those were the sixties. Behaving like that today would be considered unprofessional. And quite rightly. But things were different back then. Sex was everywhere, including in my job. And the fact is, there's a big difference in a woman's face before and after sex. She can look incredibly sexy beforehand. But afterward—she oozes sexuality.

In order to get the shots I wanted, I knew I had to present myself to my female subjects in a certain way. I provoked them with my body language, with my way of moving, with what I said, with the things I made them imagine could happen, and with what had already taken place. Only some photographers have this ability, and I was one of them. But now that I was married, I'd no idea how I could keep doing that job. Not that way, at least. I loved Claudye and no one else. But how long could I resist before I trampled on that love? And what about physical attraction? Flirting? My own libido? Everything else? Our marriage had come upon us so quickly that I hadn't had time to think about how I'd adapt.

However, Claudye knew my life very well—our life, the jet-set life. She knew that I wouldn't change overnight just because I was married now. Nor did she want me to. She'd lived with Elizabeth and Richard much longer than I had and was at ease in their carefree world. What's more, she adored being married to Gianni Bozzacchi, "the new king of the camera," much more than she loved Gianni Il Roscio from Rome. And I played my part the best I could. Claudye wanted me to grow my hair long like a rock star, so I did. She wanted me to dress better, so I did. She was prepared to ignore whatever went on in my studio in order to protect this fantasy. She never asked any questions, never put me in a position where I'd have to lie to avoid wounding her. In Italy we say, "What the eye doesn't see, the heart doesn't weep over." People probably say that pretty much everywhere. In any case, our marriage worked that way, as did many others in those days.

I also had to learn how to handle so much sudden celebrity. I came from a very simple family background. I'd never been spoiled. I was just a photographer. But Elizabeth had never had a personal photographer before. I'd been hurled into this world almost from one day to the next, and God knows how many times I wondered: "Are there other guys out there like me?" I still don't know. David Bailey married Catherine Deneuve. Many other photographers were with top models. Some became famous in their own right, and not just as a name at the end of a caption. Meanwhile, paparazzi tailed me everywhere. Articles came out about me. Had I created that character, "the new king of the camera"? No. It just happened. I was still the same person in my private life. But I learned to look after my own affairs. I dressed better. I bought beautiful things. I contrived ways of displaying class and importance in certain situations. For example, if I was just going into a restaurant for a quick meal, it didn't matter where I sat. I just went in and ate. But if I was going in order to talk about work, or thought there might be people who knew me and I wanted to make a good impression, then I'd walk differently, I'd talk with the headwaiter differently. That way people would realize I was someone significant, even if they didn't know me. They'd give me the best table without me even asking.

There was no gradual transition to this new life. Fame and reputation came out of the blue. When I left Italy I was no one. When I returned I was a member of the world's most exclusive jet-set circle. The moment my honeymoon ended, I had to start to live up to a role that I'd been thrust into almost overnight.

While Claudye and I were still on our honeymoon, Pierluigi phoned to apologize. He wanted me to join him as a business partner, principally because the clients who were calling his offices around the world were now all looking for me. I asked Elizabeth what she thought, and she told me not to accept. She didn't trust Pierluigi and thought that associating myself with him would not help me professionally. I'd never need someone like Pierluigi again. I was getting offers from all over the place. I could have chosen from among dozens of jobs that would have been the envy of any photographer. So I turned Pierluigi's offer down.

In response, Pierluigi not only refused to pay me what I was still owed for my work on *The Comedians,* but he also called the police and tried to get me arrested for stealing a number of cameras. All Pierluigi's photographers worked with his cameras. When I got fired, I still had a couple of them at home. But by the time he called the police, I'd already returned them. So then he tried to sue me for breach of contract. But that didn't work either. All he managed to do was demonstrate just how deeply envy had clouded his mind. His accusations against me were ridiculous. I almost felt sorry for him.

My agreement with Elizabeth, the attention I was getting, the interesting offers of work could all have allowed me to revel in my revenge over Pierluigi, the man who had effectively stolen my work for years. But I was too happy to get any pleasure out of his downfall. Technically, I was still under contract to him. And I still had a lot of friends working in his dying agency. Clients who for years had gone to Pierluigi were now coming to me. His business was coming apart at the seams. Without even trying, without even meaning to, I'd ruined him.

As I've said, Pierluigi was many things, but he wasn't stupid. Everyone who knew him kept telling him he was crazy to keep fighting me. The only way he could save his agency was to offer me a deal, a better deal than the previous one. When we finally sat down face-to-face, I told him I felt in his debt, but if he wanted me to continue working for his agency, he would have to change my status as well as the way he handled things. He would have to give me—and all the other photographers who worked for him— full credit for the photos we took.

Pierluigi replied that it was none of my business who took credit for what. Unfortunately for him, my sudden fame had also revealed to the world the conditions under which I used to work. Word went around that Pierluigi had signed other people's photos. This not only upset his clients, who expected authentic photos from Pierluigi (which was ironic in itself, given that an "authentic" Pierluigi photo would have been worse), but it also raised questions of copyright. Pierluigi's Hollywood clients had no desire to get embroiled in legal disputes regarding photographers' rights to "genuine" photos.

In the end, we didn't form any kind of partnership. Elizabeth didn't want our agreement to fall under Pierluigi's authority. But he did at least begin to allow his employees to sign their work, while I—out of loyalty to him and all my friends and colleagues—stayed with his agency. I allowed Pierluigi to keep representing me in order to keep his company alive as long as he could.

Meanwhile, wanting to spend as much time with Claudye as possible, I turned down a lot of offers—from movie stars and major fashion houses to production companies wanting layouts for their movies. But there was one I simply couldn't decline: when I was asked to go to Iran to photograph the shah, his famously beautiful wife, Princess Farah Diba, and their family. When I explained that I was still on my honeymoon, the shah kindly invited Claudye along too. We'd never been to Iran, so we were delighted to take the trip and, in the process, prolong our honeymoon.

By sheer coincidence, before we were due to leave, an exhibition about Iran opened on the Champs-Elysées in Paris. Claudye and I went, hoping to get some idea of what we could expect to see on our trip. We met Mehd Bushehri, the husband of the shah's twin sister, Princess Ashraf, and we spoke with an Iranian journalist. He told me that Farah would almost certainly make me wait—a lot—so I'd have to be very patient with the family. He recommended that I charge an hourly fee. I appreciated the advice.

When we got off the plane in Tehran we were met by a television crew and a local reporter, who insisted on interviewing me immediately. Elizabeth Taylor's personal photographer was in Iran to photograph the shah and Farah. It was a huge event for the Iranians as well as for the shah, who was eager to modernize his country and its image in the West.

After the interview, the shah sent a driver to collect us. We were given a beautiful suite in the Royal Hilton, and the driver was at our complete disposal. He took us to visit Persepolis, Shiraz, the bazaar. Tehran's modernity surprised me. It reminded me a lot of Milan, full of rich, well-dressed people, luxury restaurants, five-star hotels. But the moment you left the city, the scene shifted to two thousand years ago: camels everywhere, people dressed like *Lawrence of Arabia* extras drinking tea and smoking narghile by the side of the road. At one point we came upon a mountain covered with carpets. An incredible sight. There was a lake at the foot of the mountain where people went to wash their carpets, which they then laid out to dry across the ridge. As in Africa, there was an incredible disparity between the rich and poor, the urban centers and rural communities.

On my first day at work, Claudye was invited to accompany me to the palace. The shah's assistants took me to a room where I was to photograph Farah in front of a particular painting. They explained the protocol to me, how I was supposed to address Her Royal Highness, how I was never to touch her, how I had to stand at least three meters away. All those rules and formality made me very nervous. Heck, I was about to meet a full-blooded queen!

Then Farah arrived wearing a Christian Dior dress, heavy makeup, and an elaborate hairdo. Uh-oh. Daywear with evening-style makeup and hair, plus a dress that did nothing for her legs (though perhaps she thought it did). My nervousness gave way to a distinct uneasiness. I knew how to work with cinema stars and producers in order to get the best shots for selling a movie. But royalty was different. Farah's look was totally wrong. The photos would come out all wrong, to her detriment as well as mine. But how can you tell a queen that she's chosen the wrong look? I thought about just snapping a few shots and then running out of there. But my father's voice, and his high professional standards, wouldn't let me.

I switched off my flash and said in French, as politely as I could, "I'm sorry, but this situation isn't right." Having all these people around me and all this protocol made me feel very uneasy, I explained. "All right," she replied. "Let's talk about it." She invited me to take a seat and share some tea with her. I pulled out all my tact and diplomacy, and she agreed to change outfit and set. She showed me a number of dresses, listening while I suggested which ones I thought suited her best and were more appropriate for our photo session. Interestingly, although I had no idea at the time, all the dresses she showed me that I thought looked best on her were made in Iran.

During the shoot, I kept chatting with her in order to get her looking as relaxed and informal as possible. We talked about Elizabeth, the movie

Farah Diba, the queen and empress of Persia, dressed in a style that I suggested (with all due respect). Inset: She first turned up looking dreadful in Dior.

and entertainment industry, Iran. She was very pleasant company, an interesting mix of royal dignity and a worldliness acquired during her studies in Paris.

When Claudye and I left the palace, we asked our driver to take us to a bazaar. As we were parking, we were suddenly surrounded by police cars. Without offering any explanation, the police told us we had to go back and escorted us all the way to the palace. I had no idea what was going on. I thought of all that protocol, all those rules. Had I broken one of them? Was the shah angry because I'd made his wife change her dress? Had I stood two meters away instead of three? We arrived, rushed and worried, to find Farah waiting for us. "I just thought maybe you'd like to photograph me while I put my children to bed," she said. With my heart pounding nearly out of my chest, I managed to reply with a clear and calm voice that I'd be delighted to take such photos. We went to the family's royal apartments, where I photographed her saying good night to her children and tucking them in, just like any mother anywhere.

Evidently the royal family thought the photos I'd taken were sufficient, because the next day we were told we could leave. The photos proved a huge success. Farah was very happy. She'd become a superstar abroad, a beautiful, modern woman who would help her country move into the twentieth century. A couple of months later, the shah's assistants called again, asking me to go back to do more layouts. This time I went alone.

I took a few Christian Dior outfits along with me, hoping to do a little work for myself when I wasn't busy with the royal family. I wanted to do a layout with Iranian models wearing Western clothes, something along the lines of how Farah presented herself the first time, only this time done properly. My God, I saw an entirely different Tehran that second time. I met so many girls related to the royal family who had studied in Europe and returned home with attitudes and ideas about life that had little to do with conservative Islam. The women were veiled, whether they were very beautiful or hard to look at. But from what I saw, it didn't matter either way. Ugly or beautiful, they all wanted sex—immediately. Girls would come to the house I was staying in. I'd lift their veils. They'd lift their skirts. "Memiram barrat," they'd say, which roughly translated means, "I'm dying with love for you." Farah pretended (or maybe not) to know nothing about all this. When I asked her about all the loose behavior, she laughed and asked me who was "dying with love for me." Then she corrected herself: "No! No! Don't tell me." Like Farah, a lot of Iranian girls had studied abroad, in Paris, London, Switzerland. Back home they had to wear veils in the street. But indoors they dressed like Europeans. Remember, this was when the West had just discovered Mary Quant and miniskirts, French students were burning Paris, and Mick Jagger was hanging out with

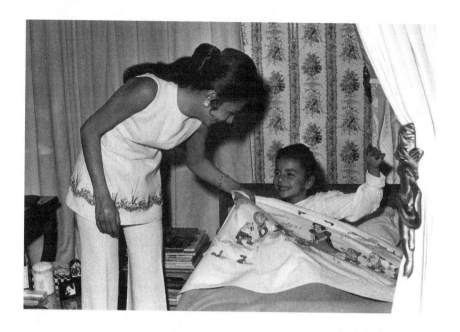

Armed Iranian guards ordered us, terrified, back to the palace, only to find that Farah merely wanted me to photograph her putting her kids to bed—thus gifting

me with these exclusive photos. *From top:* Princess Farahnaz; Prince Ali-Reza; Prince Reza; and little Princess Leila.

Princess Margaret of England. The Islamic backlash and the shah's exile after the 1979 revolution were still a decade away.

One day I met the shah in a palace corridor while I was taking more pictures of Farah. Staff had already explained the correct protocol: if you encountered the shah, you had to stop and bow, and you couldn't address him unless he spoke to you first. So I bowed in silence and waited. The shah asked how my work was going, and then added, "They tell me you like sports cars." At my assent, he took me down to his garage. I'd never seen a garage built entirely out of marble, and such an enormous place it was, full of every kind of luxury car imaginable: Ferrari, Lamborghini, Maserati, Austin Martin. Even a Bizzarrini 5300 Strada, a thrilling classic from the golden years of the Le Mans twenty-four-hour races, worth millions of dollars today. Today, I believe, it's one of many autos of the shah's collection collecting dust in a curiously neglected Islamic revolutionary museum somewhere outside Tehran. Every now and then classic car enthusiasts get a glimpse and post their sightings on the Internet.

The shah asked if I'd like to go for a drive. The police and army cleared streets in the center of Tehran, and off went the shah of Iran and I for a spin around town. I quickly realized that the traffic hadn't been blocked just to protect His Royal Highness but also to safeguard any stray pedestrian who might happen to be on the same street. I've never met a worse driver in my life.

Later I was invited for a ride in a helicopter. Two others took off along with ours. When I asked why, one of the pilots explained that, should anyone happen to be planning to assassinate the shah, they wouldn't know which helicopter he was in. That was the last time I got into a helicopter in Iran.

I photographed Farah while she worked with a number of charitable organizations—education programs, communication, poverty aid. She was very involved in modernizing Iran and her people. She laughed when I complained about the food. She said I should taste different things, and brought me a dish of yogurt and cucumber. I hate cucumbers, and cucumbers hate me. They served me caviar in the morning. And they drank vodka all day. With caviar. I wasn't impressed by their cuisine. Smoked fish, a lot of lamb, all far too rich for my stomach, which was used to simple Italian cooking.

During this visit, Farah gave orders that I be allowed to photograph any member of the family at any time. One day I asked the shah to pose for

Farah at her work desk, 1968.

Prince Reza, using one of my cameras, snaps his mom and dad on the sofa (with Princess Farahnaz and Prince Ali-Reza between them). Farah Diba later told me that it was the first time they had ever been photographed in their private apartments. The times truly were a-changin'.

a photo in the royal apartments along with Farah and their children, but not for a typical family portrait. He understood. He knew that I photographed people in a different way, that my specialty was capturing a moment, not one specific, planned moment, but whatever came along. The photos I'd taken of Farah on my first trip had been so admired that this time I had no trouble getting what I wanted. The family and his staff put themselves entirely in my hands.

One of the photos I took that day became very famous. I got the whole family to sit on a sofa while their oldest son, Prince Reza Pahlavi, stood in front of them with a camera. I then photographed him taking snapshots of his family. I'd set his camera. But he was just a kid and kept fussing with it, changing the settings, with the result that all his photos ended up out of focus. I, on the other hand, was gifted with a series of wonderfully relaxed family moments and what proved to be uniquely intimate shots of the Iranian royals at home.

On another occasion, Farah asked if I'd like to attend a gypsy wedding.

This caftan was a personal gift from Farah Diba to Elizabeth, who confessed that the solid gold and silver embroidery made it almost too heavy to wear. The photo was taken to go with Elizabeth's thank-you letter.

A military plane took us to a desert encampment. I'd dressed all in black. After five minutes in that desert, I turned khaki. The ceremony took place in the evening. I had brought a camera, of course. But they wouldn't let me use my flash because it would have ruined the atmosphere. I'd never seen anything like it. The venue had been transformed into an amusement park, packed with food stalls, game stands, a shooting range, jugglers, clowns. Once the marriage ceremony itself was over, the bride was taken to another tent where she had to weep all night. The men, meanwhile, took part in a game that involved trying to strike another man's legs with a heavy stick. I saw a couple of broken bones. When someone asked if I'd like to take part too, I hastily replied, "Thank you, but no thank you." The banquet was another matter. I heartily took part in that: simple, exquisite nomadic dishes, with succulent meat roasted in a pit dug in the sand. The party went on until 2 in the morning, with no alcohol. Women attended the party—except the bride, who had to remain alone all night crying. When I finally got back to my hotel, I was so totally covered in sand that I took a shower fully clothed.

Doing my Dior fashion shoot nearly got me killed. Literally. I had all the girls dressed in the clothes I'd brought with me and adorned with jewels from the national museum. I posed them in front of a mosque. One of them was wearing a dress with very slender shoulder straps. One of them accidentally slipped off her shoulder, revealing her breast. Suddenly the crowd of curious onlookers began to close in on us, menacingly. They wanted to beat the girl, or worse. Then I heard machine-gun fire, and the crowd dispersed. It was the Iranian secret service. I had no idea they followed me even when I wasn't with the royal family. But it was a good thing they did. They fired a few shots into the air to scatter the crowd, and the incident ended there. But it was a scary moment, to say the least. Dior and Islam clearly weren't meant to meet on the street.

A few months later, the shah's assistants called me again and I returned to Iran for a third visit. The shah wanted me to photograph a charity event being held on behalf of abandoned children. The affair took place in his palace gardens, featuring lots of food and games. The shah arrived on a 500cc MV Agusta motorbike, clearly intending to impress this humble Italian photographer. Which he did. The bike had been a personal gift from Victor Emmanuele of Savoy and Corrado Agusta himself. From her expression, however, you could tell that Farah, his passenger, was simply terrified. I understood her pain.

Later that evening, a magician came to our table. I told him I wasn't

The shah arrives at a charity event on an Agusta MV 500cc.

The shah taking part in a feat-of-strength game, 1969.

interested in that kind of stuff, but he insisted, asking all of us to take off our wedding rings and put them on a plate in the middle of the table. He covered the plate with a cloth, made some hand gestures in the air, and then whisked the cloth away. Incredibly, the rings were now all linked

The shah takes aim at a rifle-shooting booth.

together in a chain. Who knows how on earth he did it? Then I noticed Farah sitting with a fortune-teller, a gypsy woman reading cards spread out on a carpet. Farah wore a very serious expression on her face and looked uneasy. I took a couple of photos while she had her future read. I've no idea what she said because they spoke in Farsi, but it was clear that the cards predicted ugly things.

In the light of the Islamic Revolution that would later sweep Iran, and all that would happen to Farah, the shah, and their country, maybe Farah really did see her future that night. On top of whatever other hardships she would have to face, her daughter Leila would die of a drug overdose in London, and her youngest son, Ali-Reza, would shoot himself in Boston in 2011.

During all my visits to Iran, I established a friendly relationship with Farah but not with the shah. He was a man people feared. He'd given me freedom to photograph him because he wanted to show a different side of himself. But even while he was trying to project a normal impression, the shah inspired fear. You can see it in the photos I took. He tries to look as if he's having fun while shooting a fairground rifle or riding his motorbike. But actually he doesn't look happy in the least. Can you blame him? Other

Farah Diba gets her cards read by a gypsy fortune-teller. The signs seem to be predicting disaster. Time would prove them right.

powerful men would later come to me, asking me to soften their image. But none of them were in as precarious a position as the shah was in those days. I definitely left Iran with some interesting and unique photos, but I don't believe I ever managed to humanize the shah as I did Farah. And even if I had, those photos wouldn't be as honest as the ones you see. I never returned to Iran again.

But there were a few strange postscripts to my involvement with the royal family. In Rome one evening in 1971, I invited Gianfranco Piacentini, a famous Italian playboy, to dinner. He showed up with the shah's first wife, Princess Soraya of Iran. She and the shah had divorced in the late 1950s because Soraya couldn't have children, after which she lived mostly in Paris, in self-imposed exile, despite a brief foray into movie acting. Princess Soraya barely said a word throughout dinner. I have no idea if she knew that I'd worked with the shah's family, but in any case she never asked me about them and wore a very sad expression all night.

A couple of days after our meeting, I got a mysterious telephone call from the Iranian ambassador. He asked me to bring a camera and meet him under a bridge over the Tiber River. I knew the situation was unstable in Iran and that the shah was sick, so I went hoping to see either him or Farah. The ambassador arrived in one of three cars, all of which then proceeded to a secluded spot on one of Rome's seven hills. To this day, I don't know what was really going on. At a certain point, the shah's twin sister, Princess Ashraf, got out of one of the cars. She was an old-fashioned lady with old-fashioned makeup and hair, dripping with jewels. She wanted me to photograph her, in an old-fashioned way, in a beautiful Roman villa owned by the shah. The shah's entourage knew I would never have accepted the invitation if I'd known what kind of photo I was supposed to take—a bland portrait of an old woman was definitely not my line of work. And cloak-and-dagger stuff had never been my métier, whatever my old army colleagues might have said. But I agreed, out of respect for the shah and Farah. When we were through, Ashraf asked me to send the photos and my bill to the embassy. The whole situation had irritated me so much that I sent a ridiculously fat bill, far more than what I had done was worth, which they paid without batting an eye. Maybe I should have asked for more.

By now my name meant far more than Pierluigi's, and he knew it. He no longer bothered to pretend he was a photographer. He was just an agent, and I had no need for an agent. Most of my work now came to me directly, or through Elizabeth and Richard, who insisted on having me as their special photographer on whatever production they worked with. The few jobs I got through Pierluigi mostly served to keep him in business. It was an unsatisfactory collaboration, and I couldn't keep helping out Pierluigi's agency in my spare time. However, in the last few months of our association, Pierluigi did send me one fabulous job. Or so it seemed when I accepted it: a profile of Pablo Picasso.

In those days, I'd begun to exploit the fame that I'd acquired working with Elizabeth and Richard in order to dictate my conditions when I discussed prices, expenses, and other details of a job. To photograph Picasso,

I insisted on total access: 24/7, as we'd say today. I wanted to be with him full-time—when he got up in the morning, when he went to bed, and whatever happened in between. In exchange, I promised that if he, for whatever reason, didn't like a photo, he could tear it up without any explanation. Picasso's representatives agreed.

When I arrived at Picasso's house, the secluded Chateau de Boisgeloup, some forty miles from Paris, one of his assistants accompanied me to a little room, had me sit down, and put a finger to his lips, indicating that I should remain silent. So I sat there in silence. For ages. Nothing happened. Picasso didn't appear. I sat alone in that room. Every now and then assistants came and went, also in silence. Suddenly I heard noises above me, a table scraping on the floor, footsteps. One of the assistants came into the room, pointed at the ceiling, and whispered, "Picasso . . ." There was another noise: incessant sharp, unpleasant, guttural coughing. I looked inquiringly at an assistant. Should someone go and help him? He replied with a negative shake of his head. Picasso finally came downstairs. He was wearing sandals and his famous tunic. I stood up and waited to be introduced. But Picasso just sat on a chair and began smoking Gitanes Mais. After a few minutes had gone by, I decided to introduce myself. "Monsieur, my name is Gianni . . ."

"I know who you are. You're here to take photos. Go ahead." Then he started coughing again.

I got out my Leica and waited for him to stop. But he didn't stop. So I took a shot of him coughing. He sat there for twenty minutes, coughing, smoking, and coughing some more. Then he got up and walked outside. Perplexed, I turned to his assistants, who nodded, indicating that I should follow him. Picasso walked quickly, especially for an old man. Once I'd caught up with him, we strolled through the countryside in total silence. I was terrified, fearful of having given a bad impression, of not having been sufficiently artistic. Finally, I spoke: "Maestro, how does one become Pablo Picasso?"

He stopped and stared me straight in the eye. Then he turned and started walking again. Now I really felt like an idiot. Cursing myself, I followed him. Then something happened that I still don't fully understand.

We walked up to a house. A man was constructing a cement channel in his garden. "If I go and write my name in his cement, it'll be worth something, don't you think?" said Picasso, and laughed. I replied that the man would almost certainly get angry. "Quite possibly," he said, and we continued toward the house. When we got to the gate, Picasso opened it and walked straight up to the man, who looked at him in surprise. Picasso spoke to him very politely, inspected his cement work, told him he was a good artisan, and complimented him on his garden. The man stood bewildered for a moment, then began chasing Picasso out of the place, shouting and trying to hit him. He had no idea his unwelcome visitor was the famous Picasso. Given that tattered tunic and long, dirty beard, anyone might have taken him for a tramp. Picasso couldn't stop laughing. He was still laughing when he'd got out of the gate, whereupon he turned to me and said, "Does that answer your question?"

I don't know if Picasso really had answered my stupid question. Or whether he'd been joking when he talked about signing the man's cement. But of course he was right. He was already so renowned that all he had to do was sketch a couple of lines and critics would describe it as a work of genius. Over the days I spent with him, we ate in a lot of excellent restaurants. When the bill arrived, Picasso would flip it over or take a paper napkin or some other scrap of paper, scribble an animal or something else on it, and then hand it to the waiter as payment. Every restaurant accepted this without hesitation. Who wouldn't trade a couple of hundred francs for a signed Picasso?

A typical Picasso day went as follows: he'd get up late in the morning or early afternoon, cough and smoke for half an hour, then breakfast on cornflakes and poached eggs with olive oil and vinegar. Then he'd take a nap. Afterward, he'd go to his studio, sign a couple of prints, go out for lunch, and then return to his studio, where he'd take another nap. Once he woke up, he'd light a fire and start sketching. I saw more of Picasso the businessman than Picasso the artist. He had a lot of meetings with accountants and lawyers, a lot of long telephone calls in Spanish that I didn't understand. He spoke to me about the Italian artist Renato Guttuso. He said he was one of his great admirers and that I should photograph him, given that we were both Italians. I'd no idea who he was talking about, but pretended I did anyway.

Picasso intimidated me so much that I was never able to establish any kind of personal rapport. I feared I irritated him with my questions, feared that I'd asked too much when I'd insisted on following him everywhere. I never met Picasso again. And it's true I could have been more outgoing and friendly. But I don't know if the photos would have come out quite so well. Picasso inspired awe in me. And the insecurity that stemmed from that probably helped me shoot without thinking too much. My best photos have always been a candid-camera kind of shot. I remember one photo I liked in particular. Picasso was coughing, and in that moment, the light shone across his large hands, highlighting them. Photography for me has always been a question of light, and that portrait in shadow with only his hands illuminated seemed truly powerful to me.

I gave Picasso all my contact prints for approval, and he didn't discard a single one. Unfortunately, my contract didn't include any rights to my images of Picasso. I was merely paid to go and photograph him, nothing else. But I was satisfied with my work, and it seemed enough at the time. I delivered the negatives to Pierluigi, with the understanding that he'd send the photos on to *Epoca,* the Italian magazine linked to *Paris Match.* But I never saw those photos again. They were never published anywhere. *Epoca* magazine closed shortly afterward. Someone later told me that a Picasso collector had acquired all my photos from the *Epoca* archives, but I had no way to confirm this or find the presumed buyer. I'm not even sure whether Pierluigi ever really did give the negatives to *Epoca.* Maybe he sold them without my knowledge, to stay afloat. Or maybe *Epoca* sold them, or *Paris Match.* Sometimes I come across photos of Picasso from one collection or another that seem familiar to me. But I could never prove whether they really were shot by me or not.

"Does that answer your question?" I've thought about that conversation with Picasso often. He was a man who was very aware of himself and of his quality as an artist. Maybe what he was trying to tell me was, "I know who I am, but you still don't know who you are. That's why I'm Picasso. I know who I am, and I know what I'm capable of."

A couple of months later I took Picasso's advice. Back in Rome I got hold of Renato Guttuso's phone number and called him. He seemed actually honored that I wanted to meet him and take his picture. "I know your work," he said. "You're a great photographer. Picasso told me that he thinks your black-and-white photos are full of color."

With me still trying to find my way as an artist, that gave me a huge injection of confidence. Then I saw a sketch on his table showing a young woman in profile caressing her hair. The image looked familiar to me. He promptly gave it to me as a gift and wrote a dedication underneath it: "To Gianni, to his art, his likeable character and his enthusiasm. His friend, Renato." I was delighted, and even more so when he told me that the image had been inspired by one of my photos of Elizabeth that he'd clipped from

I treasure this sketch, a personal gift from the great Italian artist Renato Guttuso. He told me it was inspired by one of my photos, which he'd clipped from a magazine.

Me and Renato Guttuso, 1969. The photo was taken by my assistant at the time, Elizabeth's son Michael Wilding.

a magazine. I'm still trying to track that photo down in my archive. The magazine clipping seems to have vanished altogether.

For a long time, Guttuso's extreme left-wing views kept him from getting the recognition he deserved. He's been reappraised in recent years, and I believe many now rank him alongside Modigliani as one of Italy's— and the world's—leading contemporary artists.

Guttuso was a much easier subject to work with than Picasso, at least for me. For one thing, there was no language barrier between us. I felt much more at ease with him. And he let me do whatever I wanted. Picasso pretended not to care how he was photographed, but every now and then I caught him striking a pose. Guttuso, on the other hand, truly didn't care. He just got down to work and left me to mine. The suffering you could see in the lines in his face made him a particularly interesting subject. You could read in them all the battles he'd fought to become who he was. Picasso's face didn't display suffering. I believe this says a lot about the two men, and the two artists. And, as far as I'm concerned, I've always identified more closely with fighters.

A couple weeks later, I attended Ron Berkeley and Vicky Tiel's wed-

Me and Elizabeth, 1971.

ding. Ron did Elizabeth's makeup on a lot of her movies, so she and Richard attended too. I hadn't seen Elizabeth in a while, so we were chatting about what I'd been up to, and I told her about my experiences with Picasso and Guttuso, how meeting such great artists had inspired me but also made me feel insecure about my work. Elizabeth was very surprised when I told her how much trouble I'd had breaking the ice with Picasso.

"It is not by chance that you're sitting next to me." She looked straight into my eyes. "You have talent, but you are too humble. Show some balls."

If I had recorded that conversation, I would have listened to it over and over all day. I should have realized that Picasso had sent me a message via Guttuso, or maybe it was the other way around. Either way, "Your black and whites are full of color." Elizabeth helped me understand how huge that compliment was, and I finally took it to heart.

Chapter 8

Success, Italian Style

To some extent, the end of 1968, my honeymoon year, was also the end of my "honeymoon" with Elizabeth and Richard. The excitement of being hurled into the jet set gave way to the reality of living and working at such a feverish pace. This was now my life. I was photographed so often along-side Elizabeth, Richard, and their friends that people started to recognize me, especially after my marriage photos came out in all the newspapers. I was the center of a lot of attention. Everyone had something to say about me, even that I was possibly one of the best photographers in the world. I was young and good looking, had talent and success, and was friends with the most famous couple in the world. But that wasn't how I saw myself at all. As a kid I'd fantasized about being an actor. But I never imagined that the part I'd have to play would be "the new king of the camera." Everyone wanted to know everything about me, while I still didn't even know who I was myself.

Shortly after my photo shoot with Picasso, I visited my parents for the first time since Claudye and I had moved to Paris. Elizabeth and Richard had gone for a couple of months' holiday at their place near Puerto Vallarta, Mexico, and I had a break between jobs. In Rome I was always obliged to talk about myself, where I'd been, who I'd met, and especially, what Elizabeth and Richard were really like. It's not that I didn't enjoy the fame, the jobs, the trips, the women, but I was still far from accustomed to being the constant center of attention, everywhere and anywhere.

The street kid who'd grown up near a rail yard had now become a member of the Roma Bene, the high-society swirl of people who counted. I got more invitations than I could possibly accept: club and restaurant openings, fashion events, birthday parties, art shows. I received awards from publications and festivals that I'd never even heard of—probably sent in the hope that my participation might help improve the profile of this or

143

Claudia Cardinale was not just an amazingly beautiful woman, she was also delightful company. Not many people know she was only five feet one inch tall.

that organization. But now that I was officially one of the Roma Bene crowd, it was my duty to participate. Yet I couldn't be everywhere at once, even though everyone insisted I should be. In those circles, if you say yes to one person, you're saying no to someone else, who gets offended and tells the press you're an asshole. Or maybe you and your wife chat with some model or actress at a party. A paparazzo snaps a photo, then cuts the image to suggest that something else is going on. One day, for example, I was on a motorbike when I saw Claudia Cardinale crossing the road. Both Claudye and I were friends with Claudia, and I'd photographed her on various occasions. So I stopped for a chat. The next day photos of us were everywhere: "Claudia Cardinale steals Elizabeth Taylor's photographer!" The episode infuriated everyone concerned, including my wife, Claudia's husband Franco, and Elizabeth herself. All I'd done was stop to say hi to a friend!

And then there was the Countess Giovanna Agusta, the motorbike and helicopter heiress, who called to ask me to do her portrait. Some paparazzo shot the pair of us just as she was stepping into my studio. When I met her a couple of days later and gave her a hug, I discovered that the whole thing had been set up by her in the first place. All she really wanted was for the paparazzi to see us together. This was one of my wife's best friends. When the photos came out, I was bombarded with calls from everyone I knew, especially my mother and friends. Most just laughed it off. But others really did start taking my wife for a betrayed woman. One thing's for sure, the not-very-noble countess definitely didn't get quite as warm a hug the next time we met. I might have guessed, of course. Giovanna's particular claim to fame right then was the scandal she caused by running off with a Brazilian soccer player, José Germano—which good countesses just didn't do back then.

While all this was going on, I was still trying to find some way to make this new life my own. It was a struggle. Sometimes I'd just get in my car and go, heading nowhere in particular, just driving. It was the only way I could escape all the attention, which weighed on me like an anvil. I'd spent my childhood trying to find freedom. And when it was denied me, I fled. I'd fled from the boredom of school, from my father's darkroom. Now I fled in my car, going wherever it took me. My days suddenly felt far too short. Simply keeping up with my commitments left me no time to be myself. But if I wanted to keep working, I had no option but to play the part of a celebrity, even if, as the old Italian joke goes, you can't spell "successo" (success) without "cesso" (toilet). For me, success was a one-way door marked "Entry only." Once inside, would there be any way out, any way to get back?

What the media considered news had changed radically since the first time Elizabeth and Richard had come to Rome, but I hadn't realized just how drastic that change was until I started becoming a paparazzi victim myself. What sold now were scandals. And if there wasn't one to be had, the press invented one. How could Elizabeth and Richard live like that, under even more constant scrutiny than I, even more under siege? How do you stay sane? How can you be a mother, father, husband, wife in the middle of all that? How can you remain yourself when the public image of your personality is shaped and reshaped every morning by newspapers around the world? They had no time for themselves either. And while for me it might still be a game, for them it was real life. I didn't want to end the same way. I'd always been shy around Elizabeth and Richard's friends, and all this made me isolate myself even more.

My mother hated all the attention that was on me and our family. My sisters Paola and Ofelia loved it. My father ignored it. He'd just shake his head and say, "You wanted a bicycle. Now pedal!" which is the Italian version of "You made your bed. Now lie in it!" All this reminded me of something else I'd learned through my father, from Mao Tse-tung's Little Red Book, which every left-wing Western student would soon be reading. My father worked on the restoration of the original manuscript. Parts of it had been lost, and it was necessary to do a translation in order to restore it. I read some of the translation, and one of the things that stayed in my head was: "One day you're naked, you're a man, you look at yourself in the mirror and, naturally, your eyes go to your genitals. And after you've seen them in the mirror, you'll want to see them from behind, and you'll have to bend over. And if, when bending over, you see four testicles, don't be too impressed. It only means that someone is probably standing behind you." I was maybe only ten or eleven when I read that. But I immediately understood the double meaning, and I've never forgotten that warning against thinking too highly of yourself. It became my philosophy in life.

In any case, I was still too insecure about myself and my talent to get caught up in self-celebration, or whatever the press said about me. The "new king of the camera" sounded good. But my father's opinion was still the only one I trusted. And he didn't seem the least bit impressed by my work, or the mountain of newspaper clippings about me. "You're good," he'd say, "but you're still not there." It was his way of keeping my ego from going overboard while at the same time pushing me to stay focused on my ambitions. I appreciated that way he had of spurring me on, more now than ever.

My father only once came to watch me work in my studio. He just stood to one side and observed me. At one point, when I passed nearby, he leaned forward and said, "Have you gone homosexual?"

"No, Dad!" I replied, laughing. "What on earth do you mean?"

"You're moving in such an effeminate way."

I'd developed a body language designed to stimulate my women subjects, a certain sensuality that allowed me to understand them in order to then portray them better. My father was seeing another Gianni for the first time, a Gianni he wasn't so sure about.

Elizabeth and Richard stayed two months in Puerto Vallarta. On their return, they invited Claudye and me to join them on a cruise. We met up in Villefranche-sur-Mer, where they were delighted to see us. When we boarded their yacht, Richard asked me if I'd like something to drink. "Thanks," I said. "I'd love a glass . . ." "Oh!" he interrupted. "My, how your English has improved!" Actually it hadn't—I just felt more at ease. But the moment he drew attention to my English, I got embarrassed again. "Mr. *Barton*," I thought to myself. Elizabeth would never dream of saying something like that to anyone. It was much easier to live up to her expectations—dress well, be polite, look relaxed (even when you felt out of place). But with Richard, I still felt inferior and still wasn't convinced he even liked me.

We were docked in Monte Carlo when Harriet Annenberg Ames put her famous diamond up for public auction in New York, the pear-shaped sixty-nine-carat diamond that she'd acquired from Harry Winston. Jewelers' representatives arrived from around the world, including one of Jackie Onassis's assistants and Richard's own auction agent, Al Yugler, who followed the bidding firsthand and kept in touch with Richard by radio. From a starting price of $200,000, bidding rose rapidly. Richard, a little tipsy, got irritated at the way the price seemed to spiral crazily out of control. When it got to $1 million, he decided to pull out, convinced it would just keep rising—to $1.5 million, $2 million, $3 million . . . When Richard then discovered the diamond had gone to Cartier owner Robert Kenmore for $1,050,000, he was furious. He couldn't believe Kenmore would outbid him, given all the free publicity that Elizabeth gave Cartier. He promptly called Kenmore from the yacht to negotiate for the diamond directly, and ended up buying it for $1,100,000, on condition that the jewel be known as the "Taylor-Burton Cartier diamond." This was the world's first million-dollar diamond. Others may have previously changed hands for seven-figure sums, but this was the first to do so at a public auction, and it instantly made worldwide news.

Now, with the initial excitement over, all that was left to do was deliver the thing. However, given the huge publicity that the auction had generated, Cartier feared someone might attempt to steal it in transit. Kenmore had two copies made and sent them separately: three people with three different diamonds, two fakes and one real. I got to the yacht shortly before they arrived: three identical Cartier boxes carried by three identical bull-shaped Cartier deliverymen. Richard was drunk, and Elizabeth no less so. Richard opened two of the boxes and just started laughing uncontrollably. "One million dollars for a piece of glass," he kept saying, standing by one of the portholes juggling the two "diamonds" in his hands. Suddenly he slipped, and one of the diamonds flew out of the porthole, landed on the deck outside, and rolled into the sea. Claudye moved just in time to catch Elizabeth before she fainted. Everyone went crazy. Gaston, the chauffeur, slapped on a diving mask and threw himself into the pitch-black sea although it was the middle of the night. Elizabeth, Claudye, and Richard just kept staring at the two remaining diamonds, wondering whether either was the real one. But Richard and Elizabeth were too drunk and stunned to make any sense of the thing. They asked what I thought, which was laughable. It was the first time in my life I'd even seen a diamond close up. What would I know? Panic seemed to make them sober up. They made a string of telephone calls and eventually, with dawn breaking, decided to wake Pierre Arpels of Van Cleef & Arpels and get him to come on board and evaluate the remaining jewels. As the goddess of good luck would have it, it was finally confirmed that what Richard had tossed into the sea was merely a piece of glass. Not a $1,100,000 diamond.

The following day, Elizabeth wore the jewel to Princess Grace Kelly's fortieth birthday party. As you can see from the photo I took just before they left, Richard was now being a lot more careful with that diamond. In the end, I got a cut of its value too, given that I sold that photo worldwide.

The day after the ball, we left Monaco for Portofino, where we dropped anchor outside the port and went for dinner. When dessert arrived, Richard started telling Claudye that she was like a daughter to him, that he cared for her deeply, and that I, too, was like a son. Still burning from his "My, how your English has improved" comment, I replied, "Stop talking bullshit, Richard. You don't even like me. Don't start saying . . ." Elizabeth kicked me under the table and simultaneously my wife elbowed me in the ribs. But I really was still convinced he didn't like me, as a person or as an artist. "Elizabeth needs you" was all he'd said when he hired me, implying that he didn't need me at all. The distance I felt between Richard and me came from that little phrase.

Richard told Elizabeth to take Claudye home. He wanted a little time alone with me. And this time we finally had a real talk. And drank a lot, too. We must have stopped in pretty much every bar in Portofino. But we talked as we'd never talked before. Finally, I had the chance to confess all my fears about my new life as I poisoned a series of potted plants along the way, pouring vodka into them every time Richard offered me yet another glass. I discovered, to my great surprise, that he was afflicted by the same insecurities. We both feared getting lost in such a fabulous yet suffocating lifestyle. By the end of the evening Richard was stone drunk. But for once I didn't care. We'd finally had a real conversation. We at last understood each other much better.

We got back to the dock around 3 in the morning only to find that the

Elizabeth, Richard, and the Taylor-Burton Cartier diamond, which Richard came damn close to throwing into an ink-black ocean.

dingy that was supposed to take us back to the *Kalizma* was gone. Suddenly Richard was in the water, roaring with laughter and swimming out toward the open sea. The combination of alcohol and cold water could kill him in a flash. I could see the banner headlines already: "Burton drowns before photographer's stunned eyes." What else could I do? I leapt in after him and dragged him to the yacht. Like I said, I'm no swimmer myself. What's more, the plants hadn't had all that vodka. When we got near the yacht, the crew spotted us and helped drag us on board. I went straight to my cabin, registering three things one after the other: fear, rage, and a terrible chill. I took a boiling-hot shower and went straight to bed.

The following morning, Richard came to my cabin and asked how we'd got back on board. I just started shouting: "You asshole Englishman, you son of a bitch! What do you mean, you don't remember?! We could have died drowning!"

To which he replied, "'Welsh,' please. 'Son of a bitch,' if you insist."

Then he hugged me. I believe that was when our friendship truly began. I'd given vent to my rage, I'd exposed myself, I'd *been* myself, and Richard respected me for that. From that evening on I knew that my best man was also a close friend.

Elizabeth's next movie was *The Only Game in Town*, which was shot mostly in the Bologna Studios outside Paris, with some exteriors in Las Vegas. Frank Sinatra was originally signed to play the other lead role. But he had to drop out and was replaced by the young star of *Bonnie and Clyde*, Warren Beatty. The director, George Stevens, had already worked with Elizabeth in two of her best movies, *A Place in the Sun* and *Giant*. Paris was chosen as a location because it cost less to rebuild Las Vegas in France than to shoot the whole movie in Nevada, and for tax reasons, Elizabeth had only a limited amount of time she could work in the United States. Elizabeth also wanted to be close to Richard, who was filming *Staircase* in Paris with Rex Harrison.

One day, curious to see how Richard would play a gay man, I went to visit him on the *Staircase* set. Richard and Rex were heading to the bathroom when I arrived, and since I needed to go too, I tagged along. I was the first one to finish and went to wash my hands. Rex said, "I'm sorry I'm taking so long. I'm only peeing now by virtue of gravity." Then Richard finished and started to walk out. Rex shouted, "How dare you take a piss without washing your hands!" To which Richard replied, "Personally, I never piss on my own hands."

I tried to be friendly with Warren, but he was a solitary type. He didn't

Everyone under the sun dropped by to visit Elizabeth and Richard. Here Elizabeth is chatting with (*from left*) Queen Elizabeth of Yugoslavia, the Duchess and Duke of Windsor, and Warren Beatty.

Another alpha male who could never relax, Warren Beatty lays on a smile for a scene with Elizabeth in *The Only Game in Town*. Rumors that they had a fling were rubbish. Julie Christie, on the other hand, could melt him on sight.

Elizabeth is the photographer as we ride to Portofino in a speedboat. Claudye and I were happier to have our pictures taken than Richard.

The Olympus Elizabeth is using. (Photo by M&S Materiale fotografico.)

like being photographed. I could sense his affectations when he knew he was in a shot. He was never relaxed, and always kept an eye on me when I was taking photos, especially if I was chatting with girls on the set. Warren was highly competitive when it came to women and hated it when someone else took center stage. But whenever Julie Christie visited the set, Warren glowed, like he'd won a prize. Word went around that he was having an affair with Elizabeth, but it was totally unfounded. Warren just loved playing the part of the alpha male. On set with Elizabeth, however, he was never given the opportunity.

One day I was hanging around in the corridor outside Elizabeth's dressing room when suddenly I heard screams coming from inside. I threw open the door and rushed in. Her makeup artist, Frankie La Rue, was raving, waving his arms in the air and threatening Elizabeth with a pair of scissors. "Get out!" she shouted. "Get out, or he'll stab you too." I stepped forward anyway, at which Frankie whirled around and tried to do just that. But I dodged the blow and landed a punch. Frankie went down, struck his head on a corner of the dressing table, and lost consciousness. He'd gone out of his head, in the true sense of the expression. Elizabeth accused me of hitting him too hard, which wasn't the case. He was a heavyweight and I, in those days, a lightweight. I was questioned at length by the French police. Frankie ended up in a clinic, and Elizabeth and Richard's lawyers hushed the whole thing up.

I never did manage to establish a rapport with George Stevens. He was very detached, rather cold. As a kid I'd been a huge fan of James Dean and knew that George had directed him as the wildcat Jett Rink in *Giant*, considered by many to have been Dean's greatest performance. So I asked him what Dean had been like to work with. We were sitting on set and I was only trying to make conversation. "Was he really that good as an actor?" I asked. George just looked at me as if I'd posed the dumbest question in history, pointed at the set photographer, and replied, "Is he a good photographer?"

Elizabeth had great respect for George. Sometimes she'd sit on his lap. He was something of a father figure to her. He'd helped make her the star she was, and she never forgot it, even though she was happier with directors she could talk to, who accepted her contribution. No one contradicted George Stevens on set. He was a very old-fashioned director. He had no interest in collaborating. He knew exactly how he was going to shoot a scene the moment he got on set, and that was that. He didn't even discuss things with the director of photography or the cameraman. He'd place the

Elizabeth sits on director George Stevens's lap during a break in the shooting of *The Only Game in Town*. Right now she's furious with the photography director's choice of exterior lighting.

cameras himself and tell the actors what to do. Then he'd do an establishing shot, a straight shot, a reverse shot, close-ups, and then cut. Next scene. He never moved the cameras, never did tracking shots. His technique contrasted sharply with, for example, that of Antonioni, who discussed every scene with his actors, asked their opinions, and followed them with the camera, never just putting them in front of it like robots.

Before the production left Paris to continue shooting in Las Vegas, the Académie Française invited Stevens to give a talk, and he asked me to photograph the event. But I'd been so offended by his attitude toward me that I lied and said I was too busy.

Shooting in Las Vegas didn't last long on account of the cost. But it was plenty long enough for me. After flying for ages over desert, it was a real shock to suddenly see that insomniac city all lit up below. I'm a Roman. Aqueducts were among the marvels of ancient Rome. Looking down on Vegas from the air, I wondered where it got all its water. Once we'd landed, I continued to marvel—but not in a good way. Walking through the enormous halls of Caesar's Palace, I was unpleasantly struck by the ostentation, the soullessness: the inveterate gamblers, the waiters with lifeless eyes, the dealers who cashed their paychecks and then went to gamble in another casino, the total lack of any real history and any real culture in this extraordinary ordinary place. I was stunned by the huge size of everything. It reminded me of a joke about an Italian who goes to America, and when he comes home his family asks him what it was like: "Everything was enormous," he replies. "My room was enormous. The portions were enormous. My hotel gave me a toothbrush you could scratch your back with. Then I got an enormous cold, so I went to the hospital where an enormous doctor came and said, 'You've got an enormous cold. I'm going to give you a suppository.' To which I replied, 'Fuck you, man!' and left." That was Las Vegas. Enormous. Too much. Except I did adore the buffet breakfasts—everything you could imagine was available.

The highlight of the trip was seeing Elvis Presley live. What an exceptional artist, what a voice, what a face, even at a time in his career when he was becoming somewhat ridiculous. After the show, Elizabeth and Richard took Claudye and I backstage to meet Elvis and Colonel Parker. Elvis was dripping with sweat. It would have made a great photo, all that sweat and the strange light in his dressing room. In my terrible English, I tried to tell him that I'd love to photograph him. I said I'd like to spend twenty-four hours with him and photograph everything he did, much as I'd done with Picasso. But Elvis and his staff didn't know me, so they politely brushed me off and started chatting with Elizabeth and Richard. They thought I was just one of the crowd and didn't take me seriously. Someone must have learned better later because after we got back to Europe, Elvis's people called me to organize a shoot. Unfortunately, we were both very busy and weren't able to find a date. We decided to postpone the deal, and sadly our time ran out when Elvis died.

Shooting Elvis would have been like photographing a woman—he oozed sensuality. He was very masculine, but his face and his rosy flesh had a feminine beauty. I never understood why he hid inside those ridiculous costumes. It would have been a wonderful challenge to get beyond the sequins and rediscover the young truck driver who, all those years earlier, had sparked the sexual revolution on *Ed Sullivan*. Naturally I didn't say all that right then. But if I'd only had time to explain my ideas, I think Elvis would have welcomed my proposal. The shift of viewpoint might even have helped him recover his lost image. Who knows? "What might have been" is an abstraction.

The Only Game in Town turned out to be an entirely different movie from the one planned. It was supposed to be the story of an affair between a dancer (Elizabeth) and a pianist (Warren). But in the absence of a real dancer and a real pianist, it became a story about two failed artists, neither very brilliant in their art, whose story never seems to go anywhere in particular. Elizabeth was too old for the part, and Warren too young. But if Elizabeth wanted to do a movie and George Stevens wanted to direct it, nobody got in their way. Nobody even dreamed of saying no. A lot of bad movies get made that way, even today.

I'd been traveling with Elizabeth and Richard for almost three years by then, and had noticed something rather strange. Often, when we got to a hotel, three dozen red roses would be there waiting for Elizabeth. At first I thought Richard was sending them. Then I learned that her admirer was Howard Hughes. So I asked Elizabeth about the roses, and she explained that Hughes's lawyer, Greg Bautzer, had once called her with a marriage proposal from Hughes. Elizabeth thought it was a joke, but Bautzer insisted that Hughes was serious. He wanted to marry her—he was in love with her and would do anything to prove it. So Elizabeth replied, "I won't say yes or no. Tell Howard that if he wants to prove his intentions are serious, he must send me $2 million, in cash."

The reply arrived just two hours later: a man showed up at Elizabeth's hotel room carrying two suitcases containing $2 million, in cash. Elizabeth was flabbergasted and immediately rang Bautzer. "Please, thank Howard on my behalf and tell him I'm flattered. But I'm afraid money will never keep me warm at night . . ."

The story had the flavor of a full-on Hollywood fable, and it was the first time I doubted something that Elizabeth told me. But I was wrong. A few years later I became friends with Greg Bautzer, so I got the chance to ask him about the story, without letting on that I'd already heard it from Elizabeth. It turned out to be entirely true. I've always admired Elizabeth's romantic soul and tried to portray it in my photos whenever possible. I believe this trait explains why she married and remarried so often. She may have adored her jewels, but she never cared about money. Or fame, which she'd known all her life. She just wanted to be loved and respected. And when it didn't work out, she married again, as soon as possible. And then gave herself heart and soul to the new person she loved.

Once Elizabeth saw a story about me in a magazine. For some reason, the picture that ran with the story was of me and my former fiancée, Patrizia. When Elizabeth asked me who she was, I explained how we'd

To Richard and Elizabeth's immense delight, Charles Schulz (*far right*), the *Peanuts* cartoon creator, dropped by one day in Mexico, so totally unannounced that they almost turned him away.

been engaged before Pierluigi sent me to Africa. Elizabeth was shocked. "You mean you slept with her?" she asked. "You were engaged and you didn't marry her? Why?" All I could say was that I'd met my soulmate in Claudye. But that didn't seem acceptable to Elizabeth. "I've never had lovers," Elizabeth explained. "I always marry the men I go to bed with, sometimes before, sometimes after."

Elizabeth and Richard had time to kill before their next movie, so they decided to take the family and entourage on vacation to their place in Mexico, Casa Kimberley, near Puerto Vallarta. It was on a private beach in Bucerías, some ten miles outside the city. They had a dune buggy there that just refused to work. I spent weeks tinkering with the engine and eventually managed to get it going, which was when I taught their sons, Michael and Christopher, to drive. We had a lot of fun, and one day we were out whizzing across the desert at top speed when another buggy appeared, coming up behind us like he wanted to race. He did everything he could to get by, but I kept cutting him off. We kept this game up for a while—or what seemed like a game to me—till the guy suddenly changed the rules and pulled out a gun. That's Mexico for you. I let him pass. What a pity I didn't have a camera. He was a dead ringer for Pancho Villa.

One day I was heading out to buy milk when two middle-aged American guys turned up asking to see Elizabeth. I began trying to explain that she was unavailable when the guy doing the talking explained that he was Charles Schulz, the man behind *Peanuts,* the Charlie Brown cartoon. The moment Elizabeth heard, she and Richard rushed out to greet their distinguished guest and his friend. They were both huge Charlie Brown fans and over the moon at his visit.

Elizabeth was looking so relaxed and beautiful that she was almost unrecognizable. Free from makeup, hairstyles, and set costumes, she spent her days laughing and joking with everyone. The holiday was clearly doing her a world of good.

Elizabeth, on holiday on their Bucerías beach in Mexico, hides buck naked behind Richard, having just lost her swimsuit in the surf.

Elizabeth playing with her son Michael and one of his friends (opposite)—and enjoying the company of a local bird.

Then one day her peace and quiet were shattered. Elizabeth and Richard were out on the beach when possibly the world's most persistent paparazzo, Ron Galella, shot Elizabeth in a pose that no woman would like to get caught in. He made her look fat, with rolls on her stomach. All Elizabeth had wanted to do was relax a bit by the sea. She had no idea Galella was lurking behind a tree playing Peeping Tom. His photo went around the world, tagged pretty much the same everywhere: "The world's most beautiful woman is through!" Elizabeth was so angry she even lost her sense of humor. The truth is, she felt wounded.

In the wake of Galella's photo, everyone lost interest in my pictures of Elizabeth. Whenever I had new ones I'd send them for publication through all the usual channels. But no one published them. None of the editors believed they told the truth. "It's all light tricks and touch-ups," they'd say. "You're not telling the truth with these photos." Thanks to Galella, the only photos anyone wanted of Elizabeth now were ugly ones. No one cared anymore whether she was beautiful or not. The world just wanted to see her at her worst.

It seemed that my job, hard enough as it was to begin with, had just

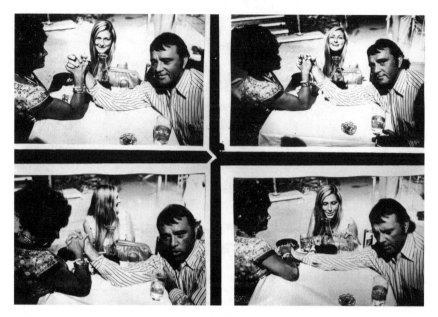

Relaxing in Mexico, my wife Claudye watches Elizabeth trounce Richard at arm wrestling, 1971. I took the photos with an Instamatic bought in a local store.

become even harder. Elizabeth trusted me to curate her image, and I had always tried to make the world see her as if for the first time. Now I had to find a way to do it all over again. Which I did, eventually. But it took time, while other affairs kept me busy.

Chapter 9

The Artist in Me

Claudye and I were living between Rome and Paris when I got hired as special photographer on the set of *Les Novices,* a French movie starring Brigitte Bardot. I'd just gifted myself with one of the Ford Mustangs used in the 1968 Peter Yates thriller, *Bullitt,* starring Steve McQueen (in possibly the most thrilling car-chase sequence in movie history). I used it to go to the set on the first day of shooting, and was just parking when I spotted Bardot on a Solex scooter with a stray dog running alongside her. I snapped these shots from the car.

She saw me, came over, and asked what kind of car it was. I explained, opened the passenger door, and in she got, wearing the most splendidly mini miniskirt. I looked at her legs and smiled. She looked at the speedometer and asked if the car really would go that fast. When I nodded that it would, she asked me to take her for a ride. Which I promptly did, pulling out all the stops, swerving into bends at the last moment. She bounced right over and hopped straight into my lap, squealing with excitement. Without meaning to, or unconsciously, one of my hands strayed, caressing her. We got to the auberge (a bed-and-breakfast of the time), where she was staying, went in, got a drink, and went upstairs. When we finally returned to the set, everyone was waiting for us. "If I give you my number, will you call me?" she asked, to which I replied by offering her my hand and a pen.

When shortly afterward we met on set, me lugging my equipment and shoulder bag, she did a double take and then looked embarrassed. She'd taken me for just another good-looking guy around town, not the special photographer. In any case, the atmosphere was decidedly grim. Everyone was irritated by Brigitte's late arrival, plus the way she was paying far more attention to me than the director. I felt so uneasy that I only stayed a couple of hours.

© copyright Gianni Bozzacchi

Brigitte Bardot took me for a nobody and took me to bed, much to her embarrassment when she later found me on her set as the special photographer for Guy Casaril's 1970 movie *Les Novices*.

I know it may sound crazy—Brigitte was one of the greatest sex symbols of all time—but I wasn't particularly attracted to her. She was intoxicated by celebrity in a way that was totally foreign to Elizabeth and Richard. After that one encounter in France, I always kept my distance, partly because I felt so guilty in front of Claudye. Whenever I did bump into her, I made sure my animal instincts were on a short leash.

Once Brigitte leaned out over my hotel balcony and said, "If I came out here naked, the whole town would stop to watch." If she hadn't been so taken by her fame, she might have become a good actress. But maybe she just loved being a sex symbol, and that was enough. What stimulated her was other people's attention, not any need for artistic expression. And I'm not sure whether she even had anything to express, besides her extraordinary beauty. I sensed in her an unsettling air of danger. During the first months of my association with Elizabeth and Richard I quite possibly might not have noticed anything other than her charm. But I was more adapted to my new life now, and had acquired a more critical eye. Watching Brigitte on my balcony, intent on only herself, I saw a hidden side to her, just as I saw a hidden side to Richard when he went on one of his drinking binges. But with Richard's self-brutalizing, I saw a deep inner conflict between his fame and his aspirations as an actor. Getting close to Bardot revealed no more than her emptiness.

Elizabeth and Richard were still on a break from work, so I had to find something to do. "Now pedal!" I thought, and got the idea of doing a photo shoot featuring Europe's leading fashion designers: Courrèges, Ungaro, Givenchy, Nina Ricci, Paco Rabanne. Deciding to start at the top, I called Coco Chanel's office, even though it was universally known that she hated being photographed. But I got an appointment to meet with one of her PR men in her atelier, where I explained that I wanted to photograph her for my agency archives because I thought she was the best designer in the world. The answer was no. He seemed unmovable. Then his in-house phone rang, and suddenly the answer changed to yes. Coco had been watching me from the upper floor. The staircase to her office had mirrored walls, which allowed her to follow what was going on below. I guess she liked what she saw because she invited me to do the shoot in her home in Switzerland. That seemed a bit strange to me, especially since I'd wanted to photograph her while she worked. But knowing just how many photographers she'd turned down in the past, I accepted.

I got to Coco's home, between Geneva and Lausanne in Switzerland, a few weeks later. She immediately started flirting openly with me and laughing almost hysterically. Her PR man looked on dumbfounded. She told him to leave. She wanted us to be alone. Coco was eighty-five at the time, still very attractive, fascinating, and sharp witted. I took a few pho-

Coco Chanel, eighty-five, did
more than agree to be
photographed—she invited me
home for a tête-à-tête.

When Coco Chanel invited me to photograph her in her chalet in Switzerland, I
hardly expected to be hugged, kissed, and asked for my hand in marriage . . .

tos. She lavished me with compliments, then sat on my lap, kissed me on the mouth, and asked me if I'd like to marry her. I hugged her the way you hug your grandmother, and she immediately invited me to dinner in her apartment in the Hotel Ritz Carlton. When I got home that night I told Claudye about Coco's proposal, and she replied, laughing, "I'll happily let her have you, but don't forget me."

The following day, Coco called and repeated her invitation to the Ritz. Claudye couldn't stop laughing. On the day of our appointment, Coco greeted me in her dressing gown. She weighed maybe eighty pounds. I believe I photographed her with more freedom than anyone else had been granted, maybe because she enjoyed the way I used my camera to provoke her. She again asked me to marry her. I again tried to laugh it off. This was a woman said to have slept with some of the world's most influential men, yet she never married a single one. When asked why she had turned down even the vastly wealthy Duke of Westminster, she reportedly replied, "There have been many Duchesses of Westminster. There is only one Coco Chanel."

I asked Coco who she thought was going to be the next "Coco Chanel." "All these women," she replied caustically, "they get dressed by men that hate them." In truth there really was no other female designer ready to take Chanel's place, and in stark contrast to today, people in the fashion industry still looked askance at the idea of gay men making clothes for women.

That marriage proposal may have been wild, but there was something serious in her tone all the same. Later, when I took Coco my photos, she treated me in a much more reserved manner, as if she were angry with me. The fashion industry in Paris was going through something of a crisis at the time. I could only figure that maybe Coco had hoped she and I would be caught in a compromising situation and thus spark a huge scandal that would generate some much-needed publicity. As it happens, Catherine Deneuve was in the building that day. Coco did everything she could to keep us apart, even though she knew we knew each other. It was as if she were jealous. I left Coco with a number of photos, and as I was leaving, she invited me to a party. I didn't go. Months later I met her again. She was very sick and didn't recognize me.

I never did finish my fashion designers shoot. After photographing Coco Chanel, I lost interest in doing any of the others. She was a legend. I'd have felt I was going downhill after her. Plus, I didn't understand that world. I've never understood haute couture, all those unwearable clothes.

Maybe I've just never possessed the necessary extravagance to work in high fashion.

Nevertheless, extravagance kept coming my way. On a brief visit to Rome, Klaus Kinski phoned. We'd met during the shooting of *A Fistful of Dollars*. He wanted me to do a photo shoot for him alone. He turned up wearing a skin-tight pair of pants—you could tell immediately that he'd padded the crotch. Klaus wanted to be photographed as a new James Dean. We went to a park where he started strutting around like a cowboy, doing a horrible version of a young American rebel. There was no way I could squeeze James Dean out of that German arrogance, that gloomy expression, that lined face. I'm a good photographer, but not that good.

Kinski showed me absolutely no respect. He kept correcting my technique, arguing about my angles and his stupid poses. "Look," I said eventually. "You're the subject, not the artist. I decide what to do." I told him that if he didn't like the photos, he could throw them away. Or whatever. I couldn't care less. There was no other way. His movements were totally out of sync with the expression on his face and the clothes he was wearing. It just wasn't going to work. When all he could do was sneer, I added, "Listen, if you follow me and do what I say . . ." But I got interrupted. "No," he said, "nobody tells me what to do." So I began packing my stuff away. At which point he blurted out, "Okay, we'll do it your way. I know it won't work, but we'll try it all the same."

In a more mature phase of my career, the shoot with Kinski would have gone better. At some stage I realized that the best way to control my subjects was to ask for a big advance. For some reason that I've never quite understood, when egocentrics like Kinski pay in advance, they let me work. It's as if they want to get as much for their money as possible. "I'll pay," they say, "but I won't lift a finger. You have to do all the work." Which is exactly what I want anyway. The less they do—pose, try to look cool, pad their crotch—the better the photos turn out. But Kinski just wouldn't listen. He had no intention of changing those stupid pants or quitting those ridiculous poses. When he saw the photos, he called to tell me that he didn't like them and that he'd probably made a mistake in hiring me. I told him he was right. I wasn't the person he needed to take the photos he wanted. I wished him good luck in finding someone more suitable.

However, maybe he didn't despise my work so much after all because a couple of weeks later he called asking me to photograph his daughter, Nastassja. I refused. The way he did things was too irritating. Over the years, I've since seen many photos of Klaus, and I don't believe he ever found the photographer he was looking for. He was no James Dean, that's for sure. Though he wasn't the only one out there trying to be.

This became clear after I got a call from the publicist for *Le Mans*, an action movie that director Lee Katsin was making based on the city's famous twenty-four-hour sports car race. They wanted to hire me as special photographer on the movie. But I wasn't interested so I submitted an exaggerated fee, much higher than my usual rate. The producers didn't bat an eye. So off I went to France. On my first day on set I saw a motorbike coming toward me. The rider was the movie's star, Steve McQueen. There—I thought—is a real James Dean kind of guy, and I grabbed my camera and took a shot. McQueen promptly told the crew to throw me off the set, only becoming even more furious when they explained that I'd been hired as the special photographer. Nobody, it seems, had asked his opinion. I told the publicist that unless McQueen apologized I wouldn't take another photo. McQueen refused. I stood my ground, gave them the only photo I'd taken, and spent the next four weeks playing cards with the cast and crew. Nobody seemed to care. I'd respected my contract with that one photo and my presence on the set, and nobody bothered to send me home.

Watching me have fun with the stuntmen and doubles, seeing me the object of so much attention, made McQueen yet angrier. I even test-drove a few of the cars used in the movie. One day I took a Porsche out on the track and overtook McQueen. He was a good driver, but so was I. I passed him and he accelerated, trying and failing to pass me. McQueen was no happier to see me spending so much time with his costar, Elga Andersen. One day I was photographing her far from the set when I saw him watching us. I snapped a shot of him and kept it for myself. That was *Le Mans*. They paid me to drive sports cars, play cards with my friends, and flirt with a good-looking actress under Steve McQueen's surly gaze. Making movies can be a weird business at times.

When I told Richard the story—that they'd paid me a boatload of money to do nothing—he found it ridiculous too. A couple of months later in Los Angeles, in our regular Beverly Hills Hotel bungalow, I saw McQueen come into the Polo Lounge. I told Richard, who called and asked to speak with Steve, inviting him to drop round after lunch. When Steve knocked, I answered the door. I could see at once that he remembered me. He stepped over to greet Richard, who immediately asked, "You've met

Steve McQueen couldn't bear having me around on the *Le Mans* set, especially when I outpaced him in a Porsche and hung out with the lead actress.

Gianni, haven't you?" Richard's sense of humor was always at its best when it came to embarrassing others, especially me. "Yes," Steve replied. "I imagine I owe him an apology." "What for?" I said. "That was the best-paid job I've ever done. I should thank you!"

Elizabeth and Richard were getting ready to go back to work. Their movies were clearly still my number one priority, so I had to find some way of cutting back on my other commitments while still giving myself a certain flexibility in case a Coco Chanel or Brigitte Bardot should call wanting a shoot. The first step was to break with Pierluigi, once and for all. I no longer benefited in any way from our association. So I opened my own agency in Rome, Forum Press Services, and hired twenty-four correspondents worldwide, just as Pierluigi had done. A lot of his employees came to work with my new company.

When Johnny Moncada heard about it, he called and offered to rent me his studio in Via Margutta, the same place where I'd once worked fixing his lights and retouching his negatives. I recalled all those hours spent with Moncada, and now I'd become as big as he was. I looked out of the amazing windows of that studio—now my own—and at the courtyard, where artists like Picasso had walked and which now thronged with my own assistants, doing the same work that I'd once done myself. Success on Moncada's level no longer seemed so impossible.

But first I had a job of my own still pending: to repair the damage that Galella's picture had done—not only to Elizabeth's image but in no small measure to her ego as well. Her next movie was *X, Y & Zee*, costarring Michael Caine and Susannah York and directed by Brian Hutton. It was being shot at the Shepperton Studios in England. Everyone on set could tell that Elizabeth had become very self-conscious about her appearance. Approaching middle age is a hard enough issue to handle for any Hollywood actress. Now Elizabeth had to deal with the whole world gossiping that she'd become fat and ugly. She desperately needed to feel beautiful again. And the world needed to see that the liar was not my camera, but Galella's.

Of all the photos I'd taken, how many revealed the artist in me? I was always photographing for reasons dictated to me by others. The artist always came last, if he even came into the picture at all. Above all, you had to satisfy the objectives of the photo shoot—whether it was publicity, a poster, or a piece of clothing that needed selling. Generally, the subject was a star or someone important. Then there was the context. Was it for a magazine? Or a poster? In which case, the subject had to be to one side of the image, because there'd be words on the other. As the photographer, you came last. If you did manage to infuse a little artistry into the photo, great. But my experience had taught me that nourishing such hopes was invariably in conflict with the aim of the image.

A true artist is free to express him- or herself completely, with no conflicts or compromises. Many of my photos were not like that. I enjoyed more freedom than a set photographer, but I had limits all the same. On set, for example, I couldn't control the lights because that was up to the director of photography. My only choice was what angle I chose to shoot from. The clothes were chosen by the director in collaboration with the costume designer. The makeup artist decided the hairstyle and makeup of whatever star I was photographing. Sure, there were a few occasions when I was able to make my own decisions and express myself. But most of the time, I had to repress myself.

But there was one shot that really did express the artist in me. I was still burned up by the fact that someone had destroyed Elizabeth's image. As her personal photographer, it was up to me to fix the damage. The idea that Elizabeth had suddenly become fat and ugly was absurd. Just look at that photo of her running out of her dressing room. It told everyone loud and clear, "Go to hell!" No one could say I'd touched anything up. That photo was as true as it gets. And technically, it was almost impossible. Just before taking it, I'd seen Elizabeth go from the set to her dressing room. Once the set floodlights had been switched off, the light was very different, very soft, beautiful. I liked the way it bathed Elizabeth's figure and wanted to be able to photograph her in that light before they put the floods back on. Using a flash was out of the question because it can destroy any atmosphere. I measured the relative aperture. The stop was on 2, so the focus would be very tight. The speed was one-fifteenth of a second, which, technically, means it should be impossible to freeze a subject in motion. But I was convinced I could pull it off.

Elizabeth came out of the dressing room running, which made everything even harder. With no time to plan, I shot without thinking. As she ran toward me, I dropped to my knees and leaned backward at the same speed that she was advancing, snapping off three shots. My movement compensated hers, creating a sense of immobility, even though Elizabeth was actually still running. There was no pose, no tricks, and the way her top wrapped around her body highlighted how well proportioned she was. And how beautiful.

Elizabeth runs out of her dressing room during a break shooting Brian Hutton's *X, Y & Zee*. The photo sold around the world and demolished rumors that Elizabeth was losing her looks. It was used on the film's publicity posters.

Many great photographers have photographed Elizabeth during her career. Why, then, does talk always turn back to me? Why not Richard Avedon or Lord Snowdon? Maybe because I never photographed only the woman, the wife, the actress or star—I also managed to photograph her as a fully authentic individual. I brought her to life. I never immortalized an immobile and inexpressive star. And I never lurked in the bushes with a zoom lens like Galella. A photographer has to be in touch with his feelings, which I believe is what made the difference between that photo and all the others. Richard liked it so much that he wrote a prose poem to go with it:

> She is like the tide, she comes and she goes, she runs to me as in this stupendous photographic image. In my poor and tormented youth, I had always dreamed of this woman. And now, when this dream occasionally returns, I extend my arm, and she is here . . . by my side. If you have not met or known her, you have lost much in life.

Everyone everywhere wanted that photo. Thousands of publications took it in a single week. No one thought Elizabeth had turned ugly anymore. And they stopped accusing me of lying with my photos. But I didn't stop there. Once and for all, I wanted to disprove all those damned articles that had made Elizabeth so unhappy. So I let a week go by, then circulated images of Elizabeth in hot pants.

I established a good relationship with Michael Caine, Elizabeth's costar in *X, Y & Zee*. He was a really nice guy, with great class. He was very enthusiastic about working with Elizabeth. The two of them got on well and understood one another perfectly. I was very struck by his kindness and the respect with which he treated the whole crew. He was in no way egocentric. He didn't demand special treatment, was always very professional, never late, always ready for the director's "Action!" call. A class act all around. One day I overheard him chatting with a number of crew members and didn't understand a word. It sounded like English, but I couldn't make out a thing he was saying. His words stayed in his mouth, his lips didn't seem to move. "Michael," I asked, "what language are you talking?" He burst out laughing and replied, "It's Cockney."

X, Y & Zee received the same poor response as *The Only Game in Town*. The plot included allusions to a lesbian relationship between

Hot pants were all the rage, and became even more so when these photos went global. Notice what happens when you move your lens: the first photo makes Elizabeth (pictured with Susanna York) look almost short; the second does wonders for her legs (and would do the same for any woman). The mirror is a liar, but my mechanical eye correctly captures my vision.

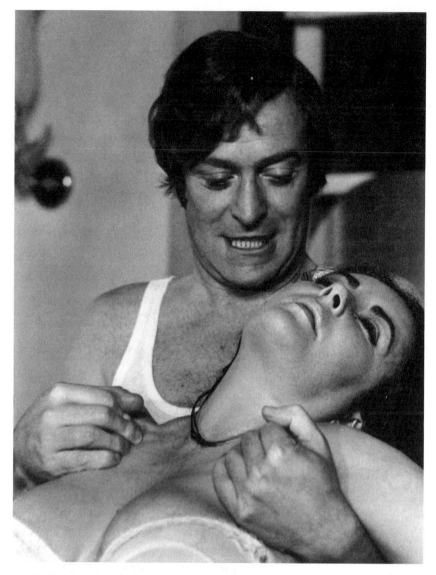

Michael Caine and Elizabeth shooting *X, Y & Zee*. Michael was a perfect gentle-man to work with, unassuming and friendly with even the lowliest crew member.

Elizabeth's and Susannah York's characters, and Columbia Pictures insisted on cutting a number of the more explicit scenes. The whole movie suffered as a result.

While Elizabeth was still busy with *X, Y & Zee*, Richard had begun

Elizabeth and
Michael play
ping-pong in the
opening credits of
X, Y, & Zee.

work on *Anne of the Thousand Days,* a Universal Pictures movie telling the story of Anne Boleyn (played by Geneviève Bujold) and King Henry VIII (Richard). That was another movie that had to battle for ages before satisfying the US motion picture production code, on account of its themes—however historically true—of adultery, illegitimacy, and incest. I never got a chance to photograph Richard on set because I was there only for the one day that Elizabeth was included in a scene, making a brief uncredited appearance in full period costume. During a break in shooting that day, she noticed someone had left golf balls and clubs lying around, so she took a club and swung. The ball whizzed off, hit a tree, and bounced back across two cars—bang, bang, bang! She was terrifically embarrassed, but I managed to snap two great shots, one before and one after.

Next door to Elizabeth and Richard's set, Roman Polanski was filming *Macbeth.* Polanski asked for an interview with Elizabeth, but she refused because she knew the movie had been commissioned by Hugh Hefner's Playboy Productions, and she didn't want anything to do with it. He snuck into her dressing room anyway and hid a tape recorder under a chair. Elizabeth rarely gave interviews, which made any scrap of conversation with her valuable. When Elizabeth returned, they started talking. But I'd seen what Roman had done, and, not wanting to make a scene, I told Elizabeth's secretary, Dick Hanley, that Polanski was secretly taping their conversation. Dick knocked on the door, asked Elizabeth to step outside, and told her about the tape recorder. She left without saying another word to Polanski. Richard then went into the dressing room, grabbed the tape recorder, and ripped out the tape. Polanski scampered away as quickly as he could.

Elizabeth and Richard's next movie, *Hammersmith Is Out,* was set to shoot in Mexico, so, shortly before leaving, I went home for a long conversation with my father. I could sense that something was wrong, and I asked him a hundred times if he was all right, if the family was okay. He assured me that everything was just fine, but I didn't believe him. Under no circumstances would my father ever ask for my help. And he never accepted a penny from me (though I'd often slip my mother some money). I remember once when he needed to go to the dentist he went to the cheapest one he could find. A disaster. I got him an appointment with the best in town, paid 90 percent of the bill up front and asked the man to simply bill my father the remaining 10 percent. He would never have allowed me to pick up his tab, and he would never have gone if he'd known what it really cost.

Dressed for a cameo part in *Anne of the Thousand Days* (1969), Elizabeth tries her hand at golf during a break and—much to her embarrassment—drives the ball smack into a row of parked cars.

Nevertheless, he complained anyway, saying the dentist had overcharged him.

My father counted every penny not because he was tight but because he earmarked every penny he earned for his family. He spent everything on us, never bought a thing for himself. Our needs always came first, his later—or never. Now that I had become so successful, I tried to repay him. But he wouldn't let me. I offered to buy him a car. He said he didn't want one. I offered to get him new clothes, but he didn't want them either. Once I went home in a brand-new Ferrari and took him for a ride. We hadn't gone far before he told me to pull over, got out, and said, "Fuck this, I'm getting the bus. This isn't a car, it's a missile! It's turned my stomach upside down!" And home he went by bus. That was my father for you.

Anyway, I knew he'd never tell me the truth if he ever got ill, so I talked to my mother about it. She confirmed that he wasn't well but said there was nothing to worry about. I had no choice but to believe her. We said good-bye and I packed my bags.

On the way to Mexico, we stopped off in California to meet with the production staff, including the movie's publicist, Jerry Pam. I knew he was one of the best in his field. When I went to meet him in his offices in the Samuel Goldwyn Studios he barely gave me time to get through the door before exclaiming, "Listen. I know you've been hired for this movie, but I don't want you. I want the photographer who took these." The wall behind him was lined with photos of Elizabeth, all taken by me. But I'd signed almost none of them, to avoid paying tax twice, a common practice at the time among photographers published around the world. So Jerry had no idea that I was the author. He was desperately looking for a nonexistent photographer. He wanted that guy and no one else. I couldn't explain why I hadn't signed those photos. It was my business. So I simply said I was sorry, but I already had a contract with Elizabeth. This only spurred him on: "No, no, no! I'll talk with Elizabeth, tell her I want this photographer. It's nothing personal, you understand."

Back at the Beverly Hills Hotel I told Elizabeth the whole story. She was outraged. "Fire the man! How dare he doubt you!"

I explained the reason for all the confusion, and she gave me carte blanche to fix the situation. When I went back to Jerry's, he made me wait forty-five minutes. I then invited him for a coffee. "I'll accept the coffee," he said, "but I'm not going to change my mind." I couldn't help but admire the guy for sticking to his guns. When I finally explained the whole thing, he looked perplexed but didn't hesitate to compliment me. We became great friends.

In California I got really sick. I couldn't digest a thing; it all came back up. I don't know if it was a physical illness or all the stress that had built up around my work and my concern for my father. I asked Elizabeth if she knew a doctor, and her secretary got me an appointment with a certain Dr. Coleman. Everyone in Los Angeles knew him. He said I had an ulcer, and prescribed a particular diet and a string of pills. Back at the Beverly Hills Hotel, I started wondering how that doctor knew I had an ulcer when he hadn't even seen an X-ray. I talked to Elizabeth about it, telling her that I didn't believe the diagnosis. She started yelling: "What do you mean, you don't believe it?! He's a luminary! Gary Cooper! Marilyn Monroe!"

Well, he couldn't be such a great doctor then, could he? Those people were dead! I went back, got an X-ray, and then a sentence: "Unfortunately, it's worse than I first diagnosed. You've got a tumor."

"Fuck!" I said. I thought I should sell everything and go have fun! I can't say I was totally convinced I was dying, because I was still suspicious of this Hollywood doctor. But I was definitely scared, and the possibility that I might be really sick hung over me for the rest of the trip.

We flew to Mexico City on Frank Sinatra's Lear jet. The landing felt really weird because, due to the city's altitude, instead of descending to land, we climbed up to the runway. My stomach was still upside down. From Mexico City, we got to Puerto Vallarta, where Dr. Coleman came to visit me on various occasions, flying down from Los Angeles in a private jet. He put me on a strange diet, prescribed strange pills, and told me to drink a lot of milk and orange juice. I didn't care what Elizabeth said. I didn't trust the guy. Secretly I slipped off to the market and bought jars of homogenized baby food, living off that throughout my stay in Mexico. I hid them in my suitcase. When everyone else went out for lunch or dinner, I invented some excuse and went back to my room to dine on baby food. I lost a bit of weight, but I felt better. I quit taking the pills.

A few weeks later we were filming outside Cuernavaca when someone spotted Ron Galella hiding up a tree. He was presumably hoping to shoot a sequel to his "fat Elizabeth" photo. Some of the crew raced over, pulled him down from his hideout, and started to beat him up. If I hadn't intervened to defend him, they'd have massacred the guy. He was a paparazzo and I didn't like him. But he was only doing his job. We were outside in a public place, and he had every right to photograph us, whether we liked it

Michael Wilding, Elizabeth, and Claudye enjoying the sun and idyllic isolation of Mexico. To tell the truth, I would have preferred the sun and sundry pleasures of a crowded Saint-Tropez.

or not. I told him to get out quick, and he didn't bother us again. Over the years, I've met Ron on a number of occasions, and he's always repeated his gratitude for my gesture that day.

Shooting *Hammersmith Is Out* was an enjoyable experience. I was delighted to work with Peter Ustinov again—he both costarred and directed—as well as meet Beau Bridges. He was about my age, newly married like me. We talked a lot about marriage and children. Work moved ahead pleasurably. We all got along and were lucky to be in startlingly lovely locations. For the final shots, production moved to Acapulco. We lodged in a beautiful hotel complex on the coast called Las Brisas. Every villa came complete with a pink rental jeep, so we all went for jeep rides down the beach. My pool was fantastic. It continued under the walls of the building, extending halfway across the living room. I used it a lot. I relaxed, and slowly beginning to feel better, to enjoy life, and even to wonder whether I wasn't letting myself get too stressed over my photography. I was

Cleaning my equipment in Puerto Vallarta one day, I noticed Elizabeth absorbed in a book and snapped this photo. Later neither of us could explain the mysterious figure you see in the background—we were both certain that nothing was there at the time.

Me in Cuernavaca, Mexico. (Photo taken by Michael Wilding.)

in Mexico with my beautiful wife and my best friends. I was being paid to do what I liked doing. And I had a swimming pool in my living room! Life wasn't really that bad, when you got down to it.

I was in that pool when Elizabeth came to get me on May 25, 1971. She was as white as a sheet. "Gianni," she said, "come and answer. You've got a phone call from Rome." It was Ottavia, my brother Giampiero's wife. My father was seriously ill. Elizabeth organized my flight through Los Angeles and New York, where Richard's secretary Valerie Douglas got a TWA flight to Rome to wait two hours for me. People were often amazed by these things, by the power that Elizabeth and Richard had—to stop planes, to go anywhere they wanted whenever they wanted, to see whomever they pleased, to work when they wished and not work when they didn't so choose. It was truly impressive, though over the last few years I'd become accustomed to that kind of clout, to their way of life, which had become mine too. But it was a way of life that had taken me to the other side of the world, far from the most important man in my life, who right then needed me.

My sisters came to meet my plane in Rome. They were crying. Ottavia had lied to me. My father was already dead. He was only sixty, and had retired just two months earlier. I was too devastated to be mad at my family for hiding the truth from me. I embraced my sisters and wept along with them. The root cause of my father's death dated to his military service in Africa during the war. He'd contracted an amoeba that never quite left him—a kind of incurable dysentery. Subsequently, he contracted hepatitis working on the restoration of books damaged in Florence when, in 1966, the Arno River had dramatically broken its banks and flooded the city. One ailment worsened the other. In the end he developed liver cancer. I'd known that my father had an amoeba that gave him trouble from time to time. But I knew nothing about the hepatitis or the cancer. My family simply didn't inform me, even though I'd told my older brother Giampiero to call me if my father's health ever took a turn for the worse. They were all so enthusiastic about my success, especially my father. He'd lived the last years of his life through my success. He'd given me photography, and he'd taught, encouraged, and challenged my talent. Now I was famous. People talked about me all the time in his local bar, at his office. My family hadn't wanted to interrupt that dream. But it took me a long time to forgive them for having kept me in the dark.

My father was Catholic but had arranged for his funeral to be held in an Adventist church out of respect for my mother. Our old friend Father Karol—now a cardinal—called my mother to give her his condolences and to thank us for the important work to which my father had dedicated his life, to the betterment of both the Polish church and Italy.

I couldn't sleep for days after the funeral. I couldn't stop thinking of my father, all alone in the dark. I'd get up at night, go to the cemetery, and sit by his grave for hours, night after night. I kept him company. I spoke to him. I knew he'd wanted a grandchild from me and felt guilty about not having given him one. I lied and told him that Claudye was pregnant. I told him that my life was going great, that I wasn't frustrated anymore, and that I knew what I was doing. Another lie.

As a boy I hadn't respected my father enough. I hadn't understood. He worked all the time, getting up at dawn and returning late at night, and all I could think was, "What kind of a life is that?" We never ate in restaurants with proper tablecloths, just paper ones. The poor guy would fold back a corner of the paper tablecloth, jot down what we'd ordered and the price on the menu, then fold it back so the waiter wouldn't see. When the bill came, he'd check it against his notes to make sure there were no mistakes. What kind of a life was that? But now I understand. He'd served his country, eleven years in the army—as an artist, not a soldier—and he'd served during wartime. He'd bicycled miles through a bombing raid just to be present at my birth, and had worked long, awful hours in a government darkroom so that we could all eat. Had I ever repaid him for all that he did for me, for all his sacrifices?

A few months later, my family told me that my father's last words had been, "I miss him, I miss him . . . I want to see my little Giannetto again."

And I wasn't there for him. Even today, more than forty years on, I still miss him.

Chapter 10

Without My Father

Many weeks passed before I was able to put my grief aside and critically analyze the figure of my father and his influence in my life. Where had that twenty-two-year-old kid found the courage to snap a photo of Elizabeth Taylor, without permission, on a movie set in Africa? From his father. He wanted to show his father that he knew how to exploit his talent and become someone. My ears still ring with what he'd tell me when someone said I was a great photographer: "You'll get there, but you're not there yet. You've got what it takes, but you're still not as good as you think you are." Meeting his standards, becoming the photographer he saw in me, was a tremendous challenge, the toughest in my career. Photographing beautiful people was easy. What was hard was taking a photo that Bruno Bozzacchi thought was beautiful.

Even though he didn't shower me with praise, I knew my father was proud of me. "You make us dream," my sister Ofelia said, "and you have no idea how much our father dreams." I believe he thought he was a better photographer than me. And he was probably right. My father was a man dedicated to art for art's sake, and he wanted to instill in me the same respect and the same devotion. He hadn't got rich and he wasn't interested in doing so. His heart was set on his work. He was an artist in the purest sense, but he was unable to ever fully express himself because he worked for the government and because he had a family to feed. He was trapped inside two vicious circles, with no way out, unable ever to do anything just for himself.

By the end of his career he was well known and highly respected by the government, the Vatican, leading museums, and many wealthy families. Once free of his government job, maybe he would have been able to do something for himself, even make a stack of money, enjoy life without having to worry too much. We'd talked about maybe working together. He

187

didn't know my business, but he knew all the darkroom techniques and he knew photography inside out. But he died before having that chance to try something new. He never received any recognition in the wider world. I was his recognition. He did so much for me. I hoped I'd done enough for him. I would have loved to do more.

I was so depressed after my father's death that I started to get terrible stomach pains. I began to worry that maybe Elizabeth's doctor was right after all. Claudye arranged for me to see the famous Dr. Rudolph Trouques in Paris. He had a whole team of specialists poke and prod me from head to toe, but they couldn't find a single thing wrong with me. When I explained to Dr. Trouques that Elizabeth's doctor in Los Angeles thought I might have cancer, Trouques dismissed this as ridiculous and fired off a letter to the American doctor, complete with all my scans and charts. We never heard back, an all-too-common story in Hollywood—doctors preying on celebrities' insecurities about their appearance, their bodies, their health, just to make money. In my opinion, Elizabeth was victimized in this way.

Elizabeth and Richard told me to take all the time I needed to recover my health. But I decided that the best thing to do was to get back to work. So Richard asked me to go ahead of him to Yugoslavia, where he was due to play Josip Broz, "Tito" in *The Battle of Sutjeska,* a movie being produced by the state cinema production company, Yugo Films. It tells the story of a key turning point in World War II when Yugoslav partisans, led by Tito, managed to break a massive Axis offensive along the Sutjeska River, regroup, and eventually emerge victorious. Tito, now the president of Yugoslavia, had personally chosen Richard to play him in the movie. Richard thought my presence would keep Tito happy until he could finish shooting in England. In addition, I'd get a chance to photograph Tito in private, which might also help Richard understand the man's character better.

When we entered Yugoslav air space, military jets surrounded our plane and escorted it to Pula airport. This was nothing like landing at JFK or LAX. It was a full-on military base, with helicopters, tanks, jeeps, and armed soldiers everywhere. From there we boarded a boat and crossed from the Istrian coast to Veliki Brijun, possibly the most beautiful island on earth, and the biggest in an amazing archipelago. It bloomed with incredible plants and flowers and featured a hotel complex and gorgeous villas alongside the presidential palace. I wondered whether someone had

When Richard was cast as Yugoslav dictator Tito, he asked me to go ahead and check the man out.

accidentally spirited me out of Yugoslavia. To some extent they had. Veliki Brijun had previously belonged to Italy, and the elegant style of the island was in sharp contrast to the rest of Yugoslavia. Had I been president, I too would have chosen it as my residence! I hear it's now become a national park, and there are plans to add a luxury tourist complex. Maybe I should revisit the place someday.

Once my bags were unpacked, attendants took me to Tito. He had a very serious air about him. He asked in what language we might communicate. We settled on a mixture of Italian and English. He invited me to take a seat, lit a cigarette for me and a big cigar for himself, and chatted with me for a bit before getting down to business: what would Richard need for the movie? I replied that I'd been sent to study his personality, the body language of the man Richard would be playing. Tito burst out laughing and gave me permission to photograph him.

The following morning, Tito invited me to have breakfast with him. He inquired about my political inclinations. I replied that I didn't have any but mentioned that my father had fought in Yugoslavia during the war.

Tito asked, "Did I kill him?"

"No."

"What did he think about me?"

"I don't know. My father never talked about you."

"Let's ask him now. Let's call him."

"He died a few weeks ago."

My answer didn't seem to fluster Tito in the least. We kept talking. I asked him what he'd do when he retired from political life. He was eighty-one. I thought it was an appropriate question. He just looked at me and shrugged his shoulders. And in the end he never did retire, of course.

Tito and Elizabeth enjoy a joke on his yacht.

Dictators don't, as a rule. Tito would die in May 1980, just three days short of his eighty-eighth birthday. His funeral is believed to have been the largest state funeral ever held in history.

Not that he was always so serious. A couple of days later he showed me a 16 mm black-and-white Yugoslav cartoon. I couldn't understand the language, but it seemed to be portraying the daily lives of common Yugoslavs. I couldn't understand anything. Tito found it hilarious so I just laughed when he did. He watched it three or four times, laughing at every joke.

When Richard and Elizabeth finally arrived, Tito wanted to show off a bit, so he drove us around Veliki Brijun in a convertible Cadillac that President Nixon had given him as a gift. Then he hit a rock, and the car ground to a permanent halt. So he took us to the zoo to show us the family elephant, all alone on a Yugoslav island. Then we went to Pula to see a Yugoslav movie about the war. It was partly in Russian and partly in German, so I didn't understand a thing and didn't recognize any of the actors. When Tito entered the theater, the audience began chanting: "Tito! Ti-to!" There are a lot of stories about the origins of the nickname Tito, though the one I heard most often explains that *ti* and *to* both mean "you," in Serbian and Croatian respectively. Broz would get up every morning at the crack of dawn to greet the crowds, addressing them in Serbian and Croatian as "ti" and "to." It helped him acquire popularity on both sides and thus work toward a united Yugoslavia. Indeed, I was struck by the deep respect both Slavs and Croatians had for him. His government was very authoritarian, but people never feared him in the way Iranians feared their shah. They loved him for how courageously he'd fought against the Germans and appreciated the socioeconomic reforms he was trying to realize.

One thing that surprised me was the extent to which the Yugoslav coast had been Westernized. It was lined with casinos, strip clubs, and lots of good restaurants and bars. Then something even stranger caught my eye. I kept seeing magazines that I'd never heard of—whose names I couldn't even pronounce—which published lots of photos of celebrities, including my own. The quality was awful, but they were undoubtedly mine. And I knew I'd never sold anything in Yugoslavia. So I rang my agent in Rome and asked him to investigate. We discovered that a company in Milan was buying the magazines, copying the photos without permission, and selling them in places like Yugoslavia, where there were no copyright laws.

Tito's wife takes Elizabeth to admire their family elephant and private zoo.

Tito, Richard, and Elizabeth chatting in Brijun, Tito's personal island resort.

Elizabeth and Richard were given use of Tito's villa in Kupari, near Dubrovnik. But they decided to live on their yacht, so the splendid villa, complete with waiters, a butler, and cook, was all mine. I wanted to do a fashion shoot in the gardens of the villa and realized I needed an electronic flash, which I had to get from Rome. So I asked my brother Renato to bring one over. He was just sixteen and believed communism was a good idea. I thought he'd be interested to see communism for real. I went to get him from the airport in a little jeep that Elizabeth and Richard kept on their yacht, and put him in a room next to mine. The following morning, I saw a servant cleaning my brother's shoes. One of his fingers came out through a hole in the sole of one of them. That was how my brother demonstrated his commitment to communism—by wearing shoes that were so old they were falling to pieces. I decided to show him another side of communist life under Tito and took him to a strip club. He'd never been in one before and here, unlike in Italian clubs, the girls stripped buck naked. That was one communism we could both agree on.

One day, while Tito had a meeting with Richard to discuss work, his wife Jovanka invited Elizabeth to visit one of their vineyards on a little island near Brijun. She was a robust woman, taller than either Elizabeth or Tito. She showed us the vineyard—its cellars lined with wine vats and bottles—and invited us to take a seat. "Let's toast our friendship!" she exclaimed, and said something in Serbian to her butler, who proceeded to bring us three strange clay cups all linked together. I'd never seen such a thing. Jovanka had a bottle opened and emptied the wine into the cups in three equal parts. Then, addressing me, she said, "You're the youngest, so you start. Drink. But if you don't finish, our friendship will break." I took the cup and started to drink, and drink, and drink. Holy smokes, it was never ending. I hadn't realized. The three cups were all interconnected. Effectively, you had to empty all three. I'd just downed an entire bottle of wine in one go. Elizabeth and Jovanka were roaring with laughter. I was stone drunk.

Richard and Tito discussed the movie with the help of an interpreter. Richard had read up on the history of Yugoslavia and respected Tito for standing up to Stalin and for uniting such a divided part of the world. Tito had only exchanged a few words with me. But with Richard he had long, extended conversations. Richard asked a lot of specific and complicated questions: about the politics of the country, the logistics of war, and the leader's psychological state of mind. Tito answered every question, through the interpreter, quickly and with authority.

As we were walking back to the villa after their first meeting, Richard marveled at how quick-witted Tito was, especially given his age. I figured, however, that Tito spoke—or at least understood—English, and said so. Richard didn't want to believe me, but that night he went to the villa's library and memorized a number of phrases in Serbian. When he met Tito again the next day, he asked a question and, while the interpreter was translating, interrupted him, saying, "No, that's not what I said." Tito smiled and replied, in English, "Mr. Burton, you're not wrong, but if you prefer, if you have the patience and accept my English, we can continue without an interpreter." He had an incredible mind. He understood everything that was going on around him, everything we said. But he'd preferred not to speak in English in order not to risk making a mistake. Which was why he'd been able to reply so promptly. He'd heard every question twice, and had had time to think.

The first day of shooting finally arrived. A huge, Russian-made military helicopter took us to the set, which was along the Sutjeska River. And that was how we came and went, or at least Richard did. Helicopters already scared me to death. Then, during one flight, our door opened and fell clean away! The helicopter started rapidly losing altitude, while my bag, with all its equipment, began sliding toward the gaping doorway. "Let it go!" Richard shouted. But I managed to grab it just in time. On another occasion, we were flying back from the set at night when, crossing over a deep gorge, we ran into a thick bank of fog. You couldn't see your hand in front of your face. Suddenly Richard looked to his left and shouted, "Watch out!" We were about to fly into a mountain. The pilot pulled back on the stick, and the helicopter went into a breathtaking vertical climb. When we finally landed in Dubrovnik, Richard fell to his knees and kissed the ground. I did the same. The following morning, I announced that I was never going to get into a helicopter again in my life. "Do as you wish," said Richard, and from then on I spent an hour and a half every day crossing the mountain by road. Richard kept going by helicopter.

Three or four days later we were supposed to shoot a scene in Sarajevo. It was too far to go by car, and I was terrified at the idea of getting back into that helicopter. I had an awful gut feeling about it. "Don't worry," said Richard. "You stay here." When they got back that evening, Richard came to find me and gave me a big hug. "Gianni, we hit terrible weather," he said. "The pilot said that we only made it back because we weren't too heavy. If you'd been with us, the helicopter would probably have crashed."

Filming was also a dangerous business, with lots of accidents. The production employed the entire army, dressing some soldiers as Germans and others as partisans. There were lots of battle scenes, with flights of German aircraft strafing Tito's soldiers. On one occasion, I was with Richard when an enormous, smoking shell case fell out of the sky right beside me. If it had hit me, it would have gone straight through my body and out my butt. Crazy! It wouldn't have helped me at the time to know that Tito himself was supposed to have survived a similar incident in the real battle. All I wanted to do was get home in one piece. Yugo Films may have been a production company, but this was no normal cinema production. It was an army obeying orders from its commander, Marshal Tito.

The day came when even the helicopter pilot, a colonel, decided the weather was too bad to fly back from the day's shooting. We spent the night in a kind of mountain refuge, an unheated cabin near the river. None of this bothered Richard in the least. He was different, as a man and as an actor. He had no need of the usual comforts. He enjoyed going without the luxuries of his life with Elizabeth. It gave him a sense of adventure. It was freezing that night. I wore every piece of clothing I had, and covered the bed with every blanket I could find, including a carpet. But Richard drank and didn't feel the cold. He'd asked for two bottles of vodka. But all they had was slivovitz, a kind of Yugoslavian grappa made from plums. I tasted it. It was awful. Pure alcohol. In fact, Richard didn't feel at all well the following morning, but he went to work all the same.

Marshal Tito only came on set once, in order to follow the progress of the final battle scene. It was extremely difficult to choreograph. A group of partisans were holding the high ground of a gorge, while German tanks advanced from below and Luftwaffe planes tried to take off and climb above the steep cliffs under partisan fire. It was the decisive moment, the one in which the partisans win the battle. The place was swarming with assistants armed with walkie-talkies, telling hundreds of extras where to go, desperately trying to synchronize the action in the middle of a deafening roar of gunfire and explosions. We shot one full take. Then the director, Stipe Delić, said we'd do it again for the president. Tito arrived, and after some moving ceremonial, Delić shouted, "Action!" The tanks advanced but didn't shoot. The planes flew much higher than required, and didn't fire. Richard observed that this was the same scene we'd just shot, only tamer. Delić promptly came over and explained, "It's for our president's safety." Richard was flabbergasted. "What?! So we're just cannon fodder?!" he exclaimed, and he was never quite so enthusiastic about the movie after that.

We also learned—much later—that shooting had been far more dangerous than we even realized. During one battle scene, it seems the props department forgot to change the live ammo for blanks and a number of soldiers died. Talk about "friendly fire"! In another scene, a helicopter with a cameraman on board hit an overhead cable and exploded in midair. If these stories are true, the incidents occurred when Richard wasn't on set, and the government did an excellent job of keeping them hushed up.

We were relieved to get out of Yugoslavia alive. Richard was paid for his work, but I wasn't. Yugo Films offered to pay me in Yugoslavian currency. But it was impossible to exchange, so I refused. So they simply didn't pay. I later sent Tito a dozen or so photos and informed him that Yugo Films hadn't paid me. He replied, "Thanks for the photos."

I never saw the finished movie, and wasn't sure it ever got out of Yugoslavia. I've since learned that it was one of the most expensive movies ever made in Yugoslavia. It was entered for Best Foreign Language Film at the forty-sixth Academy Awards, but not accepted as a nominee.

The Taylor-Burton circus moved on to Budapest, where Richard was due to play the lead role in *Bluebeard,* a movie directed by Edward Dmytryk that, to my surprise, had nothing to do with pirates (I was thinking of Blackbeard). The executive producer, Ilya Salkind, who went on to do the live-action *Superman* movies of the seventies and eighties, had called me in Paris asking me to show Richard the script. Elizabeth came with us to Budapest, but not to work on the movie. She came to keep a sharp eye on its string of beautiful costars: Raquel Welch, Virna Lisi, Nathalie Delon, Joey Heatherton, Agostina Belli, Marilù Tolo, and Karin Schubert.

I didn't see Raquel arrive on set the first day. Crew members told me she was around, but I couldn't find her. Then, taking lunch in the canteen, I saw a beautiful girl eating all alone at a table. She was wearing jeans, a T-shirt, and no makeup, had a very casual beauty, incredible skin, and one arm in a plaster cast. I went over to find out who she was. "Hi. I'm Gianni. I'm a photographer. What do you do? What's your name?"

She was highly offended by the question, and I had to apologize profusely. The thing is, before you actually met Raquel Welch, you were bound to form a certain idea of her in your mind. I'd expected some high goddess of sex. I couldn't have been more mistaken. For one thing, I couldn't get used to how tiny she was, just five foot one. She was wearing a cast because she'd broken her arm in her last movie, the physically grueling *Kansas City Bomber.* We only exchanged a few words, so I couldn't have been more sur-

Mr. Burton goes to war in *The Battle of Sutjeska*—and me too! Only later did we learn that the production used live ammo in some of the battle sequences. This explosion was so powerful even my camera shook.

prised when, the following day, I got a message from Richard's makeup artist, Ron Berkeley. He said Raquel wanted to go to bed with me and Richard together.

What actually unfolded was quite another story. Around 3 in the morning, I got a call from Richard. He was sobbing, as if heartbroken. Elizabeth and Claudye had left for a costume test, and I was terrified that Richard was crying because their plane had gone down! I dressed and raced upstairs to Richard's apartment. He was drunk and weeping uncontrollably. Opening the door to his bedroom, I saw Raquel Welch passed out on his bed, naked. "Gianni!" Richard sobbed. "I should never have done it! Never!" For a moment I thought he'd killed her. "Richard," I shouted, "what have you done?!" But he just kept whimpering. "I should never have done this to Elizabeth!" I have no idea what really happened. I'd never seen anyone more drunk. He couldn't stay on his feet. I shook Raquel awake, helped her dress, and took her to her room. Richard never told me what did or didn't happen that night, quite possibly because neither he nor Raquel could remember a thing about it.

Bluebeard was a French-Italian production with a mixed-nationality crew, and there was distinct friction between the two groups. Salkind was French and had put the French crew in a good hotel, while the Italians had been stuffed into a cheap, squalid place with a miserable daily allowance. When one of the Italian crew complained about this to me, I passed it on to Richard. He asked me to talk with Salkind immediately and tell him that everyone had to be treated in the same way, with no distinction of nationality. If the Italians weren't happy with their hotel, they could come to ours, the Hotel Intercontinental (which was even more elegant than the one where the French crew was staying). Richard had a lot of power on that set, even more than usual. He was the only reason for the movie's existence. His name had guaranteed the funding, while the costars had only accepted their parts thanks to Richard's presence. And Richard was a very fair person. He was always friendly with the technicians, never placed himself above them, and always insisted on equal treatment for everyone.

Ilya Salkind didn't want to hear about equal treatment. I relayed this to Richard, who sent me back to Salkind. The Italian crew members were to be moved to our hotel and given a suitable allowance. I passed the message on. "We'll do nothing of the sort," said Salkind. "Fine," I replied, "but I've already told the Italians to move to our hotel because that's what Richard has decided." He began shouting and stormed out of his office. I went back to Richard to tell him that maybe we had a problem. "Just go on set with Gaston," he said, referring to our chauffeur, "and tell everyone that today I have a headache. And that I'll probably have one tomorrow too. In fact, I'll keep having a headache until these differences are smoothed out the way I've requested." End of discussion. Everyone got the same allowance; everyone got the same quality of lodging.

When shooting began, Richard and I were both very struck by Raquel's talent. She was neither a doll nor a model but an excellent actress. I wanted to photograph her as the serious actress she was—aware of her sensuality but without concentrating on it exclusively, like most other photographers did. But she already had her own photographer with her, an arrogant English snob by the name of Terry O'Neill. When I asked if Raquel could do something in particular, he'd always reply, "I don't know if she'll have the time." So I decided to ignore him altogether and just go through Richard, asking him to help me get the best compositions, without saying a word to Raquel. After a while she began to get offended and asked me exactly what it was I wanted to do. I explained that my plan was to do a photo to publicize the movie. A friend of mine was painting a portrait of Richard with his eyes fixed on a woman who was supposed to be her. So I needed a good photo to get the desired result. Finally, I took it, and we finished the poster.

This little episode notwithstanding, nothing negative I'd heard about Raquel proved to be true. She wasn't a snob. She wasn't full of herself. On set she was sweet with everyone. And she took her work very seriously. Richard said she had perfect timing and was very easy to work with. Her minute body was perfectly proportioned. Shot from below, she looked like a six-foot model, and her golden skin was truly photogenic. And incidentally—as fate would have it—she very nearly became my mother-in-law. When I moved to Los Angeles in the 1980s, I dated her daughter Tahnee for ages. They were extremely similar in looks, though not in character. It was one of those love stories that began without being planned and—sadly—ended badly.

One of the members of the Hungarian crew was a big guy built like a barn door. He had a huge head and gigantic hands. He'd lift heavy set lights like they were feathers. We decided to play a joke on him. The rest of the crew began to tease him, telling him that the photographer—puny little me—was stronger than he was. For a couple of weeks, every time he came by, he'd touch my arms and laugh. The day of the joke came around, and

Raquel Welch, gorgeous off set; and dressed as a nun with Richard in 1972's *Bluebeard.*

I'll never know what really did or didn't happen between Richard and Raquel in the hotel bedroom that night, but Richard couldn't have been more impressed with her acting chops.

my accomplice told him to put his arms out straight, under my armpits, and try to lift me. He couldn't do it. Everyone then asked me to demonstrate my own strength on him. I pretended to stretch, do some deep breathing, and then, just as he'd done, I put my arms out straight and under his armpits. Without him noticing, however, my companion got behind him, grasped my wrists, and we lifted him off the ground together. He blinked, totally astonished. Every day, for the rest of the shoot, he'd come by and touch my skinny arms, trying to work out how I'd done it. Italian crews were always extraordinary, and working with them was a pleasure. Jokes and pranks were the order of the day.

However, some very serious things happened on that movie too. A number of the Hungarian crew members simply disappeared. We noticed they were invariably the ones who, always in a whisper, complained about the political situation. I talked about it at length with Richard and Elizabeth.

Edward Dmytryk had also directed one of my favorite movies, the 1958 war drama *The Young Lions* starring Marlon Brando, Montgomery Clift, and Dean Martin. In my opinion, however, *Bluebeard* was not the right kind of material for him. The authors had intended a black comedy, but Dmytryk's seriousness turned the movie into something far less enjoyable.

I believe Dymtryk invented a role in the movie for Joey Heatherton just because she was his girlfriend. She brought her choreographer along with her, and one of the crew told me he was very displeased that I was ignoring him. I couldn't understand why. He wasn't an actor; he wasn't the director. I had no idea who he was or why I should photograph him. One day he called me over and asked me to watch him, whereupon he executed a leap and pirouette and landed in exactly the same spot, an effortless, graceful, perfect movement. "I was a star before you were born," he said, informing me that he was George Chakiris, the man who'd played Bernardo, the leader of the Puerto Rican Sharks in *West Side Story*. "Okay," I replied. "So what do you want me to do? Are you a star in this movie?" No. He just looked after Joey's choreography. All the same, he felt I didn't respect him. What could I say? I apologized, told him that I was nobody too, just a photographer paid to take photos of the stars on set.

Elizabeth was very interested in Hungarian social realities that seemed linked to communism in any way. None of us could fail to notice all the young girls who would hang around the hotels where the cast and crew stayed. They were all hoping to have a love story with an Italian or French citizen, marry him, and leave Hungary; and a few did get lucky that way. Meanwhile, the government and pro-government writers didn't look favorably on Elizabeth and Richard's presence in their country, mostly because of their lavish comforts: a Rolls Royce Phantom with driver, a butler, wardrobe assistant, hairdresser, and bodyguard. The decadence and luxury of their lifestyle was all it took for them to be charged with anticommunist behavior, without them making any statement on the subject. So Elizabeth decided to make a statement of her own—and do it her way, naturally. Her fortieth birthday was coming up, so she organized a huge party and invited everyone in Budapest who counted. As well as half the rest of her universe. It was her way of telling the communists that the world should be a free place, and that no one should stop anyone from doing what they wanted.

The day before the party, our hotel went insane. Assistants, catering staff, and hotel employees swarmed all over the place, police were everywhere, journalists staked out the hotel from top to bottom. Crowds gathered in the street outside, amazed at all the private planes circling the sky and landing in Budapest. Guests included Princess Grace Kelly, Roger Moore, Fabergé CEO George Barrie, Alexandre, dozens of actors, actresses,

Elizabeth turns forty and throws a full-on capitalist birthday party in communist Budapest. This is the moment everyone sings "Happy Birthday."

Raquel Welch and Michael Caine enjoy the birthday fun.

Grace Kelly, Elizabeth, and Raquel Welch enjoy a women's moment alone.

artists, and friends, and everyone who was working on the *Bluebeard* set. A string of vans delivered the best food available in Budapest, top-quality catering and alcohol all round. Years later I learned that the Hungarian government had put Elizabeth and Richard on its blacklist. All that glamour offended the communists. Elizabeth had hit her target.

During the party I took a photo of Grace, Elizabeth, and Raquel together, three earthly goddesses: a princess, a superstar, and a sex symbol. The photo highlights wonderfully the difference between the three women. They are all beautiful but in extremely distinct ways: the perfect bearing of a princess, the relaxed elegance of a superstar, the sensuality of a sex bomb.

I wanted to take a posed photo of Elizabeth and Raquel together. But Elizabeth hemmed and hawed about the idea. Besides being possibly the world's greatest sex symbol, Raquel was younger, and Elizabeth had never completely recovered from the unflattering paparazzo photos taken in Mexico. She feared looking jaded and old alongside Raquel. Then one day she turned up on set wearing a jersey with "40" visibly embroidered across her chest while Raquel was dressed as a nun for a scene. They agreed to be photographed like that together. Elizabeth adopted a clearly sarcastic expression, as if to say that the real message on her jersey was, "Sure, I'm

Elizabeth, wearing her age on her chest, grins and bears it.

Italian actress Virna Lisi had possibly the most perfect face I've ever photographed—and also one of the kindest souls.

forty. So what? I'm still the biggest star in the world." Maybe she thought only a sense of humor could help her deal with being compared to Raquel. But the photo visibly demonstrates that she was quite wrong. And Raquel knew it, because she insisted on seeing the photo before I did anything with it.

Claudye and I were already friends with another of the costars, Virna Lisi, as well as her husband, Franco Pesci, a successful real-estate agent. We often saw them in Rome. Virna's face was an image of perfection. It was incredibly symmetrical. Once, as a joke, I printed two copies of the same close-up, one normal and one upside down. I cut them in half, pairing a normal half with an upside down one. There was no difference. Most people have a better side, one profile that's better than another. Not Virna. Her face was so perfect that sometimes it was hard to photograph. It was difficult to make any sensuality emerge from such perfect beauty. I only managed to capture her once. As friends, we were too close for me to provoke her in the way I did with other subjects. I felt intimidated photographing her. I feared that any attempt to stimulate her might be misunderstood.

Virna did everything she could to make it in American cinema. But her beauty always got in her way. She became famous for a commercial she did for a brand of toothpaste. She had two dumb lines, after which a voice-over spoke the slogan that would become a catchphrase: "With a mouth that beautiful, she can say whatever she wants." The commercial got her a role as a blue-eyed temptress alongside Jack Lemmon in *How to Murder Your Wife*. The movie had a famous scene where she emerges from a cake. She became very popular in America, but she never managed to shake off the stereotype of a blonde seductress. Hollywood producers were hoping Virna would fill the void left by Marilyn Monroe. But that wasn't what she wanted for her career, and she refused to do that. Eventually she returned to Italy. When a woman is that beautiful, often her skill as an actress takes second place. It took years before she got the recognition she deserved. She was absolutely extraordinary in the 1994 French period movie *Queen Margot,* directed by Petrice Chéreau, where her performance won her a César Award. Throughout her career she displayed unfailing professionalism. What's more, she stayed faithful to the same man and was never involved in the slightest scandal. A true lady. In this business, you don't meet many of them.

Bluebeard was the first movie where, besides being the special photographer, I also worked on the production side. I'd proposed the movie to Richard in the first place. I'd procured a role in it for Virna Lisi. We'd needed another female character, so I'd suggested another friend, Marilù Tolo, who was popular and well known to television audiences (though less fortunate in cinema). There's a title that comes with the job I did: "producer." But Salkind didn't give me a cent, nor any credit.

A few days before the end of shooting I got a request from *Playboy*. They wanted me to do a big layout with all the actresses from the movie: "The *Bluebeard* Women." It would have been fantastic, and Salkind was enthusiastic because he saw it as a big publicity vehicle. But I knew that Virna would never accept. Raquel, maybe. But never entirely naked. Plus, she would have expected a lot of money. In the end we only managed to get Nathalie Delon, Marilù Tolo, and two German girls playing minor roles. It was weird photographing nudes, and of course, *Playboy* wanted very explicit photos. I thought that playing with light and shadow would make images of a naked woman more interesting. Now you see it, now you don't. You'd see one thing in some shots, a glimpse of lingerie in others. My style was a long way away from the magazine's usual one, and I didn't want to adapt myself to the model that the editor in chief kept asking for. I did what I felt was best. We had no particular agreement about the style of the photos. In the end, however, *Playboy* only published a few shots, with no vulgar or explicit nudes.

Once the movie was over, I returned to Paris. The *Playboy* experience had been so disappointing that I decided to test myself with something ambitious, more in tune with my style. I created a wonderfully beautiful layout with Virna Lisi as my model entitled "From Eve's Days to Our Own." I had Alberto De Rossi, the best makeup artist in the world, following my instructions. The best hairdresser, Alexandre de Paris. The best French stylists, Lanvin, Chanel, Dior, Yves Saint Laurent, André Courrèges, Emanuel Ungaro, and Pierre Cardin, who all dressed her exactly as I wished. Virna flew from Rome to Paris, and we took the photos near Alexandre's country house, the same place where four years earlier I'd got married. I took the whole layout to Diane Freeland, the *Vogue* editor, who said, "Gianni, I can't publish these. What would I do next month?" She had a set standard, which she didn't want to exceed. An example of how, as I said earlier, a photographer often has to repress his or her inner artist in order to satisfy the needs of a client or editor. This time I'd tried to push beyond myself, do something important, express my own vision in something that had nothing to do with either Elizabeth or Richard. But it didn't work out.

I caught up with Elizabeth and Richard in Munich, where they were shooting a two-part television movie *Divorce His, Divorce Hers*. The story line examined the conflicting emotions felt by a couple whose eighteen-year marriage has frayed beyond repair, and I couldn't help hearing Elizabeth and Richard's own arguments in there somewhere. I never read the script, so I don't know how much of the dialogue was coincidence, improvisation, or premonition. Personally, I rarely heard them arguing in real life, even though living in the same house made that inevitable at times. Elizabeth's voice would become shrill and fast and she wouldn't stop talking; Richard would slip a word in here or there whenever he could.

Like every couple the world over, they had their difficult times. But they were also great at making up and, of course, enjoyed some options that were quite unavailable to most couples. I remember, for instance, the day Richard called me urgently from the Grand Hotel in Rome, asking me to take him to the Bulgari jewelry store. "I must get Elizabeth to forgive me," he explained. I found him already waiting outside when I got to the hotel on my motorbike. "Come on," he said, jumping on the back. "Let's go

Elizabeth and Richard working on the 1973 TV movie *Divorce His, Divorce Hers,* a film, as chance would have it, shot shortly before their own dramatic divorce.

before she wakes up." I can't remember what the visit cost him, but it sure wasn't nickels and dimes. At any rate, it won him a full pardon.

Jewels and jewelry were, of course, a famous part of Elizabeth and Richard's life, which meant they became part of mine as well—sometimes too much so. We did a shoot in London's Dorchester Hotel featuring Elizabeth and her amazing priceless collection, after which we were due to fly to Rome. But given the public exposure of such tantalizing loot, everyone was terrified at the possibility of robbery en route. So Richard came up with a solution: he and Elizabeth would take my cameras in their bags, and I'd take the jewels in mine, travel separately as an anonymous citizen, and land in Rome's Fiumicino airport, leaving them to arrive to a full media fanfare in Ciampino, south of the city. Have you ever sat inconspicuously alone at some major airport, millions of dollars' worth of someone else's jewelry in your bag, watching the departure board scroll exotic alternative destinations: Rio de Janeiro, Tenerife, Johannesburg, Bangkok, Hong Kong? I did, musing on a string of gangland options. Then I caught my flight to Rome, landed, and was asked to open my case. The whole thing took forever, and eventually Richard had to come sort out the situation. But then we had to stage a full press conference. The jewels had become even more of a security risk. I had to stand up and lie, telling the whole world that actually the baubles were all copies. Damn jewels! Those customs guys were so pissed off by the whole affair that they stopped me every time for at least a year after that.

The most heated arguments between Elizabeth and Richard always broke out when one or the other wasn't working, sparked by fear that their success or their relationship might become unbalanced. But it was increasingly Richard who sat watching Elizabeth from the sidelines. Which is why, at a certain point, Elizabeth started wanting to be known as Elizabeth Taylor-Burton, out of consideration for Richard. She knew he'd always been bothered by the idea of being desired only thanks to her, while she'd begun to resent the fact that she was no longer as much in demand as she had been after *Cleopatra*. Seeing the pair of them on-screen together was no longer a novelty. I realized all this from the drop in publication of my own photos of them together, compared to an unchanged interest in photos of Elizabeth alone. It was she who people wanted to see: in costume, wearing designer clothes, with her children. The public wanted Elizabeth. Requests for photos of both of them together, or Richard alone, began to drop off in the early seventies. Much of this could be attributed to the fact that the movies they were doing together were short on both artistic value and economic return. But Elizabeth was bigger than any box office. The success or otherwise of a movie didn't even scratch her superstar status. Richard, on the other hand, didn't enjoy such luxury.

Elizabeth and her jewels, a smoldering combination. I'm sure she and Richard must be reveling somewhere over the results of the December 2013 Christie's auction in New York: her collection sold for ten times its estimated value, raking in a cool $116 million.

Richard and Elizabeth kiss in a scene from *Divorce His, Divorce Hers*.

He had never been so at ease in the limelight as Elizabeth. At heart, he was a simple man. He hated the way that celebrity had overshadowed his acting, which he took very seriously. But understanding Richard's frustrations and insecurities didn't help much when dealing with his drunken explosions of repressed rage. Or worse still, having to watch him damage himself when, barely able to stand, he'd open another bottle. The easiest way to provoke Richard's rage was to call him Mr. Taylor, and a lot of people did just that, sometimes behind his back, sometimes from the safe distance of a newspaper article, and sometimes to his face, just to see his reaction. Elizabeth and Richard loved each other deeply, but somehow they couldn't help being self-destructive.

Divorce His, Divorce Hers was a small, penniless production. Elizabeth and Richard had agreed to do it only because one of the producers was their friend John Heyman, a man still very much in the business who—among many other claims to fame—is now credited with having almost single-handedly created "structured financing" in the movie industry. But he didn't have much financial backing that time. The production could afford so little publicity that I was only hired for two days. I spent the rest of my time working out of the Four Seasons, doing a string of fashion shoots.

Richard and Marcello Mastroianni with director George Pan Cosmatos shooting *Massacre in Rome,* a big hit in Italy but not abroad.

One day the Italian-Greek director George Pan Cosmatos came to show me a script of a movie he wanted to do, originally entitled *Retaliation* in Italian and later released in English as *Massacre in Rome.* It was about the infamous Nazi massacre that took place in the Ardeatine caves outside

Rome near the end of World War II when, after partisans killed 33 Germans, the Gestapo took a revenge multiplied by ten: 330 random victims were rounded up and slaughtered. To this day, whether the Vatican stood by and did nothing remains a controversial question. George was having trouble finding anyone to produce the project and thought that I, being Roman, might appreciate it better and bring Richard in on the project. Which is what happened. Richard didn't know the story but became interested when I explained it, coming with me to see the memorial monument that now marks the site. He ended up playing the lead role of Gestapo chief Herbert Kappler, the man responsible for the killings, and costarring with Marcello Mastroianni. The movie packed theaters in Italy, but didn't do well internationally.

Almost everything else in my life and career vanished from my mind when I came home one day and Claudye greeted me with fantastic news: she was pregnant. I felt my father smiling down on me. Even though he was no longer with us, I knew he was happy. I was so excited at the idea of becoming a father, so happy to finally give my mother a grandchild. It was one of those rare moments in my life that I truly felt was mine. Claudye and I left our house in Paris and moved to Rome in order to be close to my family. We rented a penthouse in Parioli—Rome's most exclusive neighborhood—and, while I kept working, Claudye started preparing for our new family and our new life.

Chapter 11

Another Funeral

Shortly after we moved to Parioli, I turned twenty-nine and decided to throw a big party to celebrate all the marvelous things that Claudye and I were living through. As a gift, the Countess Giovanna Agusta—with whom I'd long since made up—hired the incredible and popular steel band, Los Paraguayos, to play at the party. Once everyone had arrived—Elizabeth, Richard, all our friends and relatives—we had two hundred people eating, drinking, and enjoying music on our enormous terrace overlooking Rome. A lot of prominent government officials and ambassadors lived in the same area, and I guess around midnight one must have grown tired of all the noise because someone called the police. A very arrogant officer appeared at the door, threatening to arrest everyone on the spot. I asked him to wait and went to call one of my guests, Nino Alagna, Rome's deputy chief of police, who happened to be dancing at that moment with Elizabeth. He came straight down and told the officer to vanish. "What do you want? Get out of here!"

A little while later, two even more arrogant officers arrived, this time from the more serious Carabinieri force. They wanted me to stop the party and get everyone lined up with their identification. I was going to be arrested and fined. Again I asked them to wait a moment while I went to get Nino. They refused to even address him directly, insisting on knowing who he was. That was easy: "I'm merely the chief of Rome's police head-quarters," he said, rising to his authority. "What do you want here? This is a private party. Get out and don't let me see you again. Go! Go! Go!" And go they did. It helps having friends in high places. It definitely helps having them dancing in your house. I'm not sure quite when our party did finally wind down, but it was a great night.

Meanwhile, with Richard accepting the lead role in *Massacre in Rome*, the movie got the funding it needed. Once again, however, I got no credit.

Cosmatos never said a word to producer Carlo Ponti about how I'd been the one to convince Richard to do the movie. And if that wasn't enough to make me feel bad, he proceeded to tell me that the production couldn't afford to hire me as special photographer. He said I cost too much.

So I refused to do any kind of set photo, but I went to the set anyway to visit Richard and his costar, my old friend Marcello Mastroianni. I enjoyed watching their contrasting acting styles. Between one take and the next, Richard would sit down with the script in hand, studying the next scene, rehearsing it, smoking a cigarette. "Marcello is incredible," he'd say. "He finishes a scene, sits down, and goes to sleep. When the director calls him, he gets up and says, 'What do you want me to do?'" Marcello was a fascinating man. He had class and a beautiful presence. Women went crazy for him. He never considered himself an actor. He was just himself.

Richard, on the other hand, came from the old school of English theater, the Old Vic. He always prepared. I don't think he ever loved cinema as much as he loved theater. When he was with his old friends Rex Harrison and Peter O'Toole, all they ever talked about was theater. Playing a role in continuity for a stage production is totally different from doing cinema. Movies aren't filmed scene by scene but shot by shot, and rarely in chronological order, often for budgetary reasons. Great as he was on-screen, Richard had an incredible stage presence. Over the years I heard him give many readings and speeches, and saw him act onstage in *Equus*. What a voice. He could project it anywhere. Whether you were sitting in the front or back row of a theater, you got the same performance from Richard. And it was hard for him to find a movie that utilized those theatrical gifts to the full. It's probably no accident that all his best screen performances—*Who's Afraid of Virginia Woolf?*, *Becket*, *Anne of the Thousand Days*—were all adapted from plays written for the theater. Richard would often tell me that he earned too much from movies to be able to stop doing them. The houses, cars, staff, me—the last wheel on the cart, as we say in Italian—all cost money, a lot of it. "You have to work," Richard would exclaim. And he always took his work very seriously.

I, on the other hand, wasn't taking my work quite as seriously as I once had. Sure, I was pissed off at Cosmatos for having minimized my role in realizing *Massacre in Rome,* but not to the extent of complaining to Richard about it. He could have got me credited with a single phone call, or landed me the job of special photographer. But I didn't ask because I didn't really care, something I felt more and more frequently after my father died. That kind of work didn't attract me as much as it once had. A couple years earlier, Brian Hutton had called to offer me work on *Kelly's Heroes*. Any other photographer would have died to work with that cast: Clint Eastwood, Donald Sutherland, Carroll O'Connor, Telly Savalas, Don Rickles. I turned him down. I wasn't interested. I got to the point where in order to really be able to commit myself, I had to feel I was absolutely indispensable; otherwise I just couldn't give my best.

That mood had been there when I'd done a few days' work on the set of *The Assassination of Trotsky*. I just couldn't get excited. It was a minor production about a delicate issue and received little publicity. I'd met one of the costars, Alain Delon, in Paris, working on Jean-Pierre Melville's *The Red Circle,* but I was totally uninterested in his on-off girlfriend, Romy Schneider, who was costarring alongside him. And it would have been a pleasure to avoid having anything to do with the director, my old friend Joseph Losey. However, since Richard was playing Trotsky, I felt obliged to go, putting my own professional dissatisfaction to one side.

Everyone was delighted to see me when I turned up on set—except the set photographer, Sergio Strizzi. When I arrived in a hot new car, well

Alain Delon playing Frank Jackson in Joseph Losey's little-publicized 1972 movie *The Assassination of Trotsky.*

Richard ages to play the soon-to-be-assassinated Leon Trotsky.

dressed and brandishing the best equipment on the market, I couldn't help noticing a flash of envy in Sergio's eyes, even though we were friends. But I was used to that by now, so I decided to play a joke on him. I was sitting next to Richard showing him my new light meter, a Lunasix, while waiting for my assistant, Albertino, to get back from the car, where I'd sent him to get more film. Sergio was watching us while Richard, who had also noticed how envious he was, happily played along with the joke. Holding my Lunasix in front of my mouth, I said into it, "Albertino! Get me two rolls of 35 mm. Did you get that?" Sergio couldn't help intervening. "Knock it off!" he said. "That's a Lunasix, not a phone." Five seconds later, Albertino came back with exactly that film. Sergio was stunned. "Wow!" he exclaimed. "Can you even call home on that?" "Sure," I said. "I'll call my wife now. Let's hope she's free." Pushing a button on the light meter, I pretended to wait for the call signal. "It's engaged," I said, after a suitable pause. "I'll call back and let you know." Okay, maybe it's not quite so funny in the age of the iPhone, but it was hilarious back then.

For the shoot, the production had built a replica of Trotsky's residence on a plot of land just outside Rome. One night locals from a nearby village slipped into the place to steal equipment and set props. The production promptly built a guardhouse and hired a night watchman. He was a short, fat man afflicted with gigantism, with an enormous head and hands. They enlarged the windows of the guardhouse and built a raised platform inside. Now, when anyone approached the set, they'd see this giant of a man looming over everything. The production then proceeded to parade him through the village to intimidate the population. They put him inside a huge car on a pile of cushions so high that he had to bend his neck or his head would touch the ceiling. Then they pulled up in front of the bar in the main square, where the fake giant announced over a loudspeaker, "From now on, anyone who comes close to the movie set will have to deal with me. Okay? Do I make myself clear?" Hearing all the noise, people started coming out into the street only to see this terrifying, menacing monster who could barely fit into the car. One of the crew then got out and addressed the gathering crowd: "We've had a few problems on the set. This rather dangerous man is now our night watchman." Shouting from the car, the guard added, "Everyone had a good look, have you?" Silence fell over the crowd, and not a single theft ever occurred again in Trotsky's house. The fake giant was actually a really nice guy. He wouldn't have hurt a fly. Italian workers' sense of irony and wit is without equal in the world.

I did the shots that the production had asked for in a couple of days and then left. I'd never felt so unsatisfied with myself or my work. Something was blocked, and that something was me. I had no one to measure myself against anymore. Year after year I was getting voted "Best Photographer of the Year," author of the best photo, the most widely published photo. I had more money than my father had ever seen in his life. I earned more in a day than he had in a month. I'd photographed sovereigns and movie stars, heads of state and top models. Two of the most famous people in the world were my friends. Scores of photographers would have killed to enjoy my success, as I'd had a chance to notice on the *Trotsky* set. And yet I felt lost. What else could I achieve as a photographer? What else did I want to achieve? In reality, I'd barely debuted in show business, yet I felt I'd already made it. I had to decide whether to sit back on my laurels or keep accepting my father's challenge and push myself further.

I was increasingly interested in cinema from the production point of view. I still felt very insecure and ill at ease among those people. But I'd had fun getting Richard and my friends together on *Bluebeard*, talking about the cast with the director and producer, even smoothing over ridiculous squabbles between French and Italian members of the crew. People kept passing me scripts under the table, hoping I could interest Elizabeth and Richard. It gave me a chance to study their structure and appreciate what made a script attractive to a movie star. As a photographer, my job was to bring the best out in my subjects. Would I be capable of doing the same on a much broader scale, in the context of an entire movie and not just a single photo? While I reflected on what direction my future might take, I made myself concentrate on my work, accepting a string of fashion layouts and studio shoots whenever I wasn't busy on Elizabeth and Richard's various sets.

Federico Fellini was one frequent visitor to my studio. He'd sit on the balcony and watch me photograph actresses and models. He complained that the women I photographed were too thin. In those days he was writing *Amarcord*—a movie that would win him an Oscar for Best Foreign Language film—and he kept trying to convince me to act in one of his movies. "Gianni!" he'd say, with that thin, nasal voice of his, which I can still hear in my mind. "You shouldn't be a photographer. You should be an actor!" One day I sent him a message to say I'd be photographing a beautiful voluptuous woman, Andréa Ferréol. She was the actress who would star alongside Marcello Mastroianni in *The Grande Bouffe*, a French-Italian movie about four friends who gather in a villa for a weekend for the express purpose of eating themselves to death. Fellini dropped everything and got to the studio in a flash. Andréa was his ideal kind of woman—shapely, voluptuous, very sensual. Fellini installed himself on the balcony as usual, and during a break, I went to talk with him. "Why don't you try to get her to uncover herself a little more?" he asked. Andréa wasn't shy and posed with her breast more visible. I photographed her under Fellini's secret but attentive gaze. "There!" he said, when I went to check on him during the next break. "There's a real woman for you. I'll leave and come back in ten minutes. Then you can introduce me."

Shortly afterward, I agreed to work with Brian Hutton on the set of *Night Watch*, starring Elizabeth and Laurence Harvey. It was a small production, shot in London on a very tight schedule. Elizabeth had suggested Brian to the producer, Martin Poll. She liked him as a director and found she worked well with him. During shooting, I noticed that Brian always wore exactly the same jersey, the same shirt, the same pants, and the same orthopedic shoes, every day. He must have had dozens of each. Elizabeth's son, Christopher Wilding, was on set in those days and asked Brian if he ever took his shoes off. "Only when I wash my feet," he said. Chris gri-

The strange quirks of life! Two cronies I never photographed together, Marcello Mastroianni and Federico Fellini on the set of *Intervista*. (Photo by my friend and mentor Emilio Lari, a great photographer of cinema whose book about the Beatles has just been published in the United States.)

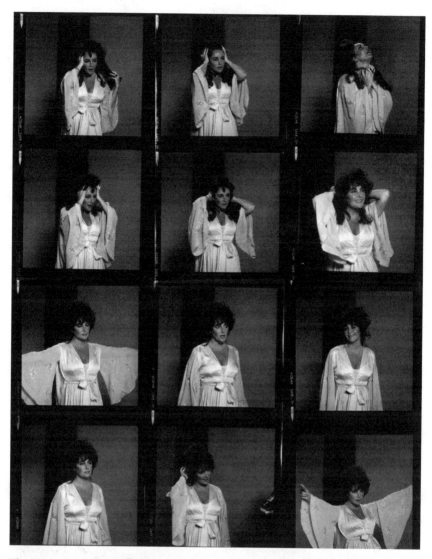

The general public usually sees only finished, authorized photos of a star. Here's a string of never-published photos of Elizabeth trying out costumes during the filming of *Night Watch*.

maced, and Brian went on, "Sure, once a month. The socks are hard to peel off because they get stuck to my feet." He had a weird sense of humor and Elizabeth loved him for it.

I realized almost immediately that there was very little I could do on

Elizabeth with director Brian Hutton on the set of his 1973 thriller *Night Watch*.

that movie as a photographer. Laurence Harvey was a nice guy, very gener-ous, a great partygoer who loved good wine and good food. But he wasn't very interesting. He was flat in real life, just as he was in his movies. This was supposed to be a horror movie. But it wasn't. I tried to do my best, and I think I succeeded with this lovely shot of Elizabeth looking out the win-dow while rain runs down the glass outside.

Ever the romantic, Elizabeth loved this shot I took of her gazing out a rain-drenched window.

Welsh to his roots, Richard takes us to visit an ancient menhir near his hometown in Wales.

Elizabeth wasn't in very good health, and Laurence got seriously sick and had to spend some weeks in the hospital. While he was recovering, the movie's insurance kept paying Claudye and me because we were under contract. Effectively that meant we enjoyed a wonderful holiday in Saint-Tropez for free.

Before doing *Night Watch,* Elizabeth and I had gone to work with Richard on a movie version of the great Dylan Thomas's radio drama *Under Milk Wood,* a production he was gifting to Oxford University. Everyone worked for free—Richard, Elizabeth, Peter O'Toole, and the rest of the cast and crew, me included. With shooting under way, we took a train from London to Richard's country house in Wales. I took Elizabeth's son, Michael, along with me as an assistant. The whole place felt very sad to me. We didn't get a glimpse of sunlight. The weather was gray, damp, and strange, even more depressing than London. But I met Richard's brothers and sisters, and we had some wonderful times down the pub. I never saw Richard so relaxed.

Peter O'Toole was a really nice guy. He'd look at me, say some word in Italian, and then smile. A while later, he'd look at me again, say another word in Italian, and smile. I began wondering whether he really was Italian. He adored joking around on set, even though he was possibly the only person who understood his jokes. His relaxing presence may have been an

Elizabeth and others rehearse for *Under Milk Wood,* the 1972 film version of the famous Dylan Thomas work that Richard gave as a gift to his alma mater, Oxford University.

influence. Or the fact that the project was private and small scale. Whatever the reason, in that movie, Elizabeth appeared more sensual than in any other.

Elizabeth loved working on that movie. It was Richard's independent project. He'd known Dylan Thomas personally. So there was no production office, no distributor to satisfy, no outside pressures. Just a movie they wanted to do. In my opinion, Elizabeth felt truly free to act and think of nothing else. It was also the only set where I saw Richard get truly jealous. There was a scene where Elizabeth and Peter were in bed together, laughing, joking, and having fun. Peter may have been one of his best friends, but Richard didn't take his eye off him for a moment—and in the end he even climbed into the bed himself.

Being with old friends in his favorite bars unfortunately brought out the worst in Richard. One night he disappeared for hours. Around 3 in the morning, Elizabeth began to worry. She figured he was probably still in the King's Pub—way after closing time, of course—and asked if I could possibly go and bring him back to the hotel. I found Richard with Laurence

225

A wildly jealous Richard improvises a threesome with Elizabeth and Peter O'Toole during the shooting of *Under Milk Wood,* principally to make sure Peter keeps his hands under control.

Harvey, Rex Harrison, and Peter O'Toole, all of them drunk. Richard stared at me and said, "What do you want? An autograph?" He was so drunk he couldn't recognize me. I dragged him to the car and took him, Laurence, and Peter home. Rex stayed behind with someone else. Richard never once apologized or thanked me for going out to find him. And the following morning, when he hauled himself out of bed, he behaved as if nothing had happened. I don't know whether or not he had any memory of the previous night's events.

Richard's dark side usually came out elsewhere, far from Elizabeth, when he was on his own with his problems and tried to drown them in alcohol. When Richard decided to go on a binge, trying to stop him only made him angrier. I did what I could to keep him out of serious trouble, and I kept him company if he wanted to talk. I was the guy who was supposed to stay sober and get him back safe and sound to his hotel or the *Kalizma* when he could no longer drag himself to the next pub or bar. I was his active listener during those demon-tormented nights. Richard's friendship was so important to me that I rarely refused when he asked me to go out with him. Unlike Elizabeth, who knew how to make everyone feel at ease, Richard was more detached. I always hoped that on these occasions we'd finally have a chance to talk and get to know each other better. But watching him get drunk every other night was definitely not the best way to make me feel close to him. He'd invariably drag me off to bar after bar, where I'd sit and watch him torture himself for long, painful hours before at last I helped him crawl into a taxi.

Those nights with Richard made me realize that people are just people—deep down, no one is better or worse than anyone else. Seeing Richard that way made him more accessible to me, more human. In Wales he quoted to me a famous passage from Shakespeare's *Julius Caesar,* which over the years I often asked him to repeat:

There is a tide in the affairs of men.
Which, taken at the flood, leads on to fortune;
Omitted, all the voyage of their life
Is bound in shallows and in miseries.

As a photographer, I was always trying to capture people's most genuinely human aspects, those moments that reveal one's true nature, whether it was Richard, Elizabeth, or any of my other subjects. First as people, and then as celebrities. With Richard and Elizabeth, fame and fortune were true distractions, a costume they wore in public. If I'd never seen Richard hit rock bottom, or Elizabeth be so tender and loving with her children, I'd never have learned to look beyond the glamour of their lives and tell the truth about them with my photos. I'd have become exactly what my father didn't want me to become: the latest in a line of paparazzi jumping out of the bushes to steal photos for gossip-hungry glossy magazines. A fascinating actress can see herself on the front cover of magazines around the world. But when she gets home and looks in a mirror, all she sees is a woman, a wife, a mother. On the other hand, a famous male actor is always and only a man. And he wants to tell the whole world when things don't go the way he wants them to.

One day Elizabeth came out with a comment that I'll never forget: "There's no better deodorant than success." I'm not sure if I'll ever quite know whether that's true or not. Who knows what odor the sweat of success has? All I can say is that I've witnessed Elizabeth and Richard producing so much all by themselves, and with their own sweat and labor creating a living for so many families and, as a result, almost a whole economy of their own.

Leaving his private life to one side, Richard was always a total professional on set. He rarely had to repeat a scene twice; he was convinced that repetition introduced a damaging mechanical aspect to the spontaneity of his performance. I was always struck by the intensity and energy of his acting. The idea that on-screen genius and a dark character somehow inevitably go together is an awful Hollywood cliché. Worse still is the tendency to idealize the self-destructive spirit that I saw in Richard, as if drinking that way was somehow praiseworthy. Almost every great actor and actress I've met has had problems. But the best, the ones that manage a long and stable career, all find some kind of balance, a certain peace. Sadly, I believe Richard never found that. And despite what anyone may say or think, drinking made him worse, not better.

Shortly before Christmas 1972, the director Larry Peerce and producer Dominick Dunne went to Rome to talk to Elizabeth about their next project, *Ash Wednesday*. Yet another movie—how many was that in just one year? Eight. It seems Elizabeth and Richard would say yes to pretty much any movie they were offered.

Anyway, Larry and Dominick threw a big dinner party in the Grand Hotel, with a lovely atmosphere, good food, and fun all round. The main topic of conversation was the challenge that the movie's makeup presented. Elizabeth was supposed to play an older woman whose husband was falling out of love with her. So she decides, in secret, to undergo major plastic surgery. What they needed was some way to make Elizabeth look old and ugly and then shoot a convincing scene of the plastic surgery operation.

At one point, Larry asked me to change seats and come and sit by him. "Gianni," he said, "don't take this personally, but I don't want you as photographer on this movie. I'm trying to find out who the new photographer is who recently did a shoot on plastic surgery. It'll be really useful for the filming." I thought he was pulling my leg at first. Then I realized he was serious. I'd done the shoot he was talking about. Dr. Rudolph Trouques, who'd cured my "cancer," was also a plastic surgeon who'd developed a way to perform breast lifts with just a simple incision under the patient's arm. In those days you'd see women on the beach with huge scars on enormous fake breasts. Face-lifts and other plastic surgery operations were becoming fashionable, and I was interested to see how they were done. I photographed a number of operations, including a full face-lift performed on

Alexandre, from beginning to end. Trouques pulled his face up so high that, for the rest of his life, Alexandre had to shave behind his ears. On another occasion, Trouques asked me to photograph a reconstruction, which he did for free. He'd met a guy at a gas station with seriously burned hands, a former race car mechanic. Trouques took nerve tissue from other parts of the man's body and used it to reconstruct his hands. When he finally removed the bandages and stitches, the man couldn't open his hands. Trouques just slapped him and shouted, "Open those damn hands!" And he did. It was an incredible scene. Trouques later fixed my brother Renato's crooked nose. But I kept well away from that one. I couldn't bear the idea of seeing my own brother's nose being whacked with a hammer. It would feel like taking the blow myself.

Anyway, Larry clearly had no idea that I'd been the author of that shoot, so I told him to come to my studio the next day. "Give me a chance to prove I'm the right guy for your movie," I said. And I did just that. When he saw all my plastic surgery photos he was delighted. He'd finally found the photographer he'd been looking for and was fascinated by every detail of the operations. "Okay!" he said. "This is the sequence for the credits: your photos!" I suggested he try filming a real operation. I called Rudolph and we found a woman who looked sufficiently like Elizabeth who, in exchange for getting it free, authorized us to film her undergoing a full face-lift. I went to Paris to film the operation myself. They used my footage as the credits sequence, so I got my first experience as a director in the bargain.

Making Elizabeth look old, ugly, and wrinkled was proving much harder than expected. They tried different techniques and a string of makeup artists, including Richard's own faithful Ronnie Berkeley. But to no avail. I, with my photos, kept condemning every attempt. Elizabeth understood immediately where I was heading. "Don't even mention that name!" she shouted. So I didn't. After all, I was only the photographer. But when yet another makeup test didn't work, she finally shouted, "All right, then, if you insist! But you call him, not me!" At that point, Larry gave me permission to call Alberto De Rossi. Elizabeth hadn't spoken a word to him since he threw that sponge in her face on the *Cleopatra* set. "You must be crazy!" said Alberto when I called. "That woman hates me!" "No, Alberto," I replied, "I assure you, she adores you. And everyone knows you're the only one in the world who can do this." Eventually I persuaded him. When he got to the set he was terrified to meet Elizabeth. Alberto was

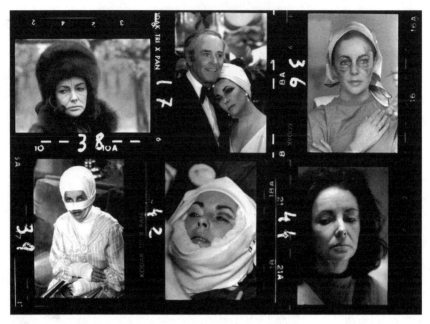

Elizabeth with Henry Fonda in the 1972 Larry Peerce movie *Ash Wednesday*. I photographed real-life plastic surgery operations before Elizabeth took the part.

a huge guy, but on our way to Elizabeth's dressing room he kept trying to hide behind me. We stepped inside. Elizabeth stood up and exclaimed, "Alberto!" He replied, "Elizabeth!" And the pair of them hugged like old friends, everything forgiven.

Alberto asked me to go with him to meet Dominick, the producer. When we got to his office, he thanked Alberto for having come at such short notice and said, "Listen, I know this is Paramount, but we've got a big problem. We've spent so much on makeup trials that I don't know what I'll be able to pay you for your work." I translated and Alberto replied, "Tell him he can give me what he wants." I reminded him that we were talking about Paramount here. But he insisted, so I passed on his reply to Dominick, who stood up enthusiastically, shook his hand, and thanked him. Then Alberto added, "Tell him I'll do the makeup in the morning and then I'll go home." I translated and Dominick replied, "Alberto, that's impossible. You have to stay with Elizabeth all day." I again translated, and Alberto got serious: "Tell this son of a bitch that if I have to stay here, I can't eat. Because if I eat, I have to take a nap. And if I can't eat and can't take a nap, then this asshole had better fucking pay me!" I gave a rough translation, and Dominick promptly conceded to Alberto the fee he deserved.

It had been ages since I'd found myself so interested in a job. I felt I was contributing personally, collaborating seriously on the movie. I made the sequences of the operation and post-op as realistic as possible. Larry even tried to entice me to play the part of a playboy in the movie, but I turned him down and the role went to Helmut Berger. I took some magnificent shots of Elizabeth, both natural and when she was made up as an older woman. I got some great ones of Henry Fonda too, who turned out to be the perfect gentleman everyone expected. I spoke a lot with Henry about our mutual friend, Sergio Leone. We agreed that Sergio had given an extraordinary demonstration of his creativity when, in *Once upon a Time in the West,* he took an actor accustomed to playing a hero and deprived him of his heroism. Henry and I even found time to spend a couple of weekends being tourists around Rome and Venice. It was an exhilarating time for me. I was involved in my work, I'd bonded with a legend like Henry Fonda, and I had a child on the way. I was happy for the first time since my father had died. Paramount Pictures even sent me a thank-you letter, something that had never happened before.

Then things changed. Richard and Elizabeth began to argue more than usual. When they were both working, they had less time to do so. But if only one of them was at work, as now, then things got worse. Shooting kept getting postponed. The movie was set in a ski resort. We spent weeks in Cortina d'Ampezzo waiting for snow. It was one of the world's most exclusive resorts. Consequently, besides Elizabeth and the other stars working on the movie, the place was packed with wealthy vacationers. The crew hated being stuck in the middle of all those snobs, working their butts off while rich kids strolled around at their pleasure. Plus there was a lot of dead time, delays and waiting. Shooting never seemed to end. Claudye had stayed behind in Rome because doctors said the altitude wouldn't be good for the baby. So I'd go home every weekend to be with her.

Richard hated all this standing around. He was already on edge because he had no other offers in sight. Elizabeth was working. I was working. He was alone in the hotel all day doing nothing. I don't believe I saw him sober once in those six months. He and Elizabeth argued often. And the enforced days off due to lack of snow didn't help things in the least. There was little else to do but sit around in the hotel all day and drink.

Elizabeth gives Larry Peerce the finger on the *Ash Wednesday* set. It was the only time I ever saw her lose control at work. They soon made up. Meanwhile, I got this splendid shot.

There's always some truth in a cliché. The popular image of Elizabeth and Richard drunk and arguing all the time is an exaggeration. But *Ash Wednesday* contributed to creating that stereotype.

During the filming of that movie was the one and only time I saw either of them let drinking affect their work. Elizabeth had a scene to shoot in a Cortina hotel with a lot of extras. She had downed significantly more than one too many the previous night and was late. Larry was furious. When she did finally arrive on set, he'd already sent the crew and extras home. He started shouting, to which she simply replied, "Dear Larry, I think I'm going to take today off and just relax." Then she gave him the finger, spun around, and returned to her apartment.

Richard came down shortly afterward—Larry hurriedly invented some excuse to leave the set before he arrived. A couple of hours later Larry apologized to everyone and we shot the scene. Meanwhile, I got that still much-revered photo.

When I got a call from our doctor to say that Claudye was about to give birth, I flew straight to Rome to be there for the event. But our daughter was born dead. By the time I got to Claudye's bedside, everything was

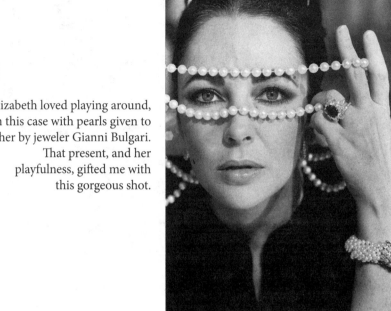

Elizabeth loved playing around, in this case with pearls given to her by jeweler Gianni Bulgari. That present, and her playfulness, gifted me with this gorgeous shot.

already over. My mother had seen the baby and told me she was beautiful, bigger than usual, with thick red curls and long fingernails. We named her Bruna, in honor of my father. My mother-in-law didn't want us to do an autopsy.

Going to another funeral was a devastating experience, especially under such circumstances. Instead of the joyful announcement of a birth, you find yourself communicating news of a death and burying someone you've never seen alive. I was worried about Claudye. She'd nourished that baby in her womb for nine months, and now the child was gone. I stayed home as long as possible, but eventually had to get back to the *Ash Wednesday* set. The tragedy actually seemed to help the cast and crew see things from a more balanced outlook, putting the problems on set in perspective. Everyone was terrifically kind to me, even though I've never been very good at accepting compassion. Shooting ended with no more melodramas. The set became a pleasant place to be again. The convalescent scenes that followed the plastic surgery operation were done in a stupendous villa, with a beautiful garden, which they transformed into a clinic. During lunch breaks, we all played soccer with the crew. Word about our

Rod Steiger, muffled in a German greatcoat as Benito Mussolini, is moments from death in Carlo Lizzani's 1974 history drama *Last Days of Mussolini*.

matches spread in Treviso, and a local team challenged us to a game. We won, 3–1.

Claudye joined me for the last scenes. She felt very bitter, and I wanted to do what I could to take her mind off our baby's death. So we left for a second honeymoon in Venice, agreeing we should try to have another child as soon as possible. Somehow, I felt I bore sole responsibility for the heartbreak, although I didn't know then and I still don't today why it seemed that way to me.

Gianni Il Roscio was still reluctant to recognize himself as "the new king of the camera," as they kept calling me. I felt I'd definitely moved forward professionally. But I felt lightweight nonetheless. Becoming a father, however: now that was a role I knew I wanted to play. I'd thought that going back to work with Elizabeth and Richard would help shake off the malaise that I'd felt since my father's death. But now there was little Bruna's death. And there I'd been, convinced that becoming a father would give a precise direction to my life, would give me an identity that I still didn't feel I had. And then I'd buried my first daughter without even having had a chance to hug her. Suddenly my life with Elizabeth and Richard appeared

Rod on set.

unstable. I felt as if I'd been in a coma again, and woken in the middle of a dream. But this time my father wasn't sitting by my bedside, waiting for me, calling me back to life. Was that dream really mine? Something told me it wasn't.

I got a call from director Carlo Lizzani. He was shooting *Last Days of Mussolini*, starring Rod Steiger as Mussolini, and had a key part that he wanted me to photograph: the moment Mussolini and his mistress, Claretta Petacci, die, gunned down by partisan commander Colonel Valerio outside the gates of the secluded Villa Belmonte, near Lake Como. Lizzani was following the official—and generally agreed-upon—version of events and insisting on accuracy. Claretta goes down first, desperately trying to get between Valerio and her lover. Valerio's gun then jams. He grabs another, and Mussolini goes down too, his head bowed between raised fists, a miserable death. The first take went fine. Mussolini crumbles to the ground. The second take went fine too, until the last moment. Steiger then suddenly raised his head, spread his arms, inflated his chest, and cried: "Go on, you bastard! I'm ready!" "Cut!" yelled Lizzani, demanding an explanation. Steiger, entirely unabashed, happily complied: "You saw how

Mussolini died," he said. "Now you've seen how Rod Steiger dies!" All actors have to get into their part. But some get in so far you wonder where they go.

It was then that I realized I wasn't acting. My life was for real. I was for real.

Chapter 12

Cinderella and Me

A photographer never has exclusive dominion over his or her own work. It's a collaboration between your vision and the subject. And my collaboration with Elizabeth and Richard was no simple matter. I was living their dream, traveling with them, following their commitments and whims from one side of the world to the other. If this dream wasn't mine, could I lose it? And what if I took an awful photo? What would happen if I woke up, this time for real?

But instead of waking up, I slipped into an even more surreal dream. Moncada's Studio Margutta had become Studio Bozzacchi, headquarters of my Forum Press Services. I adored the place. A room in front of the entrance became my office, complete with its own bathroom. To the left, a sliding door led to the twenty-seven-hundred-square-foot studio itself. A wooden staircase took you up to a mezzanine level, with the balcony that Fellini enjoyed so much. We used the space for doing finishing work, retouching, and mailing. Two rooms led off from there: the makeup room and the darkroom for black-and-white prints, which was only used for doing first-test prints. One might ask, "What would happen if that dark-room could talk?" Nothing. Whatever happened in that room stayed in that room. One day Elizabeth wandered in and, with her highly developed sense of perception—not to mention bawdy sarcasm—immediately dubbed it "la baise en ville"—fuck town. I must point out that—in her case—nothing ever happened, there or elsewhere.

The studio's courtyard was used in *Roman Holiday*, a movie I'd even tried to get work on as an extra. The star was Audrey Hepburn, whose portrait led to that rupture with my old employer, Pierluigi. Gianni Il Roscio had moved from a humble basement apartment to a luxury Parioli penthouse in Rome's most exclusive neighborhood. He could now walk out onto his own terrace and, for the first time in his life, look down on the world from above. I celebrated my success with a spin around town in my new Ferrari. I stopped at a restaurant where the headwaiter shook me by the hand and led me to a table to enjoy gourmet pasta on the house. Claudye and I got endless invitations: to movie premieres, fashion shows, dinners, and parties with the Roma Bene crowd, awash with real—though often impoverished—aristocrats. However, the more famous I became, the less enamored I was by all the glamour that came with it. I was still searching for myself and feared that those privileges, however enjoyable, would pin me down or—worse still—trap me in a life that wasn't mine. My skepticism opened the way to feelings of guilt. Shouldn't I feel grateful for the life I was leading? What photographer—what man—didn't desire a penthouse apartment, a beautiful woman, sports cars, fame, money? What more can you want when you already have everything?

Maybe this life really was my dream. I thought back to 1956, when my father had bought our first television. My father let me decide where to put it. Since we didn't have a real living room, I of course chose a spot opposite the front door where I could watch it from my foldout bed. A few months later we all gathered together in front of the screen to watch live as Grace Kelly, the Oscar-winning actress, joined hands in marriage with Prince Rainier of Monaco, becoming Her Serene Royal Highness, Princess Grace of Monaco.

Stepping from a Hollywood red carpet to a royal throne might not sound so sensational today. But back then Grace and Rainier enchanted the entire world in a way that no famous couple had ever done before. Nor would again, at least not until Elizabeth and Richard met. One of cinema's greatest stars had retired at the peak of her career to marry the man she loved and become, literally, a princess. It was the Cinderella story come true, even more magical because it took place in a land that very few people even knew existed. Until Rainier had come to the throne a decade earlier, his principality had been the exclusive resort of gambling aristocrats, with no one else welcome. Only 3 percent of its revenue came from anything other than gambling. Over the course of his reign, Rainier turned that around, and gambling now accounts for less than 5 percent of revenues. Grace would play an active role in helping him solve the tax crisis that created. But on that day we gathered around the TV, when cameras followed Princess Grace to her palace, we knew nothing of all that. The world simply fell in love with Monaco. Even on our tiny black-and-white television, the scene—sumptuous marble buildings, the broad bay dotted with yachts—looked more like a movie set than a real city. We saw carefree men and women in casual designer clothes stroll through immaculate gardens untouched by time. Or war. It all went way beyond my every infantile dream of what "glamour" might mean.

I immediately recognized Grace from one of the first movies I'd ever seen, *High Noon*, the great Gary Cooper western. My sisters analyzed every detail of Grace's look: her hair, jewels, clothes, charm, and elegance. Giampiero, with his usual sarcasm, said Grace and Rainier were not really all that different from us. Renato was struck by the fact that Rainier wore a uniform. "He must be a soldier." I kept one eye on the television and the other on my parents, who watched in silence, immobile. I don't know if they were as amazed as we were, or whether they were unhappy to see their children watching such opulence from a tiny three-room basement apartment, where stale bread soaked in water with sugar on top was the height of luxury. Like millions of other people, my family watched Grace and Rainier the way you gaze through shop windows at clothes you know you'll never be able to afford. However, for some strange reason I didn't feel that impotence. Maybe I was too young to understand, but I turned to my parents and declared, "One day I'll live like Grace and Rainier. They'll become my friends." My sisters burst out laughing. Six-year-old Renato said, "Mine too." My mother covered her face with her hand to hide a giggle. My father stroked my head, smiled, and said, "There's nothing you can't do, my boy. Remember that." Of course, that did nothing to stop Giampiero from mocking me throughout the rest of the ceremony: "Prince Gianni Bozzacchi!" As Grace and Rainier exchanged rings, my father's and brother's words rang in my ears and lodged in my memory. Now, years later, late into the night in my penthouse at the top of the world where I was living my dream of a fairy-tale life, those words came echoing back through my mind. When I finally went to bed, my head swam with images of that Cinderella and her Prince Charming.

Was it a premonition? Had the fairy tale not finished? The next morning as I opened my studio door, the phone rang and I hurried to pick it up. It was the fairy godmother herself, Louisette Levy-Soussain, personal assistant to Princess Grace, asking me if I'd be interested in doing a photo shoot for the Monaco Jubilee—the twenty-fifth anniversary of Prince Rainier's reign.

I thought it was a joke. Someone had managed to get inside my dream, or I'd spoken in my sleep. I knew that Princess Grace already had her own personal photographer, an American very close to the royal family. What's more, I could only hope the royal couple had forgotten having met me some years earlier on Elizabeth and Richard's yacht, the *Kalizma,* a meeting I'd happily forget. I'd been so embarrassed by my English and with my awkwardness among such high-society folk that I'd spent the entire party hiding in a corner, where I was obliged to speak with no one and where I knew no one would speak to me. I hadn't exchanged a single word with either Grace or Rainier, and now, speaking with their secretary, all that embarrassment came flooding back. I struggled to keep calm, and managed a brief, "Yes, I can. Why not?"

I was simultaneously excited and terrified. Claudye was pregnant again—as we'd planned—and I'd refused dozens of jobs in order to stay close to her. She was terrified that the same fate would befall this baby too. But I could hardly snub the royal family of Monaco, the only other couple as important as Elizabeth and Richard. I saw it as an opportunity to recenter my objectives. So I organized things with our relatives and our doctor, making sure Claudye wouldn't be left alone, and planned my trip with Louisette.

A few weeks later I caught a plane to Nice, arriving in the evening. During the flight I mulled over my memories of Grace and Rainier on the *Kalizma.* Louisette came to meet me, a very friendly and beautiful woman with great class. What's more, she spoke perfect Italian. My appointment was set for the following morning.

We got to Monte Carlo, where they'd booked me a suite in the Hotel de Paris, right alongside all the people who counted. If my penthouse in Rome felt like a dream, this was unadulterated magic, a fairy tale come true. Every woman dreams of meeting a knight in shining armor who'll take her to a castle in the clouds astride a white horse. And every man dreams of being that knight and of finding his princess. Maybe Grace really was living her fairy tale, just as imagined by her adoring subjects and all the tourists who flocked to Monte Carlo, hoping to catch sight of Cinderella Grace at one of the windows in her sumptuous palace, just for a moment, a fleeting glimpse, and thus feel part of the same fairy tale.

The night before my meeting with the royal family, I wandered through town looking at all the images depicting Grace and Rainier. Every shop displayed a photo: of the royal couple, their family, their children—Caroline, Albert, and Stéphanie—official shots of Rainier in uniform and photos of their wedding, all of them authorized by the family. Throughout my stroll, it was as if Grace and Rainier were watching my every step through their realm. Images of the royal family were everywhere, in the windows of every bistro, shop, and bar—even in a place of honor in pharmacies. Grace and Rainier loomed over every flower garden and picturesque café, peeping out of boutiques and offices. I stopped at a newspaper stall to buy postcards for my mother, and there they were again, smiling in glossy photos. The enchanted spell of Monaco had excited and intimidated me throughout my flight from Rome. Now I was there, and suddenly I was going to have to work for real. I thumbed through the postcards I'd bought until I nearly wore them away. From my window I could see the lights of the palace glittering in the distance. I examined those photos closely, as if trying to frame them against that background: their faces, their clothes, their style of life, the photos themselves. What for? Inspiration. Professional diligence? Whatever it was I was looking for, I didn't find it. I slept badly that night.

In the morning I took a shower, had breakfast, and took another shower. To this day I've no idea why I took that second shower. At the time it seemed of crucial importance. When a beautiful Rolls-Royce Phantom came to take me to the palace, I was in the grip of panic. I couldn't find the keys to the bags where I'd put my cameras. I'd left them in my studio in Rome. I began to think I wasn't destined to take these photos. But the porter was Italian and recognized me. "Monsieur Bozzacchi, if you'd care . . ." he said in French, with a strong Italian accent. I interrupted him. "Speak the way your mother taught you," I snapped, at which he rephrased his question in Italian: "You want me to open your bag?" He then ran to a small stockroom, grabbed a huge ring of keys, and had the thing open in a flash. "I'm the Saint Peter of the Hotel de Paris," he said in fluent Roman.

I was saved, but soaked in sweat, steam coming out of my ears. The drive to the palace was too short to allow me time to relax. When I arrived, guards at the gate gave me a military salute. A concierge helped me out of the car and welcomed me, "Bienvenu au palais, Monsieur Bozzacchi," he said.

I crossed a courtyard and climbed a stone staircase to an imposing column, where other staff and dignitaries were waiting for me, all impeccably dressed. "Bonjour, Monsieur Bozzacchi! Bonjour!" they all exclaimed, while I did a round of broad smiles and endless handshakes, proceeding through a merry-go-round of "bonjours," praying my French was a little better than my English.

Monsieur George Lukosky, the royal family's master-at-arms, led me through to the Hall of Crystals. "I'm a photographer myself, you know," he said. "If you don't mind, I'd like to stay and watch." George and I would become good friends. But that first time I wasn't very nice to him. He did everything he could to make me feel welcome, chatting a bit about work, photographer to photographer. But I couldn't concentrate on anything he said—or anything anyone else said, for that matter. I was too agitated, dazzled by that hall with its enormous arched doors, flower displays everywhere, huge windows, and crystal chandeliers glittering in the sunlight. The windows gave onto the main square, where tourists gathered to watch the changing of the guard. I recognized the famous balcony from where Rainier had presented his new wife back in 1956 and where the royal family made public appearances to announce the birth of a new child or give official statements. I'd never been in such a sumptuous place, not even on any of my travels with Elizabeth and Richard. When George left the room, I proceeded to pace up and down a thick-pile Persian carpet, my head bowed, studying every detail in its elaborate design. Except for the soft swish of my shoes over the carpet, total silence reigned in the hall.

At some point I turned and found Princess Grace standing in a distant doorway, smiling. I snapped up straight and set out toward her. When our eyes crossed my heart plunged. I had no idea what the protocol might be. No one had told me how I should address the prince and princess. Monsieur Bozzacchi, the "new king of the camera," surely knew how to do all that stuff already, right? No. I didn't. I slowed my pace, evaluating a series of options as I drew ever closer to the princess. Shake her hand, kiss it, bow, genuflect, or just keep walking clear on through to Rome? By the time I reached her, I still hadn't decided on any of them. I just stood there, frozen, terrified at the idea of not doing the right thing. Elizabeth, Richard, and all their social class filled me with awe, but this was true royalty. Grace did her best to put me at my ease. She spoke to me in French, asking me if I'd had a good flight, if I was happy with the hotel. Then she asked me about my photos, whether I needed anything in particular for my shoot.

But I interrupted her. I knew we wouldn't get anywhere until I got an answer to the question that had been haunting me throughout my trip from Rome, my wanderings through the streets of Monte Carlo, the question that had kept me awake all night. "Your Highness, please don't misunderstand me. I'm deeply honored to be here, I'm sincerely grateful to have this opportunity, but first I have to know . . . why me?"

Grace simply smiled. That one smile meant so much to me, and means even more to me today. It was her way of showing that she appreciated my work as well as my professional humility. "Mr. Bozzacchi," she replied, "I've known Elizabeth, Mrs. Burton, for some time, I might say forever. In recent years, her image has changed. Every time I see a photo of her that I like in a magazine, I check who took it. And they are all yours. You've succeeded in presenting her as a woman, mother, wife, and actress of great depth as well as a movie star. That's why I asked for you."

Prince Rainier—followed by George—entered the hall. He was a fascinating man. His contagious laugh comes back to me as I write this passage. He asked Grace something, then turned to me and said, "Excuse me, maestro." I glanced behind me, expecting to see another artist. But no one was there. I couldn't believe it. He'd addressed me as "maestro." A few moments later we were interrupted by Caroline and Stéphanie, their two daughters, aged seventeen and nine at the time. I stood to one side and watched Grace, admiring the patient and affectionate way she behaved with the two girls. For a moment I forgot I was in the presence of a movie star and princess.

That was when I got my inspiration, the angle I'd been looking for. I thought back over the official portraits I'd seen the previous night in all those shop windows, their detached, cold, severe look. I recalled other photos of Grace published in the French press, taken with so much light that they made her look icy, too immaculate. With a very beautiful, friendly, and elegant woman like Princess Grace, a precise and perfect modern Cinderella in her own right, that technique produced a publicity poster image. Worse still, a boring one. Grace came out looking beautiful, but static and perfect, too perfect. I wanted to capture that elegance and charm but without making it look too formal. I'd try something no one had dared try before: photos that would go beyond the aura of mystery surrounding the princess and reveal the Grace that Giampiero had seen during her wedding on television, the Grace that she herself saw—a person like anyone else.

I didn't take many photos during that first visit. I took a few shots of the family. Then Grace took me to their private apartments, where I caught some more intimate moments. Walking through the palace was like going on a tour of the history of Monaco, as we passed through halls dating to 1200 and on upstairs to the chic, highly modern royal apartments. At last I began to feel at ease. Grace helped immensely. She knew how to behave

Prince Rainier of Monaco and Princess Grace Kelly pose for me at home. Until Grace came to town, European aristocrats didn't do that kind of thing.

in front of a camera. Now and then, while I was getting one shot set up and measuring the light, I'd grab another camera and snap a quick photo from another angle. Grace liked those almost stolen snaps, catching her in moments when she was more relaxed, unprepared. Not knowing when I was about to shoot, she didn't have time to adopt a pose or fix her hair. All

Princess Grace poses in natural light, displaying her own natural grace.

she could do was be herself, and this created the natural look I wanted. I did, of course, do some posed shots, exploiting the room's natural light to soften her face rather than make it more rigid with artificial light. While I worked, I chatted. A photographer has to maintain an intelligent conversa-

Princess Grace shows her inimitable class, style, and genuine smile. I still remember how quickly she put me at ease.

tion in order to create a certain feeling. The composition is important in a photo, of course. But so is the extent to which you get in tune with your subject.

After developing the photos back in my studio in Rome, I returned to Monte Carlo with negatives and prints and spent an evening with Grace showing her the slides and photos. She never once said, "I don't like that," but always something like, "Maybe, though I prefer the other one. What do you think?" She was extremely kind and I knew she respected my professional opinion, which strengthened my own faith in myself as a person and as an artist. I got back to Rome very satisfied before returning one last time to complete the layout.

On that last visit I realized what a truly extraordinary person Grace was. Over a number of days, I followed her on her rounds, taking photos while she worked for the Red Cross, gave an interview to the *Herald Tribune,* visited a dance academy. I've never seen a celebrity give so much of herself to the needy, and with such generosity. I was being paid to take photos designed to give Rainier's family a friendly face. But Grace was friendly already, kind and thoughtful with every child she met, just as she

When seventeen-year-old Princess Caroline started to give me this kind of eye, it took one gesture from her father to keep mine firmly on the job.

was with her own children. She listened attentively to every worker, intervened to help when she could, and readily discussed how the royal family might assist one charity organization or another. I'd met a lot of "classy" people with Elizabeth and Richard, people who would never look a waiter in the eye or give a driver a decent tip. But watching Grace commit herself so thoroughly to improving other people's lives made me appreciate what true class really means.

I left that dance academy with six telephone numbers in my pocket. Given that I was working for the royal family, though, I didn't dare call any of them. Grace was amused by all the attention I got from young women, and as the days went by, she began letting her own hair down too. She asked me about Elizabeth, Claudye, our wedding. I believe that getting to know me better helped her relax in front of my camera as well as trust me with the task of caring for her family's image, which is something very important when you're trying to take natural photos of people accustomed to appearing highly stylized in the public eye. One day Grace asked me to photograph Caroline, who had just turned seventeen and was already breathtakingly beautiful. The way she flirted with my lens left her mother

Prince Rainier at his desk, the hub of a world within which nothing escaped his notice, including his daughter Caroline's whereabouts . . .

and me speechless. That evening, returning to the hotel, I bumped into Caroline again. There was now no camera between us, and I could see that this time she was flirting with me for real. Nothing happened, however. We chatted for a while in the lobby, and then she went home to her palace.

The following day, when I arrived to continue my photo shoot, George took me directly to Rainier's office, where I found the prince sitting behind his desk. He took one look at me and, without saying a word, shook a silent "no" with his finger. That was Rainier's power. No one in his realm did or said anything without His Highness getting to know about it. He wasn't angry. He knew I'd done nothing inappropriate. He just wanted to make things absolutely clear. I gave a nod of agreement, to which he replied, "Good. In that case, let's go get a coffee."

On one occasion, Rainier asked me to take a profile portrait of his face to be used on a Monaco coin. He wasn't someone who liked having his picture taken. But I told him what to do and he followed orders. When I showed him the prints I also offered to smooth out his obvious double chin (you'd Photoshop it today). But he turned me down. "I've never been

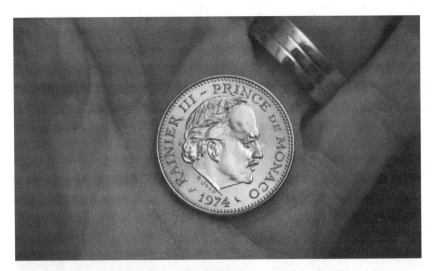

Prince Rainier told me to leave the chins in. So I did.

vain," he said. "Leave it in." So I did, and the coin duly went into circula-
tion, chins and all.

We established a good understanding, though he was never as relaxed
in front of my camera as Grace was. I just told him what to do and he did
it. He didn't remember having met me on Elizabeth and Richard's yacht,

Prince Rainier shows me his collection of cars. That's the top of my head you can see in the first photo.

which was both a sadness and a relief. I'd vowed that this time I'd conquer my insecurities and leave a good impression. Rainier loved laughing and asked me if I knew any Italian jokes. I told him one about Mussolini, in Italian. We also shared a passion for cars, so Rainier showed me his extraor-

Prince Rainier and Princess Grace in their palace gardens, 1974.

dinary collection, and we swapped opinions about the famous Monte Carlo Grand Prix that had cost Bandini his life. Before my own accident, when I still thought I might have some chance as a professional driver, I'd dreamed of flashing round bends on the Monte Carlo circuit, shouting at the top of my voice as I sped down those straights that cut through the heart of town. Now, thanks to a lucky quirk of fate, I was safely chatting about the race with Prince Rainier himself, instead of looking down on Monte Carlo from on high, alongside poor Bandini.

The moment finally arrived to take photos of the whole family together, portraits that would be put to formal use. I set up to photograph them as I would any other family: first, all of them together; then just Grace and Rainier; and, finally, just the children. Hoping to get photos with a more relaxed than usual look, I asked Rainier to put his arm around his son Albert's shoulder, instead of the pair of them merely standing at attention behind the women. Albert was just sixteen, a prince maybe, but a teenager all the same. That simple gesture was enough to make Rainier's face shine with sincere affection, and Albert's shone with that pride any boy feels when his father makes him feel important. Grace was sitting in front of them on an antique armchair, her hands in her lap, looking serene and at peace in her own home. I got Caroline to sit on one of the chair's armrests and asked Stéphanie to lean on the other. Immediately, everyone loosened up for the rest of the shoot. The end result was undoubtedly an official photo, but freed of that traditional rigid formality. It's a portrait of a royal family, yes, but also of a family that simply likes being together.

With the photo done, I let the children leave. Grace remained seated and asked Rainier to lean forward and rest his elbow on the back of her chair. She let her arm slip onto the armrest where Caroline had been sitting, rotating her upper body toward Rainier as if she were about to turn and look at him. In that moment, you sense how attracted Grace is to her husband, even though she can't see him.

These are nuances that might escape someone looking at these photos hurriedly or from a distance. However, in my opinion, their unique quality is due to just such detail. Three essential elements of a photo are: an objective, the subject and photographer being patient with each other, and an ability to adapt. I'd been asked to do portraits for the Monaco Jubilee, and that's how they appear at first glance: official portraits. But Grace also wanted to show the world another aspect of her family life, and that's what comes through in the visible affection you see between Rainier and Albert as well as in the way the girls draw close to Grace, their mother. For my part, I wanted to show the world the person behind Cinderella: a mother, a wife, a reserved woman with impeccable class.

On only one occasion did Grace assume a very stylized pose. I was try-

252

My official photo of the Monaco royal family. The usual rigid formality of such shots easily dissolved in the sincere affection they felt for each other.

ing to catch a natural expression when she caught me off guard and froze, just as any actress would for a glossy magazine. "Do you miss Hollywood?" I asked, to which she smiled and replied that the subject was taboo. In my opinion, she would have loved to do another movie. But she had children now, and was happy with her new life.

I went back to the palace later to show the family other photos, and Grace made a very singular gesture: she approved all of them. She also gave me permission to sell them, and I gave all the money they earned to Grace's favorite organization, the Red Cross. My photos were hung in every official location in Monte Carlo, including the police station—as I would soon discover.

While wrapping up the royal family portfolio, I'd also been working on a six-week project doing photos for tourist guides. It gave me a chance to get to know the palace and Monte Carlo better. One day I was out in a car with a good friend, the actor Fabio Testi. We were going to the premiere of *That Most Important Thing: Love*—a movie that would win Romy Schneider a César Award—when we were pulled over by the cops. Even though I wasn't driving, one of the officers asked for my license. Fabio and I hadn't shaved for days and looked like trouble, so they took us down to the station. A policeman asked me why I was in Monaco. I said I'd been on my way to a movie premiere. He then asked if I had a work permit, to which I replied with a nod, indicating a poster of the royal family that was hanging behind him, bearing my signature on the bottom of it. He took the gesture for rudeness, so I asked if I could use the phone, and called the palace, asking for George Lukosky. The moment the officer heard that name, he snapped to attention. I explained what had happened, and George asked to speak to the man immediately. No one asked for any more documents, and we were out of the place before you could blink.

I was in Los Angeles on September 14, 1982, when I heard that Grace had died following a car accident. She was fifty-two. Her daughter Stéphanie was in the car with her, but had survived. It was devastating news. It seemed so unjust that God should take back such an exceptional person so early. I was immediately flooded with magazine and newspaper requests to use my photos for their articles. I felt truly disturbed by the speed at which a media circus exploded around such a tragedy, and gave no one permission to use any of my photos. I didn't want to see my work under those headlines.

Grace was buried in the Grimaldi mausoleum after a requiem mass in Monaco's Saint Nicholas Cathedral. Everyone who was anyone attended her funeral, from England's Princess Diana to Gary Cooper. In his eulogy, James Stewart said: "You know, I just love Grace Kelly. Not because she was a princess, not because she was an actress, not because she was my friend, but because she was just about the nicest lady I ever met. Grace brought into my life, as she brought into yours, a soft, warm light every time I saw her, and every time I saw her was a holiday of its own. No question, I'll miss her, we'll all miss her, God bless you, Princess Grace."

I'm still very protective of my photos of Grace and her family. Sometimes I don't feel I have the right to show them. Grace put her all into everything she did, and those photos were also her work. They are photos of her dream come true. I merely had the good luck to be there in the moment. Sometimes they don't even seem real to me. I see Grace and Rainier with their children, but I'm unable to see myself behind the camera off-screen. From a basement apartment to Elizabeth Taylor's yacht, my penthouse, and the Monaco royal palace . . . If it weren't for the fact that I still enjoy the privilege of a friendship with Prince Albert and am able to observe him continue Grace and Rainier's wonderful legacy, I'd find it hard to believe I'd once played a minor role in the Monaco royal family's fairy tale. I'm still not even sure whose dream that was—whether it was also partly mine. When I and my memories revisit Monaco today, it feels even more unreal.

One small regret always brings me back to earth. The only occasion I saw Grace in her old environment was when she came to Elizabeth's fortieth birthday party in Budapest, years before I was hired to photograph the royal family. Grace came alone. I was the only photographer, and everyone knew I worked for Elizabeth, so she felt free to have fun with her old Hollywood friends. She had left "Princess Grace" in Monaco while I, as often happened, had left the famous jet-setter "Gianni Bozzacchi" in Rome. Maestro Bozzacchi was possibly too intimidated by all those stars. Perhaps he still felt ashamed by that first, embarrassing meeting on the *Kalizma*. Whatever the reason, it was Gianni Il Roscio who turned up at that party, the timid street kid who stood to one side snapping photos of Grace, Elizabeth, and all their friends, all busy sipping cocktails and telling American jokes which Il Roscio rarely understood. Then dancing on the tables. They were having so much fun I was tempted to ditch my camera for a moment. Grace danced magnificently, and I wasn't so bad in those days either. Maybe just one drink, a quick dance . . . But the moment I took my eye off the lens, an invisible wall sprang up, an insurmountable barrier between me and what I was observing. Every now and then I managed to mingle with the others without drawing attention to myself. But that evening, as on many others, I realized I could no more enter the party than I could have climbed into a painting. If I got too close, the dream would shatter.

And yet . . . I could have danced with Cinderella herself. Who turns down a chance like that?

Chapter 13

Daddy

My concern for Claudye's physical and emotional state only grew as the due date for the birth drew closer. I wanted to be near her to help her feel as relaxed as possible. Life with Elizabeth and Richard was getting increasingly difficult. They argued constantly, always over the same issues: fame and money, who was working and who not. In my opinion, we all needed our own space, Claudye especially.

So I refused a lot of offers in order to ease off a bit and stay in Rome with Claudye. We began to participate more in the Roman "scene," which Claudye appreciated but I personally couldn't stand—that whole Roma Bene thing, going to all the right parties, restaurants, and clubs just to see and be seen, to meet all those so-called friends. But frequenting these Roman society circles won me great popularity. I was bombarded with requests for interviews and photo shoots, many of which I just couldn't avoid. People knew I was in Rome and not very busy: an excellent opportunity to hire me. I stopped answering the phone, declined invitations, refused a lot of work offers. And not only because we were about to have a baby.

The less I dedicated myself to photography, the more I considered it superfluous to my life. The world still saw me as the "new king of the camera." But I wasn't. However good my photos may have been, to shoot them I had to live someone else's life—follow some star around for a few hours, or travel and live full-time with Elizabeth and Richard. I'd been photographing them for years now. How much longer could I keep it up? And if I quit working for them, what else could I hope to do? I'd never find anyone else to photograph as stimulating, interesting, and famous as they.

So . . . What if I just . . . quit?

The idea had been buzzing around in my head for some time. Drawing away from photography in order to concentrate more on my family highlighted this growing need to realize myself professionally, to do something that would be exclusively mine. On Elizabeth and Richard's last two movies I'd enjoyed going beyond my job as special photographer. I was good at bringing people together, making them my friends, and a lot of production work involves doing just that. I was honest; I inspired trust and sympathy. One day Elliott Kastner said, "Come work with me, you could be an excellent producer." I handled the directing of a number of commercials in Rome. Then, entirely unexpectedly, Luchino Visconti called, asking me to photograph a girl he wanted to hire for his next movie, *Conversation Piece*. Claudia Marsani was no more than fifteen years old. When she got to my studio I realized that what Visconti actually wanted was my opinion as to whether she'd be suitable for the part, despite her age. That was production work too. It involved giving advice, and people seemed to listen to mine. I liked working at my own pace, doing as I chose, rather than what Elizabeth, Richard, or some movie bigwig told me.

I was even offered a chance to realize my juvenile dream of acting when director Luigi Mangini presented me with a script inspired by an interview with me that had been published in installments in an Italian magazine. The script was basically an anonymous version of my life story: a shy and awkward young photographer is thrown into the jet set, where he discovers talent he never knew he had. I liked the script; it was amusing. "Why not?" I thought. Both Fellini and Leone had often said I should be an actor. Why not try? I was living at a less hectic pace and had time. It would be relaxing to be on the other side of the camera for a couple of months while waiting for the birth of my child. I met the financiers, and even though it was a minor production with a tight budget, the producers were convinced that my name would attract important actors. I accepted, and the movie was on. Claudye didn't seem all that enthusiastic, but she was feeling well, according to both her and her medical tests.

I had to go to Los Angeles for some layouts that I'd already committed to doing, and there I was stunned by the reaction that the little movie had provoked. *Jet Set* was headline news in magazines and newspapers around the world. Everyone wanted to interview me. "The photographer of the stars becomes a star" was the angle. I'd agreed to do the movie thinking it would be a relaxing job in my hometown. I'd been looking for less attention, not more. That trip to Los Angeles was already frenetic enough in its own right. Now I had a pack of journalists on my heels. I had to turn down a lot of offers and concentrate on the jobs at hand. New offers kept coming

Clint Eastwood, the actor
Sergio Leone was about
to turn down until he
saw a certain scowl . . .

in daily anyhow: a layout for Cindy Williams; one for Russ Meyer's wife, Edy Williams; another for actor Robert Stack, who said he'd love to play my father in *Jet Set*; and one for Clint Eastwood, who was so persuasive that he even roped me into doing yet another, years later, after I'd totally retired as a photographer. On that occasion, Condé Nast wanted him on the cover of *Vogue L'Homme*, the French edition of *Vogue*, and Clint called me in person. I did my best to refuse, explaining that I'd quit, was out of the business. "I don't even have a camera," I said. "Then borrow one," he replied. I got to the location an hour late. It was swarming with stressed Condé Nast staff, and Clint was delighted to see me. I took six shots and declared the job done. The Condé Nast people were outraged. Not Clint. "If Gianni's happy, I'm happy," he said, and that was that. In the end, they published a really nice cover.

However, one offer that I couldn't turn down came from Jack Painter, the MGM agent who had set me up with Al Pacino a few years earlier. Now he wanted me to photograph John Wayne. But when I got to John's Newport home, I was told that he was too sick to pose for a photo shoot. He wanted to apologize in person, so I was taken to his bedroom. He was secluded in

Rock Hudson, 1974.
He was Elizabeth's great friend
and a driving force in
her AIDS activism.

an adjoining bathroom, his voice speaking to me from the shower, saying how sorry he was to have made me come all that way, but unfortunately he didn't feel very well. So there I was. I'd been in the great John Wayne's house. I'd spoken to the man himself. But I never got to see his face. I'm sorry to say the shoot never happened.

Rock Hudson was another engagement that I accepted on that trip. I photographed him on the veranda of his home in Beverly Hills. He had a pack of German shepherd dogs, all of them male. "A couple of them are gay," he said. Years earlier Clint had told me that Rock was homosexual, but there was nothing effeminate about him, nothing stereotypical. He had great class, a certain grace, and an almost European way about him that you rarely see in the States. We spoke a lot about Elizabeth, and I quizzed him about James Dean and *Giant*. I'd only been commissioned to do a portrait, but he let me take a bunch of other photos. He was a sweet, marvelous, and fascinating guy. Years later Elizabeth would have a plaque erected in his honor on the Hollywood Walk of Fame.

I got back from Hollywood even more enthusiastic about *Jet Set* than when I'd left. I'd freed myself of all other commitments in order to concentrate exclusively on the movie, which was turning out to be much bigger than I'd ever imagined.

But Claudye didn't like the project. One evening she confronted me about it. "Our life together is already in trouble as it is," she said. "I totally don't want you to do this movie. If you go ahead with it, I'll ask for a divorce." I couldn't understand why Claudye was so dead set against the movie. But I didn't want to upset her more than I apparently already had. The weeks before the birth of our baby were anguishing. So I pulled out. Mangini was understanding about it. "If you don't do it, I'll burn the script," he said. "I'll never shoot it without you. You're the only one who can play this part." And that was the end of *Jet Set*.

Our gynecologist decided not to wait until the ninth month, a precaution considered necessary because no one knew exactly what had gone wrong the first time. With a month still to go, the baby was in good health, so they induced the birth.

The birth of my daughter Vanessa unblocked me. All my professional worries vanished, along with my irritable moods and arguments with Claudye. We were a regular Roman family. I wanted to dedicate myself totally to Claudye and my daughter. It was only then that we began to live the good life for real. We hired a driver, a cook, a nanny, and later a governess. My family became my life. I totally adored being a father. The pressures I'd been accustomed to for years—on movie sets, following Elizabeth and Richard around—vanished.

I was a father, a husband, a man who provided for his family. But my father's words kept coming to mind all the same: "Now pedal!" Sooner or later I was going to have to get back to work. However, while I was living on the fringe, concentrating on my own affairs and my family, the entertainment and publicity world was changing at a dizzying speed. Television was taking over as the principal medium for news, gossip, and publicity. One by one, the magazines that had once published so many of my photos—*Look, Paris Match, Epoca, Europeo, Stern, Life,* and many others—all began to vanish. The ones that survived the crisis were no longer interested in quality photos of stars, or in real news. Newspapers and magazines all dumbed down. None wanted beautiful layouts any more. They were all after scandals.

But I didn't want to play the game anymore anyway. I was a father now. No more ducking into the darkroom with girls at my studio, no more all-nighters on movie sets and sudden trips to the other side of the world.

Vanessa and me in 1974. I loved being a father.

Magazines and newspapers could get all the obscene photos they wanted from the new paparazzi, but they'd never get one from me. I wanted to live with Claudye and Vanessa like a regular family man. And things seemed to be working out just fine that way.

Strangely, Claudye didn't appreciate me participating more in our new home life. I tried to invite my mother and brothers and sisters around more often, but they didn't seem very important to Claudye. She only cared about her own family. All our vacations had to include a stop in Corsica. I was also expected to financially maintain Claudye's parents as well as her brother and sister. My mother never spent a single night in our stupendous apartment, but Claudye's came to stay every three months, and her sister and niece became pretty much full-time live-in guests. After a while, all this began to bother me. Her family's constant interference began to create a rift between us.

Unlike me, Claudye suffered being out of the limelight. She wanted to get back to the Roma Bene scene as soon as possible. I began to wonder whether that was why she'd stopped me from shooting *Jet Set*. She liked the "new king of the camera" just the way he was, at the peak of his career, desired, capable of bringing fat checks home for just a few hours' work—even if he didn't get any satisfaction out of it anymore. Despite the publicity, doing that movie would have meant me starting again from scratch, risking my name and reputation in an entirely new venture. What if the movie flopped? What if I proved a disaster? Would we have kept getting so many invitations to dinner? Would people still stop us in the street to shake our hands? If the king put his crown down, would he be able to pick it up again later, or would it already be riding on someone else's head?

I did a few quick calculations to work out just how long we could afford our lifestyle were I to quit photography. I figured I had time to evaluate all the options. Not much, but enough. So I took a trip to London, where I spent a week with Elliott Kastner at Pinewood Studios and watched him at work. He was incredible. Elliott was a genius. I saw him put a western together with just a couple of phone calls. He had no script, no story, but he called Marlon Brando all the same, because he knew Brando wanted to work with Jack Nicholson. Brando accepted, so he then rang Nicholson, who also accepted. The movie was done; all he needed was a director. So he then asked both actors which director they'd like to work with. Both said Arthur Penn, who happened to have a book that he wanted to turn into a western, and that was how they came to make *The Missouri Breaks*. The movie later proved a major flop—in large part due to Brando's erratic behavior on set (which included catching grasshoppers after shooting as well as taking a bite out of a live frog)—but that was tomorrow's problem. Right then, Elliott had got his movie.

He then asked me to go to Paris on his behalf. "Go convince this guy to invest in my production company," he said. I was still a photographer at that point, and Elliott probably thought that closing a business deal would be good experience for me. The guy I met in Paris was Arnon Milchan, known today as one of Hollywood's most prolific independent producers—as well as a key Israeli intelligence officer, at least until the mid-1980s. But what did I know? He was rich and wanted to invest in cinema. I explained just how good Elliott was and did my best to convince him to invest in a number of projects.

I soon began to realize that Elliott was good at doing business, but not at making movies. Some producers are also creative people who leave their own mark on a movie, on a par with the director or scriptwriter. That wasn't the case with Elliott. His talent was getting the right people together, finding the funds, identifying people (like Milchan) who could prove useful in certain circumstances. Elliott did four or five movies a year. He'd close one business deal after another. And he had fun doing it, maybe because he'd started out as an agent. But from a creative point of view, he wasn't nearly so good, especially when it came to judging the potential of a script. I discovered this in the worst possible way.

Elliott invited me to accompany him to Los Angeles, where he was shooting *Farewell, My Lovely,* starring Robert Mitchum as Raymond Chandler's immortal private eye, Philip Marlowe. With all my expenses covered by the production, I didn't even take a camera—to make sure Elliott couldn't ask me to take any shots. As we were wandering around the set, I met a young Italian American actor, a guy about my age who, until then, had had just one minor role in a single movie. He wanted me to look at a script he'd written in which he planned to play the lead role. I can still remember the expression on his face as he handed me the script: "Read it. It's monumental."

That evening I ended up hanging around my hotel. With nothing else to do, I started flicking idly through the young guy's script, and ended up reading it cover to cover straight. I fell in love with it. It reminded me of *Somebody Up There Likes Me,* one of my all-time favorite movies. I identified with the characters, with their backgrounds. Maybe it was a little too tough. The lead character, a boxer, died in the end. But it really was a "monumental" script.

I rang Elliott. He'd already heard talk of the script around Hollywood. But he could tell how passionate and enthusiastic I was, so he agreed to read it, and I took it that very evening to the house he rented in Bel Air. I was so excited I couldn't sleep. It would be my first movie as a producer, the beginning of a new career.

The next morning, I joined Elliott for a light breakfast. He was drinking prune juice and very healthy California-style food, which didn't interest me in the least. He stood up, put one arm around my shoulders and said, "Gianni, I adore you, I love you, you're a friend, you've got talent, but I think you should go back to photography. This script is a disaster. I read it because I could tell you were really enthusiastic. But I'm sorry. You don't understand a thing about scripts."

I was devastated. He made me feel ridiculous. My English was clearly still too limited, and in all the time I'd spent on movie sets, I'd obviously learned nothing about the business. I was getting this straight from an incredibly prolific and successful producer. What could I have been thinking?

The prospect of making a big leap into producing was very attractive. But I admired Elliott so much that I'd never dare doubt his opinion or his loyalty toward me. Then, by chance, I met Arnon Milchan again at the Beverly Hills Hotel. He was with Robert Mitchum. He hugged me and thanked me for putting him in touch with Elliott. That meant I'd done my work well. I'd convinced Arnon to invest in, among other things, *Farewell, My Lovely*. So I figured I'd be included in the agreement somewhere. Yet Elliott hadn't even told me he'd closed the deal, thanks—above all—to my own contribution. Following this encounter, one of Elliott's collaborators proceeded to inform me that Arnon had agreed to pay half of all script costs for every project he did with Elliott. But I knew Elliott never acquired scripts, just the options. So I told Arnon. I didn't want to be responsible in any way, even indirectly, for the scam that Elliott was running. He'd convinced Arnon to pay for half of something he didn't even possess. But maybe Arnon was just too wealthy to care. He wanted to get into the movie business, and Elliott knew how to promote movies. The pair of them did a lot of movies that way.

Clearly I had a lot to learn about the facts of life in the production world. For example, I'd even thought that some stupid script about a boxer could be a success. What did I know?

A couple of years later I was still suffering from that blow to my self-esteem when that same movie, whose script, written by Sylvester Stallone, I'd so admired, the one that Elliott Kastner had so despised, won the Oscar as 1976's Best Picture. I was happy to see Stallone had changed the ending. Rocky didn't die anymore. The movie worked much better that way. Maybe he'd even do a sequel?

Chapter 14

Breaking Up

Throughout these months, the one thing Claudye and I never talked about publicly, although it dominated—and troubled—our lives, was a story that made global headlines: Elizabeth and Richard's divorce. The news came out of the blue for us too. Neither of them released any statement or gave any explanation. We were in Rome with our daughter. They were in Switzerland, and then suddenly they were in London. We had no clear idea what was going on. Someone in the entourage spoke about arguments but nothing out of the ordinary, nothing so serious as to make you think they'd separate. Inevitably, the news became public property, and we were deluged with telephone calls from the press. We made no comment. To tell the truth, at that point the journalists knew more than we did. Elizabeth and Richard refrained from making any statements. Their staff did the same. We conformed with that silence.

It was a terrible time for Claudye and me. The "Taylor-Burton divorce" was on every front page. We were friends with both of them and didn't want to take sides in any way. What was a spicy soap opera for the rest of the world was for us a very delicate moment in the life of a man and a woman whom we cared for deeply. The speculation and misinformation was irritating, but also sometimes amusing. We learned, for instance, that Elizabeth had gone to Santo Domingo to file for divorce, when actually she'd gone to Hamburg, in Germany, with Claudye.

In the middle of this cyclone, Richard was shooting *The Voyage* with Sophia Loren for director Vittorio De Sica, while Elizabeth was busy with director Giuseppe Griffi's *Identikit*. I decided I wouldn't work with one or the other. I didn't want to find myself in the middle of whatever was happening between them. I wanted to be home with my wife and my little girl. I had no desire to be involved in that melodrama. It would be like allying myself without even knowing the reason for the battle. Richard probably wouldn't have cared. But if I'd agreed to work on the set of *The Voyage*, Elizabeth would have really resented it. I'd have gone over to the "enemy," Sophia Loren. It was a time when the two women reigned supreme, a league apart from every other actress. The superstars of the past had waned or gone, while those of the new generation were still on their way up. Whenever Elizabeth did a major magazine cover, the next second Sophia would appear on one of its rivals. What's more, they were almost opposites. Elizabeth was a beautiful woman, but she actually cared little about what she wore or how she looked, especially when she was with Richard, the love of her life. Sophia, on the other hand, cared intensely. She was deeply Italian, born in the land of the world's top designers, particularly Valentino, who made it his business to ensure that Sophia always dressed with full elegance. And right then, Richard was a guest in Sophia's house.

Elizabeth's movie was being produced by Franco Rossellini, Roberto Rossellini's cousin, who rang me one day with a problem. They'd tried four different photographers in two weeks, but Elizabeth had turned them all down. She didn't like their photos. She'd worked with me alone for twelve years. Rossellini wasn't calling to ask me to work on the movie—he said I *had* to. In my opinion, however, I didn't have to do anything I didn't want to. So I told him I'd let him know.

I went on set to meet Elizabeth, explaining how a number of American publications had asked me for photos for their articles about the divorce. "Let's do it then!" she replied, leaving me stunned, to say the least. But I agreed, and we went ahead with a layout shot in my studio.

Elizabeth understood and respected my position that I didn't want to work on either her movie or Richard's. It was obvious that she didn't care a thing about *Identikit*. It's possible that she'd only accepted the job because it was being filmed in Rome, as was part of *The Voyage*. Richard was Sophia's guest in her villa in Marino, just outside Rome. Elizabeth was constantly in bad health, suffering terrible back pains and had a nurse on hand day and night.

When a day's shooting on *The Voyage* was planned in Naples, I went down to see Richard. I was there in the Excelsior Hotel when, by chance, I met the movie's sound technician, Piero Biondi, who revealed to me the interesting shift in power dynamics on set. Initially De Sica had absolutely no control. The movie was being produced by Carlo Ponti, Sophia's husband. Sophia was worth a gold mine and very aware of her power. And Richard was Richard. But De Sica was seventy-three and shooting what

These shots, done in the "American style," were Elizabeth's answer to knowing that Richard was a private guest in Sophia Loren's villa. We did them in color. Elizabeth wanted the world to know she was single, still young, and beautiful.

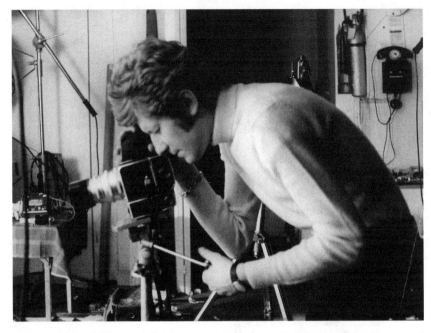

While I worked on those "Take that, Sophia Loren!" photos, Elizabeth snapped this one of me.

would be his last movie. At the end of one scene, Richard and Sophia were alone in a boat when De Sica called, "Cut." But Piero forgot to turn the microphones off—and Richard and Sophia started talking about very private, personal things to do with the previous night. Piero, who only noticed the unintentional recording later, promptly took it to De Sica, who confiscated the tape the moment he heard it. From then on, apparently, De Sica regained full control of the movie.

You hear a lot of rumors of affairs in the cinema world, and you never quite know who to believe. I don't claim to know the truth. But everyone was convinced that Richard and Sophia were having an affair—everyone involved in the movie, the press, and above all Elizabeth. Bear in mind that no one really knew what kind of relationship Sophia and Carlo Ponti had. They were married, but word was that she already had a lover in Switzerland. Carlo was her manager and her agent. They lived together, but they also didn't live together. Carlo was in Marino when Richard was there. But Richard also had opportunity to be alone with Sophia. The marriage between Sophia—Italy's beauty of beauties—and Ponti, a powerful but aging and decidedly not-beautiful man, has always been a major mystery in Italy.

I wanted to find some way to get Richard away from Sophia. I was convinced that Elizabeth and Richard still loved each other. Their assistants told me that they phoned each other daily. I told Claudye that maybe we should organize a dinner for Elizabeth and Richard and try to help them get back together. So I invited them both to our apartment. Elizabeth asked if she could bring her nurse along too, at which point I invited actor Franco Nero along with half a dozen other friends.

It was a magnificent evening. The dinner itself was nothing special, just good food. But I did everything I could to make the atmosphere enjoyable. Claudye and I shared the cooking, making all their favorite dishes: prosciutto ham and mozzarella cheese, *amatriciana* pasta, and stripped beef. Elizabeth and Richard were very sweet to each other. After dinner, in order not to bother the baby, Richard went for a smoke on the terrace and spotted our ping-pong table. First he played with Elizabeth. Then, under a sudden downpour, he and Franco had a match in the driving rain. It was a wonderfully absurd scene.

Around 2 in the morning our guests began to head home. I called the elevator, but it was out of order. We were on the fifth floor. The building had a beautiful spiral staircase, and Franco went down first. I followed, Elizabeth on my arm. When Franco got to the bottom, he looked back up at Richard, still standing on the top floor admiring the staircase. Franco stood where he was and started singing "Camelot" at the top of his voice. Richard sang back, the stairwell acting as an amplifier. When Elizabeth and I got to the third floor a woman poked her nose out of a door. "What's going on? What's all this racket?" she barked. "I'm terribly sorry," I replied, "but having Richard Burton and Elizabeth Taylor for dinner doesn't happen every day." She took one look at Elizabeth and snapped, "If that's Elizabeth Taylor, I'm Greta Garbo." And slammed the door.

A throng of paparazzi were waiting for us outside the building. A thousand photos later appeared under one headline: "Elizabeth and Richard back together!" And I could see that they still loved each other, but nevertheless they each went their own way, Richard back to Marino and Elizabeth to her apartment in the Grand Hotel.

The following day the lady from the third floor came to apologize. She was very disappointed. She explained that she'd always admired Elizabeth and would have been delighted to meet her, but, roused from sleep by "Camelot," she hadn't had her glasses on.

Richard called Elizabeth later that day. Sophia had invited her to lunch. Claudye was called in to help Elizabeth get ready, and I went along. After all those years, when it came to dressing at home or on set, Elizabeth and I understood one another at a glance. Whenever she had to appear in public in a new outfit or in something she wasn't sure about, she'd look at me and I'd reply with a return look, indicating whether I approved or not. Words were superfluous. She'd understand everything from my expression, and our shorthand avoided offense to some director or designer.

Under the circumstances, I thought I should get to the hotel before Elizabeth left, just to see how she dressed. She was still getting ready when I arrived. Claudye emerged from the bathroom to tell me Elizabeth was very agitated. The gossip about Richard and Sophia had got to her. When Elizabeth finally came out of the bathroom, I couldn't believe my eyes. She was wearing full-on makeup, an evening-wear hairdo, and was dripping with jewels from head to toe. For a lunch date? What if photographers were there in waiting? My expression couldn't lie.

"What?" she blurted. "What's wrong?!"

"Elizabeth, where do you think you're going? It's a lunch!"

"So?"

"So you look like a Christmas tree."

She let out a scream and raced back into the bathroom. Raymond Vignale, Elizabeth's personal assistant, started shouting at me. "Look what you've done!" he exclaimed. "You don't understand," I replied. "Sophia's photographer will be there, along with who knows how many paparazzi. Elizabeth will look ridiculous dressed up like that, during the day!" She emerged an hour later wearing jeans, a T-shirt, and a jean jacket. No makeup, nothing. She looked twenty years younger, a mere girl.

I didn't go to the lunch myself. But Claudye ferried Elizabeth there in a car and reported later that Sophia turned up wearing super-heavy makeup, a brightly colored caftan, and a wardrobe of jewels. In the end, it was she who looked like a Christmas tree. Photographers were there too, of course, but no photo of that lunch was ever published. It's my belief that Carlo Ponti bought them all off in order not to embarrass Sophia.

I have no idea what else went on at that lunch. Shortly afterward, however, Richard and Elizabeth invited me to go with them to Mexico. I went but spent as little time as possible with either of them. I wanted to leave them alone, give them time to talk undisturbed, to hear the echo of their words. They then left Mexico together, just the two of them. No one knew where they were going. They wanted to keep it a secret. We heard later they

This was the kiss that made Elizabeth and Richard give their marriage a second (though short-lived) chance.

were in South Africa, and that they had remarried. But it didn't last. The split became irreparable. There's rarely just one reason behind a divorce. Elizabeth and Richard had accumulated a series of conflicts over the years, and in the end the weight of them all dragged them apart.

They both had baggage from the past. They'd both been married before and had children. They needed the support of an entourage. But then they got trapped by the trappings of their life. They could no longer travel like anyone else. They couldn't walk in the street like anyone else, go to a restaurant like anyone else. There's a huge gulf between an actor and a star, an even greater one between a star and a superstar. They're no longer in charge of their own lives. They become public property. Their freedom vanishes. In Richard and Elizabeth's case, they had to buy an entire stretch of beach in Mexico just to go on holiday with their kids.

They also came from very different backgrounds. Elizabeth had lived as a celebrity all her life. Being a celebrity *was* her life. Richard, on the other hand, found the jet set suffocating. Living with a superstar, staff, and exorbitant expenses drained him. Basically, Elizabeth and Richard ended up working for everyone else, including us in the entourage, movie after movie after movie. And Richard couldn't stand it. He'd far rather have done theater instead of making movies just for the money. He enjoyed writing, reading the classics. He found celebrity a burden, unlike Elizabeth, who had been a star since age seven. Richard liked being alone, whereas for Elizabeth being "alone" meant being with her staff. But that life wore Richard down; it pushed him to drink more and more. And when he wasn't working, when his star stopped shining, he began to feel out of place in that world. I knew the feeling all too well myself.

In the end they became two people who'd stopped facing their lives in a rational way. I don't think they ever planned how to manage their careers or their lives, how to maintain some kind of balance. I never heard Richard or Elizabeth discuss critical reviews of their movies. Sometimes they talked about box office returns because that influenced future projects. Richard would often say, referring to *Where Eagles Dare,* "I earned more money with that stupid movie than with all my other movies put together." But there's a huge difference between what the Hollywood industry considers a success and recovering costs, making a simple profit with a movie. Elizabeth's and Richard's movies always sold. And if $1 million wasn't a success for Hollywood, it sure was for whoever got a cut.

The trouble with Elizabeth and Richard was that, despite all their talent, they needed those profits, and that need compromised their artistic satisfaction. Looking back, it's strange to realize that two of the world's biggest stars didn't participate in the most exciting and innovative period of modern American cinema. They never worked with any of the legendary "New Hollywood" directors: Scorsese, Altman, Spielberg, Coppola, Ashby, Rafelson. Oscars and good critical reviews are all well and good. But they don't pay for a yacht, a string of homes, a personal photographer. You hear about a lot of actors these days who are very careful not to inflate their image, who hire teams of PR experts to make sure the public doesn't get tired of them. Elizabeth and Richard, on the other hand, did movies, together and alone, every single year for nearly a decade. Richard would often say, "If we keep doing movies together we'll end up like Laurel and Hardy." Which is pretty much what happened. Did the industry just get tired of them? By the end of their relationship, were they obliged to accept whatever they were offered? *X, Y and Zee* was supposed to star Richard alongside Elizabeth. But the production called in Michael Caine instead. *Night Watch* was written for the pair of them, but Elizabeth ended up costarring with Laurence Harvey. Then Richard really wanted to play the lead role in *Under the Volcano*, but director John Huston wasn't interested because of the circus that Richard dragged behind him.

That circus became too much for both of them and provoked some of the epic arguments you so often hear people talk about. But I've only one word to say about all that: nonsense. I was there. It's true they argued. But just like any other couple. The press exaggerated everything. Their love had no room for the kind of furious arguments it's alleged they had. Gossip by people who weren't there has no value. From their first meeting until they finally separated, Elizabeth and Richard lived one of the greatest love stories of all time. It's just that sometimes history gets the better of people. When their relationship began, the press adored them. You would read about how in love they were, how beautiful, how happy. You heard about their charity work. Even when serious publications gave way to the gutter press, Elizabeth and Richard were still the greatest love story on earth. They were beautiful alone, and even more so when they were together. But in order to sell the new kind of magazine, the plot had to change. Elizabeth and Richard had to become two violent drunks who did nothing but argue. If she left a party because she was tired and he stayed behind for a drink with his friends, the following day the newspapers all said they'd gone separate ways because they'd had a vicious argument. All nonsense, just nonsense. But the myth sold, and it still sells today.

For twelve years I had shown the world the truth: a man and a woman who loved each other intensely, wholeheartedly, in the middle of a show that most of us would have trouble even imagining. But now that love story was over, and all that was left was the show, for the use and abuse of magazines, newspapers, journalists, TV crews, and the public. In fact, anyone who felt like it—which definitely wasn't me. My place in that story had ended.

I wanted to grow. I was a married man and a father. I wanted to do something for myself. It's easy enough to photograph some Mr. Nobody. But when you're photographing important people, when you look after their image as I did for Elizabeth and Richard, every photo has to have a reason to exist. Merely having an impulse to take a photo was never reason enough for me. What satisfaction can you get from that? If I'd felt greater artistic satisfaction, I'd have believed I'd made more of myself. But the photos I took and the satisfaction I took in them were often in conflict. I was fed up with always having to put my own ambitions as an artist in second place. Today I can appreciate the quality of my photos, their art, their personal style—which I didn't think I had back then—much more than I ever could when I was thirty. Because back then I just saw them as a job done for others, not as a creative act.

What else could I achieve as a photographer? Where should I go next? The magazines I'd worked for in the past had shut down or changed. Ugly photos paid more than beautiful ones. When I tried to do something new, different—like my Virna Lisi layout—I couldn't get it published. If I tried to innovate, using unusual lenses for a fashion shoot, my efforts weren't repaid. I attempted other work—cinema posters, advertising—with the same sense of invention, the same quality that I always demanded of myself. I did a poster for a documentary entitled *The World by Night* for which I did twelve shots on the same negative, each time moving the position of the model to give the impression that she was actually moving inside the picture. It looked like a good job of editing, only it wasn't editing—it was one photo, painstakingly shot piece by piece during the course of a single day. But it was all pointless. People just weren't interested. Quality no longer had any importance. Beauty even less so. Standards had plunged. You wanted to advertise a movie or sell a product? You just had to do a poster and print it a thousand times, far faster and cheaper.

What could I do? How much further could I push my photography career? If I'd wanted to, I could have earned a fortune working in advertising or fashion. But whenever I did a commercial, my photos had to be whatever the client or PR agent said. Or, worse still, whatever a team of PR agents said, plus an art director. And usually fashion magazines and designers have a specific design they want you to adhere to. I was at a fork in the road. I could keep repeating myself, or I could try something new. That's when I hung my camera on a hook and decided to move to Los Angeles.

Claudye didn't want to come with me. She tried to make me stay in Rome, keep working as a photographer, keep going to all those Roma Bene parties. She wanted to revive all the attention she got when I was famous. But I'd escaped from that life. I didn't allow anyone to ask me about Elizabeth or Grace Kelly or whoever else it was they asked about when my latest photos came out. I'd turned my back on all that—those elite clubs, restaurants, and society folk. But Claudye hadn't. She adored that life. She loved being Mrs. Bozzacchi, the queen of the "camera king." But I wanted to grow, do something big as a producer, take more risks, see if I could maybe succeed and find satisfaction.

We began separation procedures, first in practice and then legally. All the while, though, I still felt sure that once I'd settled in Los Angeles, Claudye would understand that my new life could be as stimulating as my old one. I didn't want a divorce. I never did. Sadly, however, we weren't even given a chance to reconcile. Claudye had a fear of needles, and, following a dental operation, she refused the prescribed antibiotics. Septicemia flared one night, and she died on the spot, in her sleep. I flew back for the funeral in Rome, and we buried her in her hometown in Corsica. Then I settled down for a while in Rome, where my first priority became my daughter Vanessa.

I don't know what would have happened if Claudye hadn't died so suddenly. While I watched our marriage collapse, I began to wonder whether she'd actually been far more in love with the life she'd had with Elizabeth and Richard than with the one she had with me. All the same, I'd wanted to share this new phase of my life with her, begin a new one that would be ours alone. Claudye didn't want that. And then she lost any chance of joining me. She left, and I had to face the change alone. The man once dubbed the "king of the camera" put down his crown. And Gianni moved to Los Angeles, taking the Redheaded Devil from Rome with him.

Epilogue

I thought retiring from photography would be simple. I was done taking pictures. The end. But nothing in life is ever that easy, of course. No one believed I was serious. I insisted that my retirement was real, and my camera hung idle. The truth only set in when I sold my black-and-white lab to my printer and my studio to another photographer. After only thirteen years, and with an apparently endless career ahead of me, I was done.

Which is when the whispering started: "Bozzacchi's burned out," they'd say. "He's lost his eye, doesn't have what it takes anymore." What other reason could there be? Then I began getting a new kind of phone call: magazines around the world offering a ton of money for me to gossip about Elizabeth and Richard. "He doesn't work for them anymore, so we'll pay big and he'll tell all" was how they figured it. I turned them all down.

Everyone thought I was crazy to leave photography, making a huge mistake. But my transition into producing over the next decade was so rapid that I didn't have time to weigh my decision in terms of "good" or "bad"—things just kept happening, both personally and professionally.

Vanessa continued her schooling, first in Rome, then in Corsica. Right after I sold my studio, I was back with Elliott Kastner shooting *The Missouri Breaks*, then premiering it at the Cannes Film Festival. The next thing I knew, I was prepping *China 9 and Liberty 37* with director Monte Hellman, followed quickly by *Together*, starring my friend Jacqueline Bisset. I was a real producer, making movies! But my next couple projects didn't work out as planned.

Sergio Leone called me and asked me to help him produce *Once upon a Time in America*. I'll never forget what he told me when he handed me the script: "Read, you'll see with this film we give the answer to *The Godfather*." I started working for Greg Bautzer, described by the press as "the man who seduced Hollywood," the former attorney of Howard Hughes, and the current attorney of Kirk Kerkorian, owner of MGM. Greg and I helped Leone promote the project and started his partnership with MGM. Studio executives didn't like the title, so I suggested a new one, "In

PREMIO CINEMATOGRAFICO SERGIO LEONE
XIV EDIZIONE
RASSEGNA "CINEMA A MEZZOGIORNO"
VII EDIZIONE
TORELLA DEI LOMBARDI
28 LUGLIO - 5 AGOSTO 2006

TARGA SERGIO LEONE

A GIANNI BOZZACCHI

Torella dei Lombardi, 4 agosto 2006

The plaque that the Leone family gave me, presented as an annual prize given in Sergio's hometown, Torella dei Lombardi, Avellino.

Gold We Trust," which Sergio also liked. After several attempts to edit, even halve the seven-hundred-page script, the project was ultimately rejected by MGM. I found Leone a deal with financier-producer Arnon Milchan. But I was under contract at MGM, so I was greatly disappointed to be unable to produce the film. My contribution was forgotten by both Sergio and Arnon, most notably in the credits. *C'est la vie.*

Around the same time, I had begun to collaborate with Michelangelo Antonioni, who with the help of Tonino Guerra had completed a screenplay titled "To Suffer or Endure." It was an extremely complicated story addressing the problem of faith in a traffic jam of love in search of truth. It was very well written, but—I have to be honest—I did not understand much. Mick Jagger was interested in playing himself in the film. I went to meet Mick, who was very nice and an excellent businessman, and I managed to work out an agreement.

Many scenes of the film were to be shot inside Vatican City. I made an appointment with one of the secretaries of Pope John Paul II, who to me was still my dear Father Karol, to try to get permission. The answer was fast and precise: "No!" At that time, if the Vatican said no, what it really meant was: "This movie cannot be made at all!" And sure enough, "To Suffer or Endure" was never made, and it's never even mentioned in the biographies written of Michelangelo Antonioni.

Michelangelo at the time wrote short stories for the newspaper *Corriere della Sera,* including one entitled "The Boat Drunk," inspired by a true, mysterious story involving a yacht drifting in Australian waters, three men locked up for days in the hold, and a captain who climbs out on deck and disappears. I wanted to make a movie out of that story. We started to develop the project with a new title: "The Crew." Mark Peploe and Antonioni wrote a beautiful script. L'Ente Gestione Cinema and Cinecittà were interested in financing the film, believing it might be Antonioni's last. Michelangelo agreed, on the condition that I produce the film. After analyzing the project, I realized that the budget was too high for L'Ente Gestione Cinema and Cinecittà. I asked the American company Orion to co-produce the film, and they agreed.

Michelangelo and I traveled around the United States and Mexico scouting out locations and picking the cast. We spoke with many actors—Robert Duvall, Joe Pesci, Robert De Niro, Matt Dillon, Roy Scheider, Dustin Hoffman, Sean Connery—and all of them were excited to work with Antonioni. We were confident we could put together a great team with great names on the marquee. Mexico's president, José López Portillo, even made his personal plane available for our research, and we found the remains of a small port destroyed by a hurricane, perfect for the end of our film.

At Cinecittà, production designers Dean Tavoularis and Ferdinand Scarfiotti and cinematographer Carlo Di Palma began preparing the film. Everything was going at full speed when Michelangelo was hit by a devastating stroke, losing the ability to speak. Gone was the voice that used to speak famous quotes like: "Loneliness is the lack of words around us."

We tried various solutions to get the movie made anyway, including employing Martin Scorsese as standby director, but unfortunately he did not at the time have dual citizenship, and therefore he couldn't work in Italy. This project, unfortunately, was shelved.

Meanwhile, I wrote a semi-autobiographical script, *I Love N.Y.,* and then found myself directing it, alongside my soon-to-be wife, Kelley. We married, moved to Wisconsin, and had a beautiful new baby, Rhea. Then Kelley got sick with cancer. We battled that for five years and more before she finally left us, by which time a full decade of my life had gone by.

Michelangelo Antonioni and I discuss plans for his film *La Ciurma,* which unfortunately never materialized.

Whether or not I should have quit photography had become irrelevant, which probably means I made the right decision. But nonetheless, Kelley hadn't been wrong when she urged me to revisit and share the celebrated works of my past. I'd been so determined to create a new career beyond photography, entirely separate from Elizabeth and Richard, that I never bothered to take stock of everything I'd accomplished during my jet-set years. I'd wanted to find my best so badly that I overlooked the best I'd already achieved.

Meanwhile, the old dissatisfaction began to set in again. I was making movies because I could, but not because I truly wanted to make them. My mind kept returning to a challenge my father had posed: "Gianni," he'd say, "when art and science traveled together, there was a pure sense of logic. If you grow up to be who I think you'll be, you should do something about it." Which is why I decided to put the true history of the Renaissance on film, to dramatize, in Shakespeare's words, that "brave new world," the rebirth of civilization, many of whose priceless documents I had watched my father lovingly restore in his work. Researching the project, I visited the archives of all the great Renaissance families in Italy, many of whom still live in the very same palaces their ancestors did five hundred years ago. My studies made me realize just how much we've lost the sense of logic that reigned in the Renaissance, the logic my father had spoken of.

Today we call it common sense . . . though what's common often doesn't make sense. And it's definitely not logic. When religion and politics embraced each other, the meaning of the word *logic* changed. I want *The Renaissance* to show the world that we need to get back to basics, start over from where we went wrong. What's true remains true, after all. When Galileo was condemned for teaching the "heresy" that the earth revolves around the sun, he is said to have muttered, "Yet still it moves."

The world keeps spinning. Your life keeps changing. You change with it.

These days I always wake up very early, even after a harder day than usual. I go to my study, its walls lined with so many precious mementos and photographs, and stand at the window, inviting the light to enter, that light which has always been my companion and the master of my life's itinerary. When you choose the light, you have to embrace the changes it brings, the metamorphoses, allowing life to take the shape of a circle, the way a beam of light, if uninterrupted, will go on forever, until finally it will circle back on itself, creating a circle with no circumference whose center is everywhere, constantly repeating and renewing. That's where I sit now,

Directing my 2015 documentary *We Weren't Just Bicycle Thieves: Neorealism.*

at that place where the light of my present stretches ahead of me until it touches my past, leading me forward, brightening my future, and exposing every memory before my eyes. Finally, I now know who I want to be when I grow up.

As the great Leonardo da Vinci said, "What is beautiful and mortal passes, but not art" (Cosa bella e mortal passa e non d'arte), and I for one could die happy if even one of my photos, a single shot, were considered a work of art.

I never wanted to write this last chapter, but everything has a meaning, even things that are almost impossible or too painful to make sense of. And life has, sadly, made me something of an expert in this art. So let's proceed.

Elizabeth was afflicted by endless ailments, many of them physical, some dating as far back as her famous fall from a horse while shooting *National Velvet.* The last years of her life were, for her, a terrible ordeal. I spoke to Elizabeth on February 27 for her birthday and then again, for the last time, on March 7. She was confused and didn't want to talk, or maybe didn't have the strength to.

When I hung up, I couldn't help but think about the upcoming date of March 13, and I felt a shiver of fear run down my body: what else might this day have in store for me? I started thinking, short of breath. I lost my first daughter, Bruna, on March 13, 1973. More than ten years later, her mother joined her on the exact same day. Yet that very special date had also brought me joy: Kelley, my second wife, was born on that day. Was there meaning in all this?

March 13 arrived, and as always, I tried to call Elizabeth. But I couldn't get through, and a certain fear set in. Was fate playing with me again? Would I have to face yet another terrible loss? Later that night, I managed to speak to Christopher Wilding, her son. He had grim news. "She's in hospital with serious heart problems," he said, and all I could gasp was, "No! That's impossible." I couldn't bear the thought of losing her.

On March 23, 2011, the last star faded, and with her died a very special part of my life. I'd known her as Baby Boobs. The world knew her as Liz.

Dear Baby Boobs, thank you. You always loved to play and joke about everything. You just loved having fun, always amazing me with new surprises. And the biggest surprise of all was the very first. To this day, and every day, I still wonder why a woman who could have had anything and anyone chose me, way back then in Africa. During the many years we spent together, I may have found an answer, and I'll try to explain it shortly.

But first a word about Elizabeth. She didn't just work in cinema: she *was* cinema, the essence of cinema. Hers was a seventy-two-year mission strung with sixty-two movies, beginning in 1939 (when she was not yet seven) with *There's One Born Every Minute,* followed immediately by the hugely successful *Lassie Come Home.* The times were difficult, scored by the uncertainty of war. Yet before those two movies had even come out, Elizabeth was signing for two more: *Courage of Lassie* and, of course, *National Velvet,* which is when the world truly witnessed the rising of a new star.

I smile at my memory of the last time we spoke, only a few weeks before she died. Elizabeth had a wonderful sense of humor and a predilection for jokes tinged with bawdy innuendo. And she was a great audience. I'd tell her my stories, describing people and events, and she'd listen with her whole body. She always used to ask for the latest jokes, and made no exception on that last occasion.

"Gianni, do you have a new one?" she asked, her voice weak.

"Of course," I replied. "I saved this one just for you."

"What are you waiting for then?"

"We're in a small town in Sicily, you understand?"

She was already laughing at my heavy voice and Sicilian Mafia accent.

"Two old men, very old men."

Here's looking at you, Baby Boobs!

"Vecchi!" she said, which means "old" in Italian.

"Yes," I replied. "Vecchi! Well, these two old guys are sitting outside a bar in the center of town. 'Have you heard about this new medicine?' says one to the other. 'It's a blue pill, blue like our sea . . .' 'What are you talking about?' 'Viagra!' 'Ah, Viagra, and what does it do?' 'Well, they say it keeps your dick hard for a full two hours!' 'Okay, so it's a sedative.'"

Elizabeth burst into laughter. "You don't happen to have that second guy's number, do you?"

And that is just how I want to remember Elizabeth Taylor . . . What a woman! Honest, unpredictable, charming, affectionate, sensuous, and so beautiful it was impossible not to stand in awe of her. Those penetrating violet eyes could touch you so deeply you'd drown, not knowing how to react. Nothing seemed appropriate. You turned to stone. Believe me, I'm not exaggerating.

Elizabeth was all this, plus everything else from the universe of women. She was stunning. Yet, as I've already said, I never once considered the idea of us getting together. Quite why I couldn't say, though I know in my heart I could never have agreed to be Mr. Taylor. The story may possibly have been different for her, as some people have had occasion to speculate.

After Kelley's death, Elizabeth was very kind and affectionate toward me. She let time soothe my pain and then called me. "Why don't you visit sometime and introduce me to your daughter Rhea Bianca?" she asked. Elizabeth had wanted to be Rhea's godmother, but Kelley had demurred, fearing the media pressure. I agreed to visit, of course. But when we arrived at her Bel Air home she was with a Chinese doctor, right in the middle of an acupuncture session.

286

"Come on in," she called, while Rhea stood timidly at the door, absorbing the rather curious scene: Elizabeth stretched out flat, almost naked, a dozen needles stuck in her body while her white-coated acupuncturist stood beside her. "Don't be scared, Rhea Bianca," she said. "Come closer."

I was standing close behind Rhea when the conversation suddenly got a lot more complicated.

"You're so beautiful," said Elizabeth. "You look exactly like your mother. And your dad tells me you are also as smart as she was."

"Thank you," Rhea replied.

"Listen, my dear. Your father is now a widower, and I am single . . . So now we'll get married and we can keep each other company."

At this, Rhea flashed back without a moment's hesitation: "No!! My dad is my dad!!" She then spun round and left without another word.

It was a surreal situation, but whatever it meant, it ended like that and I kept my memory of that weird day to myself, sure it would remain our own little secret forever.

Then Elizabeth died, and people started calling, swarms of agencies wanting to know about something that had never happened. The Chinese doctor, it seems, had talked. A CBS journalist was the first to ask: "So, you're the one that got away, right?" I didn't get what he meant at first. But the story was already out. "Well, you refused to marry Elizabeth when she proposed to you; otherwise you'd have been her ninth husband."

I was tempted to explain that the person who'd actually turned down Elizabeth's proposal had been my daughter Rhea. But I knew that wasn't entirely true, so I kept my peace, a half smile on my face, musing on the acupuncturist who couldn't keep his mouth shut.

However, as I've promised, I'd like to try to explain my own idea of why Elizabeth chose me that day long ago in Africa. But in order to do so, I have one last story to tell.

My relationship with paparazzi and journalists has always been very peculiar, to say the least, because in a way I belonged to their group, while at the same time I belonged to Elizabeth's. I was more than just her personal photographer, and for that reason I represented a potential gold mine of information for anyone wanting to know about her—which was often half the world. I've always respected the fact that paparazzi are just doing their job. But I've also always protected everyone's privacy. Which is why, on many occasions, I've been reluctant to answer certain questions. For example, I've been asked so often to describe just how tumultuous

Giulia Fanchin Bozzacchi. I am happily married to this beautiful creature, and as Elizabeth might say, I'm a "pain in the ass" to her every day!

Elizabeth and Richard's relationship really was. My answer has always been the same: silence, accompanied by a small smile. Finally, I decided to end the questions and answer once and for all: "How could I possibly know how tumultuous their relationship was? I never spent any time in their bedroom."

Respect has always been of paramount importance to me. Elizabeth, my dear Baby Boobs, I really believe you chose me when I was still a nobody because you looked deep into my eyes and saw not only my talent but my moral integrity.

It was an honor to photograph her, always so genuine, joyful, and sexy, with a sensuality that I like to believe was emphasized by my trustworthy presence. Looking back at those photos today, reliving those moments, I'm even more convinced that, in trying to draw out her sensuality, I witnessed her light up in photo after photo until, in the end, she opened like a flower. And in the process, while taking my photos, always following my instinct, I grew too, picture by picture.

So long, Elizabeth "Liz" Rosemond Taylor, my darling Baby Boobs. I've always loved you and will always love you for the rest of my life.

There is a postscript to my story of that young Japanese American couple I photographed on the Pincio, the girl and boy to whom I had so naively given my Leica, the companion of my entire career. They returned my camera, asking only that I sign the photos I had taken. I was very happy—the camera had been a gift from Elizabeth.

My eyes, and my camera, will always see the world in black and white. But now, for the first time, my life is in color. Photos like these are how I express myself today.

Index

SCREEN CLASSICS

Screen Classics is a series of critical biographies, film histories, and analytical studies focusing on neglected filmmakers and important screen artists and subjects, from the era of silent cinema to the golden age of Hollywood to the international generation of today. Books in the Screen Classics series are intended for scholars and general readers alike. The contributing authors are established figures in their respective fields. This series also serves the purpose of advancing scholarship on film personalities and themes with ties to Kentucky.

SERIES EDITOR

Patrick McGilligan

BOOKS IN THE SERIES

Mae Murray: The Girl with the Bee-Stung Lips
    Michael G. Ankerich
Hedy Lamarr: The Most Beautiful Woman in Film
    Ruth Barton
Rex Ingram: Visionary Director of the Silent Screen
    Ruth Barton
Conversations with Classic Film Stars: Interviews from Hollywood's Golden Era
    James Bawden and Ron Miller
Von Sternberg
    John Baxter
Hitchcock's Partner in Suspense: The Life of Screenwriter Charles Bennett
    Charles Bennett, edited by John Charles Bennett
My Life in Focus: A Photographer's Journey with Elizabeth Taylor and the Hollywood Jet Set
    Gianni Bozzacchi with Joey Tayler
Hollywood Divided: The 1950 Screen Directors Guild Meeting and the Impact of the Blacklist
    Kevin Brianton
Ziegfeld and His Follies: A Biography of Broadway's Greatest Producer
    Cynthia Brideson and Sara Brideson
The Marxist and the Movies: A Biography of Paul Jarrico
    Larry Ceplair
Dalton Trumbo: Blacklisted Hollywood Radical
    Larry Ceplair and Christopher Trumbo
Warren Oates: A Wild Life
    Susan Compo
Crane: Sex, Celebrity, and My Father's Unsolved Murder
    Robert Crane and Christopher Fryer
Jack Nicholson: The Early Years
    Robert Crane and Christopher Fryer
Being Hal Ashby: Life of a Hollywood Rebel
    Nick Dawson
Bruce Dern: A Memoir
    Bruce Dern with Christopher Fryer and Robert Crane
Intrepid Laughter: Preston Sturges and the Movies
    Andrew Dickos
John Gilbert: The Last of the Silent Film Stars
    Eve Golden
Stuntwomen: The Untold Hollywood Story
    Mollie Gregory
Saul Bass: Anatomy of Film Design
    Jan-Christopher Horak